VITAL LIES, SIMPLE TRUTHS

THE PSYCHOLOGY OF SELF-DECEPTION

DANIEL GOLEMAN, Ph.D.

BLOOMSBURY

First published in Great Britain in 1997
Bloomsbury Publishing Plc, 38 Soho Square, London, W1V 5DF

A CIP catalogue record for this book
is available from the British Library

ISBN 0 7475 3413 6

10 9 8 7 6 5 4 3 2

Printed in Great Britain by Clays Ltd, St Ives Plc

(*continued on page 269*)

FOR TARA
"OM, TĀRE, TUTTĀRE, TURĒ, SWAHA!"

It seems plain and self-evident, yet it needs to be said: the isolated knowledge obtained by a group of specialists in a narrow field has in itself no value whatsoever, but only in its synthesis with all the rest of knowledge and only inasmuch as it really contributes in this synthesis toward answering the demand, "Who are we?"

—ERWIN SCHRODINGER

ACKNOWLEDGMENTS

In the spring of 1978 I had the pleasure of visiting with Gregory Bateson. Although Bateson was wheezing badly because of the lung cancer that would end his life several months thence, his spirits were high, his mind as alive as ever.

Bateson was reviewing his intellectual odyssey. A breakthrough had occurred for him just after World War II, at the Macy Foundation conferences where Norbert Wiener's group developed cybernetics. "Then," said Bateson, "I got on the right track: I could see more clearly the properties of whole systems, of the interlinked patterns that connect things."

He abandoned then-fashionable views of behavior: "Those theories of man which start from his most animalistic, maladapted, and lunatic psychology turn out to be improbable first premises from which to approach the psalmist's question, 'Lord, what is man?' And this narrowness led us to a failure to discern the pattern which connects."

"What," I asked, "is the 'pattern which connects'?"

"The pattern which connects," said he, "is a 'metapattern,' a pattern of patterns. More often than not, we fail to see it. With the exception of music, we have been trained to think of patterns as fixed affairs. The truth is that the right way to begin to think about the pattern which connects is as a dance of interacting parts, secondarily pegged down by various sorts of physical limits and by habits, and by the naming of states and component entities."

A dance of interacting parts. The pattern that connects. The ideas stuck with me. Over the next few years they gave shape to a search of my own.

I had long been intrigued by a range of facts and insights that all seemed to point to the same pattern, but from widely divergent angles. My training in clinical psychology at Harvard had put me in the midst of patients whose very disorders seemed to protect them from some deeper threat. A seminar with Erving Goffman, the sociologist of ordinary encounters, led me to see how the ground rules of face-to-face interaction keep us comfortable by ruling some zones of awareness out-of-bounds. Research on the psychobiology of consciousness showed me how cognition—and so our experience itself—is the product of a delicate balance between vigilance and inattention.

These disparate bits of evidence struck me as clues to a pattern, one that repeated in complementary ways at each major level of behavior—biological, psychological, social. As I reflected and gathered more evidence, the pattern became more focused.

The pattern is a dance with attention and anxiety as partners. In this minuet, there is an exchange of skewed attention for a feeling of security.

This book describes that pattern, as best I see it.

Along the way many people have been important in offering pieces of this puzzle, parts of the pattern. Conversations with the following, all experts in one or another domain touched on in this book, have been particularly helpful: Dennis Kelly, Solomon Snyder, Monte Buchsbaum, Floyd Bloom, Richard Lazarus, R. D. Laing, Donald Norman, Emmanuel Donchin, George Mandler, Howard Shevrin, Ernest Hilgard, Carl Whitaker, Karl Pribram, Robert Rosenthal, Irving Janis, Freed Bales, Anthony Marcel, and Robert Zajonc. Aaron Beck, Matthew Erdelyi and Ulric Neisser gave invaluable advice on the manuscript.

While each has helped me with a piece of the pattern, the synthesis is my own, as are any distortions or blind spots in thinking.

I am particularly indebted to Richard Davidson, Shoshona Zuboff, Kathleen Speeth, and Gwyn Cravens for thoughtful readings, frank remarks, and close friendship. Inspiration has also come from several teachers and colleagues, notably David McClelland and George Goethals.

A. C. Qwerty showed outstanding patience, diligence, and perspicacity in the preparation of this manuscript.

And Alice Mayhew helped me follow the thread of thought with an unswerving sense of what this book could be.

CONTENTS

FOREWORD

We live at a particularly perilous moment, one in which self-deception is a subject of increasing urgency. The planet itself faces a threat unknown in other times: its utter destruction.

Whether that death be the quick one, from nuclear war and the catastrophic changes that would follow, or the slow ecological one, from the inexorable destruction of forests, arable land and usable water, the human capacity for self-deception will have played its part.

Consider the rapidly growing ecological deficit—soil erosion, shrinking forests, grasslands turning to desert, depletion of the atmosphere's protective ozone layer, and the poisoning and drying up of water tables.

Our habits of consumption, on a worldwide scale, are destroying the planet's resources at a rate unparalleled in history. In effect, we are destroying the planet for our own grandchildren, simply by our heedlessness of the links between how we live and the effects on the planet.

The virgin rain forests of the Amazon, for example, are being destroyed at an incredible rate, to make room for cattle to graze. Those cattle are raised, in the main, to feed the world's hunger for beef.

How many hamburgers does the destruction of an acre of virgin Amazon jungle yield? We do not know: the answer could be determined, but that bit of homework has not been done.

And that is the point: we live our lives oblivious to the consequences for the planet, for our own descendents, of just *how* we live. We do not know the connections between the decisions we make daily—for instance to buy this item rather than that—and the toll those decisions have on the planet.

It is feasible to weigh, more or less accurately, the specific ecological damage involved in a given act of manufacturing. And having done so, to generate a standard unit that would summarize how much ecological damage has gone into the making of a car, say, or a box of aluminum foil.

Knowing that, we would be able to take more responsibility for the impact on the planet of how we choose to live on it. But there is no such information available, and even the most ecologically concerned among us do not really know the net effect on the planet of how they live. And, for most of us, being oblivious to that relationship allows us to slip into the grand self-deception, that the small and large decisions in our material lives are of no great consequence.

The question, then, is what can we do to break out of these self-deceptions, and the others that have us in their web?

The answer this book proposes is to understand, first, how it is that we are caught at all. For self-deception, by its very nature, is the most elusive of mental facts. We do not see what it is that we do not see.

Self-deception operates both at the level of the individual mind, and in the collective awareness of the group. To belong to a group of any sort, the tacit price of membership is to agree not to notice one's own feelings of uneasiness and misgiving, and certainly not to question anything that challenges the group's way of doing things.

The price for the group in this arrangement is that dissent, even healthy dissent, is stifled. Take the case of the shuttle explosion. The night before the launch two engineers strongly objected, saying that the seals on the propulsion rocket were not designed to bear up in cold weather. Their objections were never passed along to those at higher levels, many of whom already knew of the danger, but had chosen to discount its import. There had been several delays already, and people were questioning whether NASA could ever make the shuttle work well enough to pay its own way.

In the inquiry after the disaster, when the same two engineers testified about what had happened, they were demoted. And yet what they had done was in the highest interests of the entire mission. Had they been heard, the tragedy would not have occurred. Only after a public outcry were the engineers reinstated.

Therein lies the lesson for those who want to break through

the cocoons of silence that keep vital truths from the collective awareness. It is the courage to seek the truth and to speak it that can save us from the narcotic of self-deception. And each of us has access to some bit of truth that needs to be spoken.

It is a paradox of our time that those with power are too comfortable to notice the pain of those who suffer, and those who suffer have no power.

To break out of this trap requires, as Elie Wiesel has put it, the courage to speak truth to power.

INTRODUCTION

My topic is hard to explain to you, although it is something with which we are all intimately familiar. The difficulty is that we have no precise words for it. That very fact is, in part, why it intrigues me so: there are, it seems, vital parts of our lives which are, in a sense, missing—blanks in experience hidden by holes in vocabulary. That we do not experience them is a fact which we know only vaguely, if at all.

Those blanks in experience are my topic.

Our failure to experience these aspects of our lives appears due to causes deep within our consciousness. It results in an incapacity to bring attention to bear on certain crucial aspects of our reality, leaving a gap in that beam of awareness which defines our world from moment to moment.

My subject is, then, how we notice and how we *do not* notice.

In other words, a piece missing from awareness. A hole in attention. A lacuna.

The blind spot is an apt physiological metaphor for our failure to see things as they are in actuality. In physiology, the blind spot is the gap in our field of vision that results from the architecture of the eye.

At the back of each eyeball is a point where the optic nerve, which runs to the brain, attaches to the retina. This point lacks the cells that line the rest of the retina to register the light that comes through the lens of the eye. As a result, at this one point in vision there is a gap in the information transmitted to the brain. The blind spot registers nothing.

Ordinarily what is missed by the one eye is compensated for by overlapping vision in the other. Thus ordinarily we do not notice our blind spots. But when one eye is closed, the blind spot emerges. To see your blind spot, close your left eye and hold this book at arm's length with your right hand while focusing on the cross. Very slowly, move the book toward you and back again. Somewhere between ten and fifteen inches away the circle will seem to disappear.

It is instructive to see one's blind spot: it offers a concrete instance of a far more subtle, psychological parallel.

Let me give you some examples, drawn from various realms of life. They all suggest the pattern I mean to get at.

Take the case of a woman in therapy who recalls having heard, as a child of five, her mother crying at night. The memory comes as a surprise to the woman; it does not fit at all with her conscious memories of that period of her life, just after her father had moved out. While the girl's mother made long calls to the father pleading with him to come back, in the girl's presence she portrayed her feelings very differently: The mother denied missing her husband and put on a carefree and unconcerned air. After all, they were happy, weren't they?

The daughter understood that her mother's sadness was not to be mentioned. Since the mother needed to conceal these feelings, her daughter too was to deny them. The daughter repeatedly heard a version of the divorce that fit the image the mother wanted to convey; the story became an established fact in the daughter's memory. The more frightening memories of her mother crying at night faded from memory, not to be retrieved until many years later, in psychoanalysis.

The theme of the devastating impact such buried secrets can have is so familiar in literature that it suggests the universality of the experience. The story of Oedipus revolves around the device, as do Ford Madox Ford's *The Good Soldier* and several of Ibsen's plays. Indeed, Ibsen called this sort of secret a "vital lie," the family myth that stands in place of a less comfortable truth.

Such vital lies are not all that uncommon. For example, a psychiatrist reports having overheard a woman who, at a dinner party, remarked: [1]

> I am very close to my family. They were always very demonstrative and loving. When I disagreed with my mother she threw whatever was nearest at hand at me. Once it

> happened to be a knife and I needed ten stitches in my leg. A few years later my father tried to choke me when I began dating a boy he didn't like. They really are very concerned about me.

The denial evident in this reminiscence is a hallmark of the vital lie. If the force of facts is too brutal to ignore, then their meaning can be altered. The vital lie continues unrevealed, sheltered by the family's silence, alibis, stark denial. The collusion is maintained by directing attention away from the fearsome fact, or by repackaging its meaning in an acceptable format. A psychiatrist who treats families with problems like incest and alcoholism observes how vital lies operate:[2]

> Clues are minimized, joked about, explained away, or called something else. Semantics plays a big part in minimizing what is actually occurring; euphemisms are employed to hide what is really going on. A "good" drinker, marital "disputes," or "stern disciplinarian" can mean alcoholism, spousal violence, or child abuse. Explanations of "minor accidents" are gratefully accepted to explain the bruises and broken bones of child or spouse abuse. The "flu" excuses drunken behavior.

Or, as the now fully grown child of an alcoholic put it, "In our family there were two very clear rules: the first was that there is nothing wrong here, and the second was, don't tell anyone."

A different kind of example. Jesse Jackson, recalling growing up in South Carolina, tells the following tale about an encounter with a man named Jack, the white owner of the local grocery:[3]

> This particular day I was in a hurry, because my grandfather was outside and he gave me a nickel to get some Mary Janes and cookies or something. There were eight or ten black people in there, and I said, "Jack, can I have a cookie?" He had been cutting bologna or something. I whistled for his attention. Suddenly, he was on me with a gun pointed at my head. He said "Never whistle at me again!" The thing that stood out in my mind was that the other blacks who were in the store acted as if they didn't see it. They stayed busy. They had a deep and abiding fear. I was not so much afraid of the gun as I was of what my father would do. He had just gotten back from World War Two, and I knew he had not only a temper but a mind that had been opened up after being exposed to Europe during the war. He had become more resentful of the system. I knew that if my father heard about it, he'd either

kill Jack or get killed. So I suppressed it. It came out many years later. But that was the nature of life in the occupied zone.

The flip side of that story, in a sense, is told by Barney Simon, a South African playwright, reflecting on an unspoken truth about apartheid. If in America blacks suppress rage toward whites, in South Africa whites repress tenderness toward blacks:[4]

> All white South Africans are brought up in early childhood by black women. I remember the one in our house, Rose. . . . You spend your first years on the black woman's back. You spend your first years with your cheek pressed against her neck. You hear her songs, her vernacular. You go to the park with her and sit among other black women like her. You go into her room and maybe her lover is there. You develop this knowledge of each other. But at a certain point, South Africa tells you that knowledge is obscene, and a crime—worse than a crime, a sin. You are told to forget what you already know.

Military history is rich with another variety of what I am trying to get at—take, for example, cases of outright refusal to believe the truth:[5]

- In the First World War, a week before the Germans launched their first attack with poison gas, a German deserter brought a warning that such an attack would occur. He even brought along one of the masks that the German troops had been issued to protect them. The French commander who received the message dismissed it as absurd, and rebuked his messenger for not having gone through proper channels.
- In World War II, Herman Göring was told that an Allied fighter had been shot down over a German city, the first that had ever been seen that far behind the Axis lines. This meant the Allies had developed a long-range fighter that could escort bombers over Germany. Göring, a pilot himself, "knew" such a development was impossible. His reply: "I officially assert that American fighter planes did not reach Aachen. . . . I herewith give you an official order that they weren't there."
- In the same war, on the day the Germans began their offensive against Russia, a Soviet frontline unit sent the message to headquarters, "We are being fired on. What shall we do?" To which headquarters responded: "You must be insane."

For another case in point, from a vaster arena, ponder the future of mankind. "Nuclear weapons," says an item in *The Wall*

Street Journal, "are accumulating at a cost of $1 million a minute world-wide, with the stockpile exceeding 50,000 weapons." At the same time, according to the World Health Organization, fifty million children die each year from diarrhea, the world's biggest killer —and one preventable by the simplest sanitation and nutrition.

Psychiatrists give the name "nuclear numbing" to the widely observed inability of people to let themselves feel the fear, anger, and rebelliousness that fully grasping the human predicament—notably, the arms race—might bring them. People seem to anesthetize themselves, as though the danger were too vast to arouse concern.

Lester Grinspoon, a psychiatrist, notes how, in nuclear numbing, people "avoid acquiring information that would make vague fears specific enough to require decisive action"; how "they contrive to ignore the implication of the information they do allow to get through." In other words, they treat this—everyone's problem —as if it were someone else's.

These diverse instances all exemplify the power of a skewed attention to hide a painful truth. What connects them is that, in each case, in some way, a looming anxiety is appeased by a twist of attention.

Attention is the gathering of information crucial to existence. Anxiety is the response when that information registers as a threat. The intriguing part of this relationship is straightforward: we can use our attention to deny threat, and so cushion ourselves from anxiety.

In some ways that is a useful self-deception. In others it is not.

In the Soviet Union every publication has its own censor. But the journalists and editors who work there rarely confront the censor's pen: they perform his task for him automatically, applying his standards as they do their work.[6] Lev Poliakov, a Russian emigré who worked as a freelance photographer in Russia, tells of his going to a city near the Caspian on assignment for a children's magazine. The city had two large facilities, one a science center, the other a labor camp. He was met there by a local party official, who said to him, "Look, you're busy and I'm busy. Let's make it easy for both of us. Whenever you see barbed wire, just turn your back and *then* shoot."

Another emigré photographer, Lev Nisnevich, took a photo of members of the Writers' Union voting on a resolution. Included in the shot was a KGB man watching closely as the union members voted. When the picture ran in the widely read *Literaturnaya Gazeta*, the KGB man was cropped out, leaving only the voting members holding up their ballots. The visual impression was of a spontaneous unanimity, with no hint of other forces at work among the membership.

Such heavyhanded censorship is obvious. It is not so easy to see a similar editing in our own awareness. The incident of the cropped picture is a particularly apt metaphor for what goes on in our own minds. What enters our attention is within the frame of awareness; what we crop out vanishes.

The frame around a picture is a visual directive focusing our gaze toward what it surrounds and away from everything else. It defines what is in the picture and what is out. The framer's art is to build margins that blend with a picture so we notice what is framed rather than the frame itself.

So with attention. It defines *what* we notice, but with such subtlety that we rarely notice *how* we notice. Attention is the frame around experience.

Except in special cases—say, a gilded, baroque monstrosity—we don't notice the frame. But just as the wrong frame intrudes and ruins the picture, a distorted attention warps experience, inhibits action.

A skewed awareness can be disastrous. One theme of Greek tragedy is the sorry chain of events begun by a slight flaw of perception at the outset. Hannah Arendt, the social philosopher, described how the mix of self-deception and free will allows us to do evil, believing it good.

The deadening of one's pain through the warping of awareness may be an affliction to which the modern sensibility is particularly vulnerable. John Updike, in a review of Kafka's works, states it well:[7] "The century since Franz Kafka was born has been marked by the idea of 'modernism'—a self-consciousness new among centuries, a consciousness of being new. Sixty years after his death, Kafka epitomizes one aspect of the modern mind-set: a sensation of anxiety and shame whose center cannot be located and therefore cannot be placated; a sense of an infinite difficulty within things, impeding every step; a sensitivity acute beyond usefulness, as if the nervous system, flayed of its old hide of social usage and religious belief, must record every touch as pain."

Blind spots are especially tempting to a mind-set hypersensitive to pain. They offer easy solace from the flow of facts that prick that pain, whether the source is deeply personal, such as the memory of a childhood hurt or this morning's rebuff from a spouse, or public—tortures and murders by unjust regimes; nuclear perils.

Some filters on awareness are essential by virtue of the flood of data available at each moment to our senses. The cortex, the newest part of the human brain, expends much of its energy picking and choosing among this flood. "Indeed," suggests the neuroscientist Monte Buchsbaum, "filtering or coping with the tremendous information overload that the human eye, ear, and other sense organs can dump upon the central nervous system may be one of the major functions of the cerebral cortex."

Perception is selection. Filtering out information is, in the main, for the good. But the very capacity of the brain to do so makes it vulnerable to skewing what is admitted to awareness, what rejected. Buchsbaum goes on to point out that the differences in what people filter out "would then appear to produce a different consciousness of the external environment, each person biasing his admission or rejection of sensory signals."

The ways in which our attention is biased have profound effects. As William James put it, "My experience is what I agree to attend to. Only those items I notice shape my mind." But, he adds, "Without selective interest, experience is utter chaos." For James, attention was an act of will, the choice of what to admit to mind a conscious one. For Freud, it was shaped in crucial ways by forces in the unconscious mind, a realm out of the reach of conscious choice.

Both James and Freud had part of the truth. Attention is ruled by forces both conscious and unconscious. Some are innocuous, such as the limits on capacity set by the mehanics of the mind. Some are crucial, such as the bias introduced by saliency, where what matters at the moment takes the foreground of awareness. Some, as I will show, can be self-defeating. Foremost among these is the self-deception induced by the trade-off between anxiety and awareness.

THE TRADE-OFF

The trade-off of a distorted awareness for a sense of security is, I believe, an organizing principle operating over many levels and realms of human life. My intent is to sketch this attention-anxiety link, which I see as part of a complex web embedded in the workings of the brain, the texture of mind, and the fabric of social life.

My focus is on how information flows, and how that flow is skewed by the interplay between pain and attention. The notion of the link between pain and attention is not new. Freud elaborated it with brilliance. But recent theory and research, particularly in the field of information-processing, offers a more articulated view of the mind's inner dynamics, one that can be extended to the structure of group life and the social construction of reality.

Neither Freud nor any other student of the mind could have made that leap in this way before the last decade. In recent years cognitive psychologists have developed a model of how the mind works which is far more detailed and solidly based than any we have had before. That model allows us to gain a new sense of how our experience is shaped, and of the hidden forces that sculpt personal and social reality.

That terrain—the stretch from the mind's mechanics to social life—is the domain we will explore here. Our journey begins, though, at an even more basic level: in the brain's system for sensing pain. At the neural level lies the cardinal model for the trade-off between pain and awareness. The brain, as we shall see, has the ability to bear pain by masking its sting, but at the cost of a diminished awareness.

That same organizing principle is repeated at each successive level of behavior: in the mind's mechanics, in the makeup of character, in group life, and in society. In each of these domains the variety of "pain" blocked from awareness is successively refined, from stress and anxiety, to painful secrets, to threatening or embarrassing facts of social life.

My thesis, in sum, revolves around these premises:

- *The mind can protect itself against anxiety by dimming awareness.*
- *This mechanism creates a blind spot: a zone of blocked attention and self-deception.*
- *Such blind spots occur at each major level of behavior from the psychological to the social.*

This book is in six parts. The first sketches the trade-off between pain and attention, showing that interaction at work in the brain and in the mind's handling of anxiety and stress. The neural mechanism for the trade-off involves the opioids, the "brain's morphine," which numb sensations of pain and dim attention. An analogue of this neural trade-off is a psychological one: soothing anxiety by withdrawing attention.

The second part elaborates a working model of the mind, to show the mechanisms that allow the attention-anxiety trade-off. Two key concepts here are the crucial role in mental life of the unconscious, and the notion that the mind packages information in "schemas," a sort of mental code for representing experience. Schemas operate in the unconscious, out of awareness. They direct attention toward what is salient and ignore the rest of experience—an essential task. But when schemas are driven by the fear of painful information, they can create a blind spot in attention.

In the third part, this model of mind brings us to a new understanding of psychological defenses—the quintessential self-deceptions. This section recasts psychodynamics in light of the links between attention and schemas, showing how, in the mind's design, inattention to painful truths shields us from anxiety.

When such soothing inattention becomes habit, it comes to shape character. Part four traces the ways such habits of avoiding anxiety through inattention are passed on from parent to child. As personality forms, a given set of protective schemas dominates, and with them the blind spots and self-deceits they lead to.

The fifth part describes group life—using the family as a prototype—showing how shared schemas guide group dynamics. The same anxiety-attention trade-off operates here, carving out blind spots in a group's collective awareness.

The sixth part uses the same template to explore the social construction of reality. Shared schemas are at work in the social realm, creating a consensual reality. This social reality is pocked with zones of tacitly denied information. The ease with which such social blind spots arise is due to the structure of the individual mind. Their social cost is shared illusions.

This is a groundbreaking expedition, a quick survey of terrain in several domains of experience. It stakes out a territory to which I hope to return another time for more detailed mapping. I must ask the lay reader's forbearance with my reviews of theory and research. They make, at times, for difficult going. My hope is that the reward for the reader will be a new understanding of his own experience.

I also must ask expert readers—fellow psychologists, cognitive scientists, psychoanalysts, neuroscientists, sociologists, and any others upon whose territory I infringe—to forgive my hurried reconnaissance of these rich subjects. I have much ground to cover, and can only skim the surface of each area in passing. For example, I do not explicitly address the work of Ruben Gur and Harold Sackheim, psychologists whose focus has been how self-deception is at play in mental disorders such as depression. My general approach is compatible with theirs, though from a different perspective.

The extrapolation I attempt from an information-processing model of the mind into the domains of personality, group dynamics, and social reality has not, to my knowledge, been attempted before. I do so here in the service of a specific hypothesis, namely that our experience is shaped and limited by the pain-attention trade-off. This unified model of behavior at all levels makes my task easier. But I propose such a grand synthesis with an equally grand trepidation.

This is not a book of easy answers (I suspect there are none), nor a profile against which to measure oneself. It simply offers a new map of experience, with particular emphasis on some of the more shadowy patches. The topic is how things work, not what to do about them. The new understanding of the mind that science has come to, I trust, can offer insights into our personal and collective mental lives.

My intent is to give the reader a clearer look through a veil or two at the margins of awareness. These veils are most apt to take over in those realms that matter most to us: in our innermost thoughts, in our crucial relationships, in closely knit groups, in constructing a consensual reality. I mean to suggest how those veils come to exist. But I do not pretend to know how best to pierce them nor indeed to know exactly when they should be swept away.

There is a peculiar paradox when it comes to confronting those ways in which we do not see. To put it in the form of one of R. D. Laing's "knots":

> The range of what we think and do
> is limited by what we fail to notice.
> And because we fail to notice
> *that* we fail to notice
> there is little we can do
> to change
> until we notice
> how failing to notice
> shapes our thoughts and deeds

Gregory Bateson coined a germane usage. He used the word "dormitive" to denote an obfuscation, a failure to see things as they are. "Dormitive" is derived from the Latin *dormire,* to sleep. "I stole the word from Molière," Bateson once explained to me. "At the end of his *Bourgeois Gentilhomme,* there is a dog-Latin coda in which a group of medieval doctors are giving an oral quiz to a candidate for his doctoral exam. They ask him, 'Why is it, candidate, that opium puts people to sleep?' And the candidate triumphantly replies, 'Because, learned doctors, it contains a dormitive principle.' " That is to say, it puts people to sleep because it puts people to sleep.[8]

The coinage "dormitive" is applicable here. To steal the word from Bateson, dormitive frames are the forces that make for a waking sleep at the margins of awareness.

In the catalogue of factors that shape awareness, my special focus is on the dormitive frame—the bends and twists insinuated into attention by the urge for security. If we can glimpse the edges that frame our experience, we are a bit freer to expand our margins. We may want to have more say over them, to consider whether we want the limits on thought and action so imposed.

My aim is to ponder our collective predicament: if we so easily lull ourselves into subtle sleep, how can we awaken? The first step in that, it seems to me, is to notice how it is that we are asleep.

PART ONE

Pain and Attention

THOUGHTS ON BEING MAULED BY A LION

David Livingstone, the Scottish missionary of "Dr. Livingstone, I presume" fame, was once attacked by a lion. The incident haunted him for years; he had come close to dying. Recalling it some twenty years later, Livingstone was struck by an oddity. In what should have been a moment of utter terror, he felt a curious detachment:[1]

> I heard a shout. Starting, and looking half round, I saw the lion just in the act of springing upon me. . . . He caught my shoulder as he sprang, and we both came to the ground below together. Growling horribly close to my ear, he shook me as a terrier does a rat. The shock produced a stupor similar to that which seems to be felt by a mouse after the first shake of the cat. It caused a sort of dreaminess in which there was no sense of pain nor feeling of terror, though [I was] quite conscious of all that was happening. It was like what patients partially under the influence of chloroform describe, who see the operation but feel not the knife.

Why should we be able to respond to pain by numbing its effects? Dr. Livingstone's encounter with the lion offers an exemplary event for considering this question, and a seminal jumping-off point for exploring the nature of our reaction to pain and what its dynamic might mean for the rest of mental life.[2]

My premise is that the brain's basic design offers a prototype of how we handle pain of all sorts, including psychological distress and social anxieties. These neural pain mechanisms embody patterns that operate also in our psychological and social life—or so I will argue.

Consider pain. Though not ordinarily thought of as such, pain is a sense, like seeing or hearing; it has its own tracts of nerves and neural circuitry (balance, in this regard, is another slighted sense). As with other senses, the psychological experience of pain depends on far more than the simple strength of nerve signals: fear of the dentist's drill and the joy of childbirth each alter pain, in entirely opposite directions.

The brain has discretion in how pain is perceived. Our view of the neural plasticity of pain is based on evidence which has come to light only in the last few years, mainly from research on animals. For decades researchers had misgivings about the relevance to humans of findings based on the reactions of laboratory animals. Animals were thought to have a very simple pain system, while humans had a complex one intertwined with the higher, distinctly human brain centers. Veterinarians, though, had long known that stroking an animal's head made probing a wound easier—animals, too, had a psychology of pain.

A closer analysis of the pain tracts in humans and animals revealed that the system had taken shape so early in evolution that animals as primitive as snails and mollusks shared with humans the basic design. This discovery meant that experiments on animals could offer us an understanding of the human pain response; a flood of research in the last decade on the neurology of pain has been the result of that discovery.

While direct stimulation of nerves in many parts of the pain tract evokes pain, stimulation of other parts of that tract does quite the opposite: it eases pain. The effect is so strong that stimulating a certain brain site in a rat will allow it to stay calm during stomach surgery without anesthetics. Analgesia, the soothing of pain, is as much a property of the system as is the perception of pain.

Pharmacologists had long assumed that a neurotransmitter existed with the capacity to numb pain. But it was not until the late 1970s that Solomon Snyder at Johns Hopkins (as well as other brain researchers working independently) showed that the brain tracts where morphine acted had cells with receptors that were specifically fitted to the shape of opiate molecules, like a lock to a key.

What were these sites of action for? As one researcher notes, "It seemed unlikely that such highly specific receptors should have evolved in nature fortuitously only to interact with alkaloids from the opium poppy."

The subsequent discovery of "endorphins," a group of neurotransmitters that act like opiates in the brain, resolved that question. The pathways where morphine could evoke analgesia are precisely the site of action of the endorphins. Endorphins, which have been called "the brain's own morphine," are a natural pain balm.

The endorphins are part of a larger class of brain chemicals known as "opioids."* Opiates like morphine and heroin have their effects because their molecular structure imitates the opioids in the brain. Endorphin, like the drugs that imitate it, also produces a euphoria, the "high" feeling of well-being that appeals to users of opiates.

The discovery of the endorphins led to a wave of research on what conditions trigger the release of these soothing chemicals. At first a variety of physical stressors were tried. Thousands of laboratory rats have had their tails singed or feet shocked to elicit endorphins; hundreds of human subjects immersed a hand in a bucket of freezing water.

Then a new discovery was made: mental stress alone could trigger endorphins. More precisely, apprehension in volunteers waiting to get a shock during a pain study led to endorphin release. So, too, with other kinds of psychological stress. For example, students taking final exams were reported to have higher endorphin levels.

It stands to reason that purely psychological stress should trigger the same brain response as biological pain. In nature, pain comes delivered in an envelope of stress. The threat of pain is the essence of stress: an animal fleeing a predator is aware of the danger long before it experiences pain, if it does at all. The winning design in evolution, it seems, is for the pain response to be part of the total package of reaction to danger.

That package as a whole is what Hans Selye, the pioneer of stress research, dubbed the "stress response," or "general adaptive syndrome." Selye's use of "stress," though it has found its way into common parlance with several loose connotations, has a very precise meaning.[3] He described a series of neurophysiological changes that the body undergoes in response to injury, the threat of harm, or life's minor ordeals. Selye proposed that the stress re-

* Since the discovery of the endorphins, other opioids have turned up which are even more potent in numbing pain. One of these, called dynorphin, has a chemical action two hundred times stronger than morphine. Another pain-relieving hormone was discovered in an unlikely source: it was first isolated from the camel pituitary. Called B-lipotropin, its main function was at first thought to be breaking down fats (a common chore for hormones). The later discovery of the endorphins led to a more thoughtful look at B-lipotropin; it was found to contain within it a sequence of amino acids identical to one of the endorphins. While the molecule as a whole had no pain-relieving properties at all, no less than three of its constituents proved to be active pain relievers. Many other substances have since come to light which also seem to suppress the pain response. There are certain to be more: Snyder, who discovered the endorphin pathways, conjectures there may be as many as two hundred different neurotransmitter systems in the brain. We now know of between two and three dozen or so.

sponse is a universal reaction by the body to threats and dangers of all sorts, ranging from burns and bacteria to bears and bad news.

In brief, when a person perceives an event as a stressor, the brain signals the hypothalamus to secrete a substance called CRF, or "cortico-releasing factor." CRF travels through a special gateway to the pituitary gland, where it triggers the release of ACTH (for adrenocorticotrophic hormone) and opioids, particularly the endorphins.*[4] Presumably, early in evolution this brain alarm went off when a saber-toothed tiger came into view. In modern times, a meeting with the accountants will do.

In sum, whether physical or mental in origin, pain registers in the brain via a system that can dampen its signals. In the brain's design the relief of pain is built into its perception. That is a clue to Livingstone's numbness in the lion's jaws—a clue to which I will return. But there is more to the story. Consider the role of attention in all this.

* Not all stress evokes endorphins, although the stress response invariably involves ACTH. It was ACTH that Selye thought of as the prime brain chemical underlying the stress response. There are several others, but few neurotransmitters had been identified at the time he was formulating his theory. The endorphins, for example, were completely unknown.

THE PAIN-ATTENTION LINK

Now to eat if one cannot the other can—and if we can't the girseau Q. C. Washpots Prizebloom capacities—turning out—replaced by the head patterns my own capacities—I was not very kind to them. Q. C. Washpots underpatterned against—bred to pattern. Animal sequestration capacities and animal sequestered capacities under leash—and animal secretions . . .

This passage has an almost Joycean ring. There is an appealing lilt to "Now to eat if one cannot the other can"; it would not be out of place in *Ulysses*. But it was written by a diagnosed schizophrenic in the ward of a mental hospital. Textbooks on psychopathology enumerate many similar examples; clinicians take language patterns like these to be one diagnostic indicator of schizophrenia.[5]

These florid language patterns are unintentional, not efforts at poesy. Schizophrenic language is a symptom of an underlying problem, disrupted attention. Schizophrenics are easily distracted —by noise, by movements, by ideas. Most significantly for their odd language patterns, they are distracted by their own background thoughts and mental associations.

A focused attention is one that can tune out or ignore distractions, or at least mute them. For the schizophrenic, though, distractions intrude into the focal zone of awareness with the same force as the primary thread of thought. This sabotages the effort demanded to construct a sentence.

Constructing a sentence is a complex attentional task which seems simple because it has become automatic. As a train of thought is transformed into an utterance, a chain of words and associations comes to mind. The word "stock," for example, could lead by association to bonds, Wall Street, dividend; or to cattle, barn, and farm; or to theater, summer company, and so on.

Ordinarily the mind sorts through these associations and chooses only those that complete the thought we want to express. For the schizophrenic, though, a faulty capacity to inhibit irrelevant thoughts lets associations stray into the sentences he manufactures. Such lapses signify a breakdown in the ability to attend.

Attentional breakdown in schizophrenia has been well recognized for at least a century. But only recently has this deficit been linked to another odd characteristic of schizophrenics: they have a higher than normal tolerance of pain.

A series of experiments by a psychiatrist, Monte Buchsbaum, and a group of co-researchers at the National Institute of Mental Health make the case that both the schizophrenic attentional deficit and heightened tolerance to pain are due to an abnormality in the endorphin system.[6]

Several lines of evidence point to an endorphin abnormality in schizophrenia. One study, for example, compared a group of seventeen hospitalized schizophrenics with a normal group matched for age and sex. Both groups went through identical procedures to measure their reaction to pain. Researchers administered a carefully regulated series of mild electric shocks to a point on the forearm of each subject in the study. The shocks varied in intensity from a barely noticeable tingle to levels most people would feel as sharp pain.

The schizophrenics were less sensitive to pain than were the normal people in the control groups. That fact alone suggests that the schizophrenics may have heightened levels of endorphins.

The Buchsbaum team went a step further. They gave schizophrenics doses of naltrexone, which blocks the activity of endorphins in the brain. If doses of naltrexone reverse any particular behavior, it is a good sign the behavior was due to the action of endorphins on the brain. When the schizophrenics—all of whom were rated as pain-insensitive—took the dose of naltrexone, their pain sensitivity increased threefold. This result strongly points to heightened endorphin levels as the cause of schizophrenics' pain insensitivity.

The naltrexone had another intriguing effect on the schizophrenics: it improved their capacity for paying attention, even normalizing it. The Buchsbaum group pursued this lead through another route. They compared a schizophrenic and a normal group on the ability to attend. The schizophrenics did poorly—until they got naltrexone. But the real surprise came when the researchers administered naltrexone to the normal groups; for them, too, the endorphin-blocking drug improved attentional capacity significantly. Endorphins seem to hamper attention.*

The interplay between pain and attention involves another neurotransmitter, ACTH. There is an intriguing complementarity between endorphins and ACTH, both of which are released at the onset of the stress response. Endorphins ease pain, and thus allow it to be ignored for the time being. They also lessen attention, an effect which may make denying the urgency of pain all the easier. ACTH, however, has just the opposite effect.

The Buchsbaum group gave ACTH to patients who were being tested on their alertness to tones and lights. ACTH *enhanced* their attention, *just as had the endorphin-blockers* in a previous study. Other researchers, Buchsbaum notes, have found that in rats ACTH *increases* sensitivity to pain.

ACTH, then, is somehow keyed to dampen endorphins. ACTH and endorphins, it seems, have opposing actions. ACTH heightens attention and sensitizes the nervous system to pain, while endorphins do just the reverse.

Endorphins and ACTH are split off from the same master molecule—they are, literally, part of the same neurochemical package for confronting danger. The interaction between ACTH and endorphin is orchestrated, in part, by timing. During the stress response, both these brain chemicals are triggered by the pituitary. But ACTH streams into the body more quickly; its effects can be seen in humans within the first thirty seconds of a stress alarm. Endorphins, though, have a slower rate; their effects don't show up until after two minutes or so. The first response to an alarm alerts us to the danger; the second stroke allows an obliviousness to pain.

Both ACTH and endorphins course through the brain during

* The link would be more convincing if there were centers in the brain where these two mental functions—selective attention and pain sensitivity—come together. Buchsbaum found some, using a computer-averaging of brain signals to pinpoint where in the brain a given mental task goes on. This method renders a topographical picture of the brain with scaled shadings reflecting the degree of activity. The result is a view of the brain rather like a map color-coded for elevation, which at a glance reveals where the mountains and valleys lie.

Using these brain maps Buchsbaum found that there was major overlap between brain areas most active during selective attention and those active in pain perception. While the data from this technique is still sketchy, it points to the frontal cortex and a section toward the rear, in the sensory cortex, as key to both attention and pain. Most of the effects he studied—such as the ability of naltrexone to affect the schizophrenics' ordinary level of attention and pain—showed changes in these areas.

There are at least two other brain sites where the action of endorphins may directly suppress attention.[7] One is the locus coreleus, the other the raphe system. Each is a major nexus of cell assemblies essential for attention. The endorphins inhibit their activity.

the stress response. But the relative ratio of each will determine to a large degree how attentive and how pain-sensitive we are. These two elements of experience—the numbing of pain and dimming of attention—seem to have a common purpose: dimming attention is one way to numb pain. That these neurochemical systems should be linked attests to the elegance of the brain's design.

The conceptual split between pain perception and attention may be more artificial than we realize. The brain does not necessarily parse mental functions as we do in experience. Buchsbaum makes the point that the scientific study of pain and of attention has been separated by virtue of the different disciplines that study them. These recent findings about the intimate tie between attention and pain, in his words, "indicate that this separation is artificial, since the same neurotransmitters, anatomic structures, and information-processing systems" may modulate both pain *and* attention.

The endorphin system, then, is rigged to reduce attention as it soothes pain. Pain relief and selective attention share common pathways through the brain, although their relationship is one of mutual exclusivity: as endorphins activate, pain lessens and attention dims. The increased attention that accompanies ACTH enhances pain sensitivity.

Such an arrangement is permanently fixed in the brain; the neural networks that cause this relationship between pain and attention have come about through millions of years of evolution. Consider again the "dreaminess" Livingstone felt in the lion's grip. Might it offer a clue to the evolutionary basis for the curious connection between pain and attention?

WHY DIMMED ATTENTION SOOTHES PAIN

Ever the missionary, Livingstone wondered if his detachment in the lion's mouth might have a role in some divine plan. There must, he thought, be some higher purpose for what he called "this peculiar state." This condition, Livingstone conjectured, "is probably produced in all animals killed by the carnivora; and if so, is a merciful provision by our benevolent creator for lessening the pain of death."

While there is a sentimental appeal to Livingstone's proposal, a different interpretation seems more compelling. Evolution favors responses that allow an animal to survive and procreate. A gene that fosters peaceful dying would have little chance to be passed on by those for whom it operates best.

Pain ordinarily prompts responses that aid recuperation and healing—withdrawal, rest, a slowed metabolic rate and lessened activity. This round of recuperation, though, has zero survival value if one is about to be eaten, needs to defend one's young, or should run. In such instances a means to bypass the urge to attend to a painful wound is essential. The endorphins allow just that.

The pain-numbing response to severe emergency—the attack of a predator being the prime case—is an even more elegant design for survival than it is for peaceful, resigned death. Utter terror is paralyzing. But a predator's threat calls for action, for a response that rallies to the challenge. What better than to numb the pain and terror of the moment, while inducing calm? That permits a life-saving response, one based on an assessment of the situation less clouded by fear and panic. This is precisely the state Livingstone described.

The stimulation of certain parts of the endorphin tract also evokes aggression and defensive maneuvers, at least in laboratory animals. For instance, after doing battle for territorial dominance, rats show a strong post-fight analgesia, indicating elevated endorphin levels. This suggests that the pain-numbing system is closely linked to those designed for handling danger and threat. It seems reasonable—though, admittedly, speculative—to suppose that the pain-numbing system evolved as part of a package that allows the brain to rally to the challenge of a physical threat.

This, then, is the alternative to Livingstone's theory: Fitness for survival falls to members of a species who, when events warrant, are best able to ignore their pain while dealing with the threat at hand. The high survival value of pain-numbing would explain why it is found in primitive brain areas, which humans share with more ancient species. Indeed, opiate receptors have been found in every species examined, including those with nervous systems as primitive as leeches.

Another line of research supports the notion that the endorphin response is tailored for handling emergency, not for recovery afterward. A UCLA research team found that inescapable foot shocks—but not escapable ones—heightened endorphin levels in rats.[8] Shocks that can be escaped, they found, trigger a nonopioid release; escapable shocks are less of a threat than inescapable ones.

This precise difference in reactions to types of stress, they observe, is also found in tumor growth. When laboratory rats with cancer tumors get an inescapable shock, the tumor growth rate quickens. When they can escape the shock, the growth rate does not change. Endorphins may be the culprit: when tumorous rats are given opioid antagonists like naltrexone, their tumor growth rate slows and they survive longer. This pattern suggests that the opioids, while they dull pain, interfere with healing.* The broader implication is that the endorphin pain-suppression system, while it may be of vital survival value in handling emergencies, is not the response of choice when recuperation is needed.

The pain-numbing system needs to discriminate somehow between those times when it pays to relieve pain and those when it does not. Some wounded soldiers, for example, have reported experiencing a state like Livingstone's. But for many, their pain remains an agony. The pain-numbing system switches on selectively.

* To find out why, the UCLA group examined the effects of these different shock patterns on the rat's immune system function. The rats subjected to the shock pattern that triggers opioids had impaired immune function on two counts: the antitumor response of both T-lymphocytes and "natural killer" cells suffered. But there were no such immune system deficits in a group of rats treated with naltrexone (an opioid antagonist) and subjected to the same inescapable, opioid-stimulating shocks. When the endorphin response was suppressed, the immune system was unimpaired. The conclusion: "opioid peptides are significantly involved in the effects of stress on cancer and the immune system."

Although there are rational guidelines for when it pays to ignore pain and when not, the endorphin system seems to follow its own imperatives. Just what they are is still a mystery: we do not know how a mechanism as phylogenetically primitive as this distinguishes between the lion and the mortgage payments.

But there is little doubt that, in the long run, it pays a species to have the capacity to override pain in special instances. There is survival value both in the perception of pain and in its numbing. But why should soothing pain diminish attention? Such a response to emergency would seem on first glance to have little survival value. What positive role in evolution might dimming attention play? We can only speculate, of course. Livingstone's lion suggests one solution.

A serious wound is a life-and-death matter. It should get full attention, become the primary focus, to ensure care. Survival should dictate a reflexive, involuntary attention to a pain. Indeed, the pain system is constructed to compel attention to the source of pain—in most cases.

But in those instances when a greater danger looms, an animal whose attention is compulsively pulled to the wound rather than to the lion is as good as dead. Attention must swing in a wider arc: To override the reflexive attention to pain, awareness must somehow be wrenched away. Endorphin is the chemical agent capable of loosening attention in that way. While attention suffers thereby, the evolutionary bottom line—survival—shows that the outcome makes the bargain worthwhile. The pain system is a fixture of our neurological legacy. Its antiquity attests to its success as a strategy for survival.

My premise is that the pain-attention trade-off marks a pattern which has found a niche in both the psychological and social domains. For modern man, physical pain is a relatively rare event. Far more common is psychological pain—affront to one's self-esteem, apprehension, loss. We meet these pains with an alarm system tuned by millions of years of more primal threats.

The brain's tactic for handling physical pain through muting awareness offers itself as a template for dealing with psychological and social hurts as well. Whether these brain mechanisms are the actual root of the numbness that operates when we brush up against mental pains, or are simply analogues for it, is an open question. My goal here is more modest: to point out a pattern that connects. The perception of pain includes the ability to numb pain by tuning it out. That pattern, as we shall see, repeats itself again and again, in every major domain of human behavior.

MENTAL PAIN MAKES COGNITIVE STATIC

Just once in my life have I been paralyzed by fear. The occasion was a calculus exam during my freshman year in college for which I somehow had managed not to study. Looking back, it was a minor event, but that day it loomed enormous.

I still remember the room I marched to that spring morning, with feelings of doom and foreboding heavy in my heart. I had been in that lecture hall for many classes: history, humanities, physics. It was a large amphitheater with bolted-in wooden straight-backed chairs, each with a fold-up arm for note-taking. Its large windows looked out over a vista of hills and woods. I had gazed out those windows, lost in thought, while one professor or another droned on about the Carthaginians, Henry James, or Planck's constant.

This morning, though, I noticed nothing through the windows and did not see the hall at all. My gaze shrank to the patch of floor directly in front of me as I made my way to a seat near the door. I don't recall looking up as the tests were handed down the rows, as I folded out the arm, as I opened the blue cover of my exam book.

There was a smell of old lacquer from the wooden floors, there was the thump in my ears of heartbeat, there was the taste of anxiety in the pit of my stomach. There was the blank page of the exam book.

I looked at the exam questions, once, quickly. Hopeless. For an hour I stared at that page, the green lines thinly etched on white. My mind raced over the events that had brought me there, unready, and over the consequences I would suffer. The same thoughts repeated themselves over and over, a tape loop of fear and trembling.

I sat motionless, like an animal frozen in mid-move by curare. My hand held its pencil poised, but still. My eye studied the blank exam page, straying nowhere else.

What strikes me most about that dreadful moment was how constricted my mind became. I did not spend the hour in a desperate attempt to patch together some semblance of answers to the test. I did not daydream. I simply sat fixated on my terror, waiting for the ordeal to finish.

At the hour's end I rose, a zombie, leaving my blank exam book still open on the fold-up arm.

Anxiety is cognitive static. The essence of anxiety is the intrusion of distress into physical and mental channels that should be clear. A nagging worry invades sleep, keeping one awake half the night. A persistent fear imposes itself into one's thoughts, distracting from the business at hand. When anxiety crescendoes into panic, as happened to me during that calculus exam, its intensity completely captures thought and action.

Anxiety is a particular blend of emotion and cognition. It melds the arousal pattern of the emergency response with the cognition of threat. The forms of anxiety are multiple, for it expresses a complex melange of biological and cognitive events, any one of which can manifest itself most prominently as the key symptom. A mental preoccupation is, in this sense, the functional equivalent of heart palpitations. Both signal the same underlying dynamic, a stress response run amok.

It is not danger, but rather the *threat* of danger, which most often primes the stress response. The central characteristic of the information that signals stress is uncertainty. Uncertainty calls forth an early warning, an alert to check for the possibility that a threat looms. A stirring in the bushes may or may not be a predator. But those small primates that startled into action at the first stir were the ones whose descendants have survived to write books about it.

In the most general case, anything new or novel, anything unfamiliar or out of the routine, bears scrutiny, if only in passing. The new, by definition, is unknown; novelty is the essence of uncertainty, which in turn is the harbinger of possible threat.

The brain confronts novelty by calling the stress response into readiness (but not total engagement)—just in case. The stress response has a dual link to attention: Attention triggers that response in the first place, and attention centers are in turn activated by the stress alert. If the possibility of threat is confirmed, then the stress response will go into high gear.[9] The exhilaration of the new and novel can be traced to this neural hookup: novelty gears the body to act by engaging a low-grade arousal.

The universal response to novelty in animal species is the

"orienting response," a combination of increased brain activity, sharpened senses, and heightened attention. The quiet alertness of a cat watching a bird indicates orienting. So does the person straining to hear if a strange sound by the window is a burglar or the cat.

If the event that triggers the orienting response registers as familiar and nonthreatening (it's just the cat), then the brain and body subside into a lower state of arousal. But if the information registers as threatening (burglar!), then orienting leads to a stress response.

The degree of brain arousal depends on how great the mismatch is between what is expected and what found. When events are routine, the hippocampus—a center in the midbrain—keeps the level of arousal low; events are noted and taken into account, but with evenmindedness. The hippocampus registers familiar stimuli without the rest of the brain having to orient to it. It does the drudge work of handling the mundane routines of life.

An account of the neurology of attention describes the hippocampus's role in these terms: [10]

> When welcoming someone at our doorstep, we need not consciously process the walls, door frame, etc.—but these inputs to our senses nonetheless guide our behavior. Should an earthquake occur, we immediately *pay* attention to these previously unheeded stimuli.

The importance of the hippocampus in these cases can be seen when it has been surgically removed. Then, "every environmental change takes on earthquake proportions. . . . Inputs intrude, distract, and so disrupt the active encoding processes . . . that guide behavior." The hippocampus, then, keeps the brain from making every event an emergency, and keeps the routine from intruding on awareness.

In the stress response, part of the brain circuit that triggers the ACTH release is via pathways that ascend from the brain stem through the hippocampus.[11] These pathways prime attention as well. The net effect is that attention and stress arousal are intertwined: some stress steroids are released whenever the brain rouses attention above a certain threshold.

The total bath of brain chemicals in the stress response elegantly prepares a person to deal with danger. In early evolution, this meant either fight or flight. After the danger passed, the body could relax. But with the advent of civilization, neither fight nor flight are called for with any regularity, if at all. More often than not, we are left to stew in these juices.

As pain enters the psychological domain, its source becomes

more abstract and diffuse. A lion's bite is specific; it can be dealt with decisively: flee, or, if trapped, flood the brain with endorphins. But mental pain is elusive. Financial woes, an uncommunicative spouse, existential angst—none of these stressors necessarily yields to a single simple solution. Neither fight nor flight is satisfactory; the fight could make matters worse, the flight even more so.

While stress arousal is a fitting mode to meet emergency, as an ongoing state it is a disaster. Sustained stress arousal leads to pathology: anxiety states or psychosomatic disorders such as hypertension. These diseases are end products of the stress response, the cost of an unrelenting readiness for emergency.

That response is in reaction to the perception of threat. Tuning out threat is one way to short-circuit stress arousal. Indeed, for those dangers and pains that are mental, selective attention offers relief. Denial is the psychological analogue of the endorphin attentional tune-out. I contend that denial, in its many forms, is an analgesic, too.

ANXIETY IS STRESS OUT OF PLACE

Anxiety is the extreme end of the ordinary continuum of arousal. Grappling with a tough mental problem or returning a tennis serve both activate arousal. This increased arousal is fitting and useful; such tasks require extra mental and physical reserves.

But when the arousal does not fit the task at hand—more particularly, when it is too great—then it becomes anxiety. In anxiety, arousal that might be fitting for confronting a given threat intrudes into another situation, or occurs at such a high pitch that it sabotages an appropriate response.

During an anxiety state, attention can cling to the source of threat, narrowing the range of awareness available for other things. The narrowing of attention under stress is amply documented. For example, in a classic study volunteers were put through a simulated deep-sea dive in a pressure chamber.[12] The dive, done under water, was dramatic, with real changes in pressure and oxygen. Because of the oxygen changes there were some actual, but minor, dangers involved, and the volunteers learned some emergency procedures. During the dive simulation, the volunteers had to perform a central tracking task and at the same time monitor a flashing light. As the dive proceeded and the volunteers got more and more anxious, they could continue with the central task, but lost track of the light.

The notion that anxiety narrows attention is not new. Samuel Johnson said it pithily: "Depend upon it, Sir, when a man knows he is to be hanged in a fortnight, it concentrates his mind wonderfully."

When the stress response drives attention, it focuses on the threat at hand. This is fine when attention and bodily arousal are poised to deal with a threat and dispatch it on the spot. But stress situations in modern life rarely allow for that option. Most often we have to continue with life as usual while dealing with some ongoing situation of threat: carry on at work during a drawn-out marital fight, do the taxes despite a child's worrisome illness.

Attention primed to focus on a threat dominates even when other matters should be more pressing; thoughts of the threat intrude out of turn. The operational definition of anxiety is, in fact, this very intrusion.

The role of intrusion in anxiety is most thoroughly described by the psychiatrist Mardi Horowitz.[13] "Intrusion," Horowitz writes, refers to "unbidden ideas and pangs of feeling which are difficult to dispel, and of direct or symbolic behaviorial reenactments of the stress event." This squares well with an attentional definition of anxiety: unbidden thoughts and feelings impinge on awareness.

Horowitz showed how anxiety impinges on awareness with a simple experiment. He had groups of volunteers watch one of two stressful films—one showing ritual circumcision among teenage Aborigines, the other depicting bloody accidents in a woodworking shop (both are mildly horrifying)—as well as a neutral film of a man jogging.

After seeing the films, the volunteers undertook a task in which they rated whether a tone was higher, lower, or the same as the preceding tone. This task, though boring, demands a focused, sustained vigilance. Between segments of tones, the volunteers wrote a report of what had been on their mind during the task.

Not surprisingly, the volunteers reported far more intruding film flashbacks during the tone task after seeing the films on circumcision or accidents than after the film about running. The more people were upset by the films, the more intrusions.

Based on a detailed investigation of dozens of patients with stress-based symptoms, Horowitz has been able to enumerate many of the guises and disguises anxious intrusions take. His list is wide-ranging and particularly instructive: every one of the varieties of intrusions is some aspect of the stress response carried to an extreme. These include:[14]

- *Pangs of emotion*, waves of feeling that well up and subside rather than being a prevailing mood.
- *Preoccupation and rumination*, a continual awareness of the stressful event that recurs uncontrollably, beyond the bounds of ordinary thinking through of a problem.
- *Intrusive ideas*, sudden, unbidden thoughts that have nothing to do with the mental task at hand.
- *Persistent thoughts and feelings, emotions or* ideas which the person cannot stop once they start.

- *Hypervigilance*, excessive alertness, scanning and searching with a tense expectancy.
- *Insomnia*, intrusive ideas and images that disturb sleep.
- *Bad dreams*, including nightmares and anxious awakening, as well as any upsetting dream. The bad dream does not necessarily have any overt content related to a real event.
- *Unbidden sensations*, the sudden, unwanted entry into awareness of sensations that are unusually intense or are unrelated to the situation at the moment.
- *Startle reactions*, flinching or blanching in response to stimuli that typically do not warrant such reactions.

Anxiety, as this list shows, can intrude in many forms apart from the obvious. Whatever its guise, when anxiety swamps attention, all performance suffers. The antidote at hand, as we shall see, is attention itself—more precisely, *dis*attention, or denial. To see how denial can erase anxiety, we need first to understand the key role of cognition in the stress response, particularly the cognition of threat.

THREAT IS WHERE YOU SEE IT

A tiny cable car wobbles swiftly over the steep ravines leading up to a peak in Poland's Tatra Mountains. Inside a dozen people are packed tightly, including a traveler who describes the various reactions:[15]

> To the old Polish grandmothers with babushkas on their heads, it seems just another weekend distraction. To three or four young children in the car it is high adventure. To my wife, who shudders even at the tram ride to Roosevelt Island in New York City, it is very nearly heart-stopping. And to the conductor, of course, it is all too familiar even to pay attention; he sits by a terrifyingly open window and reads his newspaper.

Events are what one makes of them. What delights a child bores the conductor; what is a bother to a grandmother strikes terror in a Manhattanite. How one construes events determines whether or not they will be stressful. This is a major tenet of an especially instructive view of stress and how people cope with it, a model developed by Richard Lazarus, a psychologist at Berkeley.

Stress, in his view, occurs when the demands of the environment in a person's eyes exceed his resources. The operative phrase is "in the person's eyes." It is not just that an event is in and of itself overwhelming; whether it is so or not depends on how the person construes it. A given event—divorce, job loss, childbirth—can be seen as a threat, as a challenge, or as a relief, depending on the person's circumstances, attitudes, and sense of resources.

The nature of threat is highly subjective. It is not the event *per se*, but its meaning that matters. When events are *seen* as threats, the stress response is triggered. Stress is the product of a cognitive act, appraisal.

Once a person has defined a situation as a potential threat, his stress response will fluctuate with his appraisal. For example, in Lazarus's lab, students in an experiment sat waiting for an electric shock for periods varying from 30 seconds to 20 minutes.[16] Stress varied with how threatening the student found the situation:[17]

> For example, one minute was long enough for the subject to assimilate the threatening idea that he was going to feel pain when the shock came, but not long enough to develop doubts about the threat. However, if the subject had five minutes to think about it, he began to reflect on or reappraise the situation, saying to himself, for example, "A college professor surely would not expose me to severe pain," or "I had a shock before in a laboratory and it was hardly anything to worry about." At 20 minutes, the dimensions . . . changed. Subjects commonly began to feel anxious, perhaps thinking that so long a wait must portend something of major import.

Such rumination, alternating reassurance with worry, is familiar to us all. No matter the specifics of the matter at hand, the substance of such private monologues boils down to: How much of a threat is this? The search for that answer engages the orienting response. Depending on the answer at a given moment, the orienting mechanism will elevate or dampen the stress response accordingly.

As Figure 1 shows, an event leads to the stress response only if it is appraised as a threat. That appraisal starts a spiral, where events that might otherwise have been seen as neutral take on the negative flavoring that anxiety lends, biasing their appraisal. The mechanism can be seen at work in an anxiety attack of the sort

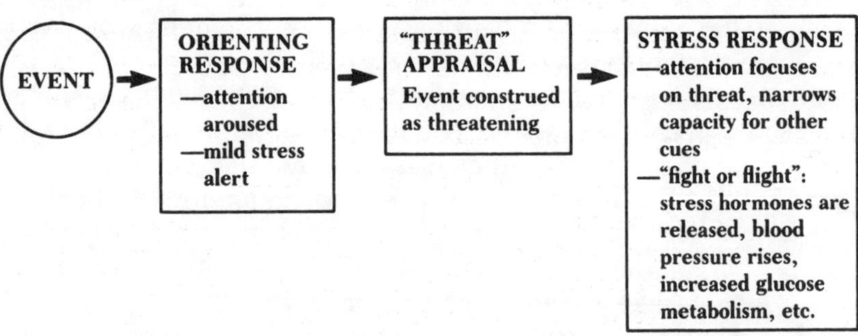

FIGURE 1. Prelude to the stress response: A novel event evokes an orienting response, which is appraised as threatening. That appraisal triggers the stress response.

Aaron Beck, a psychiatrist, describes in one of his patients, a forty-year-old man who was brought to an emergency room in Denver in an acute state of distress, and whose severe anxiety continued after he returned home to Philadelphia:[18]

> . . . He recalled that, when he had reached the top of the ski lift, he noticed he was short of breath (this was probably due to the rarefied atmosphere). He remembered having had the thought that his shortness of breath might be a sign of heart disease. He then thought of his brother who had had shortness of breath and had died of a coronary occlusion a few months previously. As he considered the thought of having a coronary occlusion more seriously, he became increasingly anxious. At this point, he began to feel weak, perspired a great deal, and felt faint. He interpreted these symptoms as further evidence that he was having a heart attack and was on the verge of death. When examined at the emergency room, he was not assured by the normal electrocardiogram because he believed "the disease might not have shown up yet on the test."

Had he not been in a state of stress arousal, preoccupied by his worries about heart disease, the man might have been able at some point to reappraise his initial reaction as a normal response to high altitude, not a sign of heart attack. But his continued anxiety led him to read every piece of information as confirming the appraisal of threat. Only weeks later, when Beck pointed this out and the patient was able to see that his "heart attack" was a false alarm, did his anxiety abate.

Reappraisal is often relied on to vanquish a threat. If the threat can be reappraised as a nonthreat (the fire alarm was only a drill; the letter from the IRS was a refund, not an audit notice), then the stress arousal that accompanied that appraisal ceases. We remind ourselves that the plunging roller coaster is only an amusement ride, that a scary scene is only a movie. A famous instance of a scene that calls for the latter reappraisal is in Luis Buñuel's early surrealist short *Un Chien Andalou*, in the scene in which a young woman's eye is sliced open with a razor blade. A reviewer writes:[19]

> People still gasp when this scene is shown. There is no way of reducing the intimacy of its violence. The fact that the same young woman appears soon after in the film, both eyes happily intact, and the fact that the sliced eye on inspection can be seen to be that of an animal . . . are not as consoling as we might hope. I don't gasp anymore, but I do have to sit tight in the cinema, energetically reminding myself that the eye being sliced is *not* the woman's, that it is neither human nor alive.

Appraisal begins at the initial instant of orienting and initiates a chain of cognition aimed at finding the most finely tuned response. When reappraisal fails—the threat does not evaporate—then other strategies are needed.

THE SERENITY TO ACCEPT THE THINGS I CANNOT CHANGE

In 1962 the psychiatrist Robert Lifton spent several months in Hiroshima doing intensive interviews of *hibakusha*, survivors of the A-bomb:[20]

> I found the completion of these early interviews left me profoundly shocked and emotionally spent. . . . But very soon—within a few days, in fact—I noticed that my reactions were changing. I was listening to descriptions of the same horrors, but their effect upon me lessened. I concentrated upon recurrent patterns I was beginning to detect in these responses, that is, upon my scientific function, and while I by no means became insensitive to the suffering described, a more comfortable operating distance between *hibakusha* and myself quickly developed. This distance was necessary, I came to realize, not only to the intellectual but the emotional demands of the work.

Lifton, a psychoanalyst, recognizes his response as "psychic closing off," a form of coping. Technically speaking, "coping" is the term for a range of cognitive maneuvers that relieve stress arousal by changing one's own reaction rather than altering the stressful situation itself.

A homily used by Alcoholics Anonymous bespeaks the two main coping alternatives: "God grant me the serenity to accept the things I cannot change, the courage to change the things I can, and the wisdom to know the difference." One can take some action to remove the threat—call the insurance agent, get to the emergency room, pay the overdue bill. Or, one can try to calm oneself.

Lazarus refers to the first of these alternatives as "instrumental" and the second as "emotion-focused" coping. Instrumental coping is straightforward: there is something one can do to remove the threat. In the primal situation, that action typically was fight or flight. In the modern world, such options are rare.

More often than not, the person is left to handle a situation that is ambiguous, uncertain, and ongoing. When the appraisal of threat has led to a stress response, this means he is stewing, both in the brain's stress hormones and in his worries about the threat. That stew is what we call anxiety.

While a threat can call forth any of a range of emotions, from anger to depression, anxiety is the most pervasive reaction. Emotional coping generally means calming anxiety. If anxiety goes unallayed, it will intrude on attention in one or another of the many guises Horowitz describes.

Those intrusions can interfere with the whole range of cognition, in ways we will investigate later in more detail. For now, it will suffice to point out that anxiety spews cognitive static, which makes reappraisal difficult. Anxiety itself can hamper the reappraisal that might allay the sense of threat.

If reappraisal fails, one or another form of denial may work. In the natural course of recovery from a devastating event like the death of a loved one or loss of a job, there seems to be a spontaneous oscillation between denial and intrusion. Mardi Horowitz, the psychiatrist who enumerated the varieties of intrusion, proposes that following any serious life event, intrusion and denial come and go in ways that suggest basic phases of adjustment.

Horowitz offers as extensive a list for the varieties of denial as he did for intrusion. The forms of denial include:[21]

- *Avoided associations*, short-circuiting expected, obvious connections to the event that would follow from the implications of what is said or thought.
- *Numbness*, the sense of not having feelings; appropriate emotions that go unfelt.
- *Flattened response*, a constriction of expectable emotional reactions.
- *Dimming of attention*, vagueness or avoidance of focusing clearly on information, including thoughts, feelings, and physical sensations.
- *Daze*, defocused attention that clouds alertness and avoids the significance of events.
- *Constricted thought*, the failure to explore likely avenues of meaning other than the obvious one at hand; an abbreviated range of flexibility.
- *Memory failure*, an inability to recall events or their details; a selective amnesia for telling facts.
- *Disavowal*, saying or thinking that obvious meanings are not so.

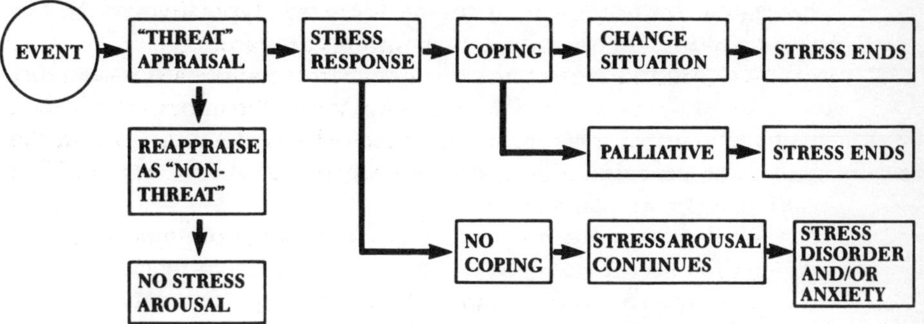

FIGURE 2. Options for short-circuiting stress: If an event appraised as a threat can be reappraised as a non-threat, the stress reaction will not begin. Once begun, the coping options are external—change the situation to make the event no longer a threat—or internal—soothe the arousal. If these fail or are not tried, stress arousal can lead to stress-based diseases and/or anxiety states.

- *Blocking through fantasy*, avoiding reality or its implications by fanciful thoughts of what might have been or could be.

The operative principle that unites these forms of denial is that they all betoken a way of blanking from awareness a troubling fact. These tactics are countermoves to the intrusions listed previously. Denial and intrusion are the two sides of attention, the one an avoidance, the other an invasion. Neither is healthy; both skew attention. While the multiple forms of denial do not lead to a more realistic appraisal of what is actually happening, they can be powerful antidotes to anxiety.

Lazarus lumps such intrapsychic maneuvers with taking drugs or drinking to ease anxiety. All are palliatives: they reduce anxiety without changing the status of the threat an iota. Such a strategy, says Lazarus, is normal: "For many serious sources of stress in life, there's little or nothing that can be done to change things. If so, you're better off if you do nothing except take care of your feelings . . . healthy people use palliatives all the time, with no ill effect. Having a drink or taking tranquilizers are palliatives. So is denial, intellectualizing, and avoiding negative thoughts. When they don't prevent adaptive action, they help greatly." [22]

Palliatives are intrinsically rewarding, just by virtue of their easing anxiety. What is rewarding is habit-forming. There is ample proof that a person's palliative of choice, whether Valium or Jack Daniels, can be addictive. So also, I contend, are the mental maneuvers on which we rely to ease our private anxieties.

The cognitive palliatives fall, by and large, within the range of what Freud describes as "defense mechanisms." The potency of the defenses is in their allaying anxiety. As Lazarus points out, palliatives are the norm; all healthy people use them to some degree. But as Freud observed, all normal people use defense mechanisms to a degree, too.

Mental palliatives skew one's ability to see things just as they are: that is, to attend clearly. When anxiety is at large in the mind, even if capped by an artful mental maneuver, there is a cost to mental efficiency. Denial compromises full, unflinching attention.

We have only recently begun to know enough about the mind as a processor of information to understand how anxiety and the defenses we erect to contain it operate, and the mental cost of their operations. To comprehend the dimensions of that cost, we must first look at the contemporary model of the mind at work. Then we can use that model to analyze the trade-off between anxiety and attention, and the self-deceit that trade-off promotes.

PART TWO

The Machinery of Mind

FREUD'S MODEL OF THE MIND

As was the case for so many ideas in psychology, the first to anticipate a contemporary view of the mind's mechanics was Sigmund Freud. In 1900, in the seventh chapter of *The Interpretation of Dreams*, Freud set forth a model of how the mind handles information.[1] Freud's model is remarkable in how well it anticipates what has become—over the intervening three-quarters of a century—our best understanding of the processes through which the mind takes in, uses, and stores information, and how those processes are prone to bias by the trade-off between anxiety and attention.

There is a series of way stations in Freud's model. The two he posits at the outset and end are in keeping with the physiology of his day, which had as a recent triumph mapped the neural basis of the reflexes. The reflexive stimulus-response sequence was well accepted and widely known, and Freud borrowed it. The first point in Freud's psychic apparatus was "Perception," the point at which the mind takes in sensory stimuli. The last point was motor activity, the "Response."

This simple sequence from sensory to motor end is akin to the "stimulus-response" of the reflex arc, which became the working model of behavior for behaviorists from Pavlov on. Pavlov and Freud could have agreed about the nature of behavior if Freud had stopped there. The behaviorists, however, went on to regard everything in between stimulus and response as a "black box," impervious to scientific observation, and so unworthy of learned conjecture. But that terrain was Freud's favored domain. Dauntless, he filled in the spaces in the black box between stimulus and response.

The psychic apparatus, said Freud, has a sense of direction; as we would say now, information "flows" (see Figure 3). In

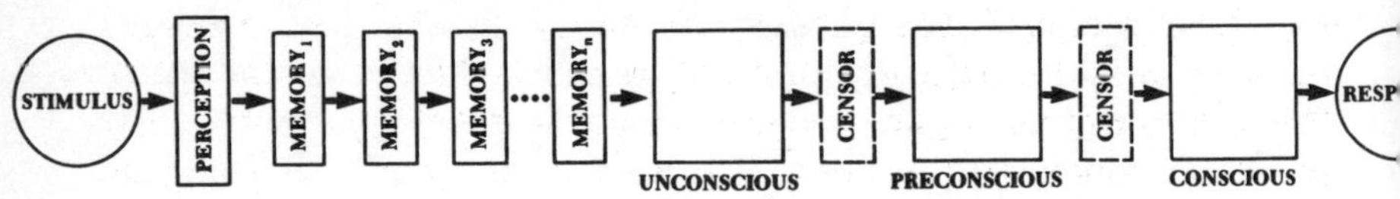

FIGURE 3. Freud's model of the mind, adapted from *The Interpretation of Dreams:* Information is sorted through various memory sub-systems, then finally passed on from the unconscious and preconscious, through censors, to consciousness. A response may follow.

Freud's model, information flows linearly, from initial sensation to final response. As it passes through the mind, information is not merely transmitted—it is transformed. What the eye senses is an array of waves; what the ear senses is a form of vibration. By the time sight and sound become memory, they have gone through radical changes in the kind of information they embody.

At each point in the transmission of information, there is selection; some aspects of what has been received are not passed on, while others survive. From perception, the first way station, information moves to a first "Memory System." This memory, though, is quite fleeting. $Memory_1$, as we might call it, transforms sensations into memory simultaneously with their registering, and passes them on almost immediately.

Freud's prescience is exemplified in his positing a perceptual capacity that has no memory of its own, takes fleeting note of the sensory world, but stores no lasting impressions. He saw that the functions of *receiving* sensory signals and *registering* them are separate, a fact later borne out by the neurophysiology of the sensory cortex. It was not until 1960 that his description of perception found a scientific basis with the experimental discovery of what we today call "sensory storage," a fleeting, immediate impression of our sensory world.

$Memory_1$ passes its information on to a subsequent chain of numerous such memory systems, as shown in Figure 1. These memories, said Freud, are unconscious. We are not aware of them until a later stage in the flow of information. Nevertheless, he contends, they can have effects on us while they remain out of our awareness:[2] "What we describe as our 'character' is based on the memory-traces of our impressions; and, moreover, the impressions which have had the greatest effects on us—those of our earliest youth—are precisely the ones which scarcely ever become conscious."

For a memory to rise into awareness in Freud's model of the mind, it must pass from a memory system into the realm he labelled the "Unconscious." The unconscious has no direct access to awareness. Material from the unconscious passes next to the realm called the "Preconscious." The preconscious is the gateway to awareness, or "Consciousness" in Freud's model. If the mental energy invested in a thought in the preconscious becomes strong enough, then it will burst into consciousness and become the focus of attention.

This passage is a perilous one. If the thoughts coming into awareness are neutral, fine. But if they are in some sense "forbidden," then, said Freud, they are likely to be tampered with as they pass from the unconscious through the preconscious and on to consciousness.

At this juncture in the mind, Freud saw, there are censors of sorts at work. Particularly during our waking hours, censors bar forbidden thoughts from consciousness. But during the night, the censors can be bypassed. Freud formulated this model of mind to explain how dreams express embargoed information. In dreams, Freud felt, forbidden thoughts leak through to consciousness in disguised forms.

No information, said Freud, gets from the unconscious into awareness without passing through censors. It is at this point that material which would arouse anxiety is filtered out. The memories may be quite recent or from long ago—a wilting glance a child has just received from her mother or a chain of hurtful looks a woman recalls from a childhood long past. Whichever the case, it is at this point that the flow can be impeded in the service of keeping threatening facts and ideas from awareness.

There are two sorts of censors, in Freud's view. The first selects out unwanted memories from entering the preconscious. A second, between the preconscious and the conscious mind, serves as a backup. Although threatening information may have leaked into the preconscious, and thus may stand on the fringe of awareness, the second censor can still weed out facts not easily faced.

Modern research shows that, if anything, Freud was too cautious in proposing points where biases could sidetrack the flow of information. What he did not realize is that the flow of information is not linear, but is intertwined among mutually interactive subsystems. The mind does not pass information along a single track, like a train going from town to town. Rather, information flows in and about circuits that loop like New York City subways or Los Angeles freeways. The possibilities for bias in such a system are even richer than Freud's model suggests.

Nevertheless, his model makes several key points, all now accepted in the contemporary view, each of which offers insights into how the mind can skew attention:

- Information flows, and is transformed during its passage, between interlinked subsystems.
- Information is unconscious before it is conscious.
- Filters and censors select and distort information.

THE INTELLIGENT FILTER

What words do these fragments suggest to you?

s_x
shi_
f_ _k

Reading these, you should have no trouble completing them, more likely than not, as suggestive or off-color words. But imagine yourself in a room with a stranger, repeating aloud the words you make of these fragments. Your responses might take another turn, if only to avoid embarrassment. Your thoughts might, too.

Over more than two decades following World War II, researchers conducted a gargantuan number of studies to test ways in which what one perceives can be muted or heightened depending on its emotional salience. Several hundred published studies dealt with this question, for the most part without resolving anything. The problem was not so much with the studies themselves, as with the then-current understanding of how the mind processes information.[3]

Take the words in the list above. If I ask you to complete the fragments and you tell me they represent the words "six," "shin," and "fork," I can surmise that you either did not allow yourself to *perceive* the more suggestive alternatives, or that you suppressed *reporting* them to me. In more technical terms, the question is one of the locus of bias: is it in perception or in response?

If the bias was in your response, then I can assume the suggestive words first came to mind but you quickly thought of more acceptable alternatives. But if the bias was in your original perception and you *never* were aware of the suggestive words, your mind somehow engineered its censorship outside your awareness.

The implications for how the mind's workings are orchestrated are quite different for each of these alternatives. Bias in response suggests that this is merely an instance of social dissembling—nothing very startling. But a bias in perception implies an unconscious center at work in the mind, imposing its judgments on all we perceive, shaping our experience to fit its priorities.

For many years these two possibilities vied with each other as mutually exclusive alternatives. An exhaustive review in 1966 of two decades of experimental results pro and con was unable to resolve the debate.[4] The reviewer's conclusion, after failing to settle the battle, was a conciliatory suggestion: since the two possibilities are not incompatible, perhaps, just perhaps, both may be correct. There may be censors in perception as well as in response.

That suggestion fits well with what is today the commonly accepted view of how information moves—and fails to move—through the mind.

There was a half-century lapse before experimental psychologists seriously addressed the proposals Freud made in the seventh chapter of *The Interpretation of Dreams*. From the 1920s on, the ascendancy of behaviorism made what went on within the mind a taboo topic for most psychologists. When the mechanics of mind finally re-entered psychological research, one immediate impetus was most unlikely: the rise of aviation.

The next major volley in the debate over how the mind handles information was fired in 1958 by Donald Broadbent, a British psychologist.[5] His interests were very different from Freud's. Broadbent worked with the British Royal Navy in the years after World War II. Because of the explosive growth of aviation in that era, the volume of air traffic beseiged controllers. The controllers, Broadbent realized, took in far more information through their eyes and ears than they could deal with. He wondered just how the mind sorted out this barrage.

Broadbent, like Freud, used a flow chart to describe how the mind handles information. His chart showed that people receive more data through the senses than they can handle (see Figure 4). This information gets to a short-term store—akin to the sensory store—and then flows on to a "selective filter," where most of it is weeded out. This filter somehow blocks all but those messages that merit fuller attention. The passage is seemingly instantaneous. But the few thousandths of a second it takes allow ample time for the mind to sort through the mass of data in sensory storage and filter out irrelevancies before the information passes into conscious awareness.

Broadbent assumed that the mind needs to filter the informa-

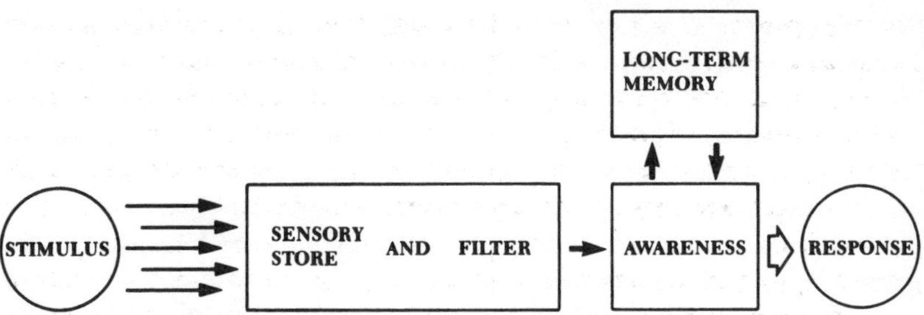

FIGURE 4. Broadbent's model of the mind, slightly modified: Sensory stimuli are analyzed as they reach the sensory store and sorted and filtered on their way to awareness (or short-term memory).

tion that impinges on it through the senses because it has only a limited capacity. The selective filter, he believed, is essential here because of a bottleneck: there is a sharply limited channel capacity at the next stage of processing, often called "short-term" or "primary" memory.

Primary memory is the region of perception that falls under the beam of attention. For our purposes we will call it "awareness." The contents of the zone of awareness are what we take to be "on our minds" at a given moment; it is our window onto the stream of consciousness. This zone is quite fragile, its contents fleeting.

The traffic between awareness and long-term memory is two-way, according to Broadbent's model; what is in long-term memory can be called into awareness, what is in awareness finds a place in memory. Only information that reaches awareness, he proposed, will be retained for very long—that is, we remember only what we first pay attention to. Awareness, then, is the gateway to memory, and a filter controls what enters awareness. But what controls the filter?

For Broadbent, only the gross physical aspects of a message—its loudness or brightness, say—determined whether it would get through, not its meaning. That view was put to rest soon after he proposed it by experiments on the "cocktail party effect." At a cocktail party or in a crowded restaurant there is typically a din of competing conversations, all carried on at high volume within earshot of the others.

Contrary to Broadbent's prediction, you don't hear simply the loudest voice. For example, if you are stuck listening to a bore recount the gruesome details of his last vacation, rocky relationship, or nearly consummated deal, it is easy to tune him out and tune in on a more interesting conversation nearby—particularly if you hear your own name mentioned. During the course of these tune-outs and tune-ins, the *sounds* coming to your ears may be identical in volume. What changes is the focus of your *attention*.

This means that information is scanned for *meaning* before it reaches the filter, contradicting Broadbent's assertion that the filter tunes in or out based solely on physical aspects of a message. The filter seems to have some intelligence; it is tuned by the importance to a person of the message.

This has major consequences for how the mind's architecture must be arranged. In order for an intelligent filter—one that reads meaning—to operate during the few moments of sensory storage, the arrangement of the mind's elements must be modified in a critical fashion. If the filter is intelligent, then there must be some circuit that connects the part of the mind that cognizes—that recognizes meanings—with the part that takes in and sorts through initial impressions. A simple, linear model such as Freud and Broadbent proposed would not work.

Meanings are stored in long-term memory. What is required is a *loop* between long-term memory and the earlier stages of information processing. That loop is shown in Figure 5. Such a feedback loop allows for the sensory store to sort its contents by drawing on the vast repertoire of experience, on the meanings and understandings built up over a life span, stored in long-term memory. The judgment "salient" or "irrelevant" can be made only on the basis of the knowledge in long-term memory. With access to the mind's lifelong store of experience, preferences, and goals, the filter can sift through the mass of impressions that assail it at each successive moment, and immediately tune in or out what matters.

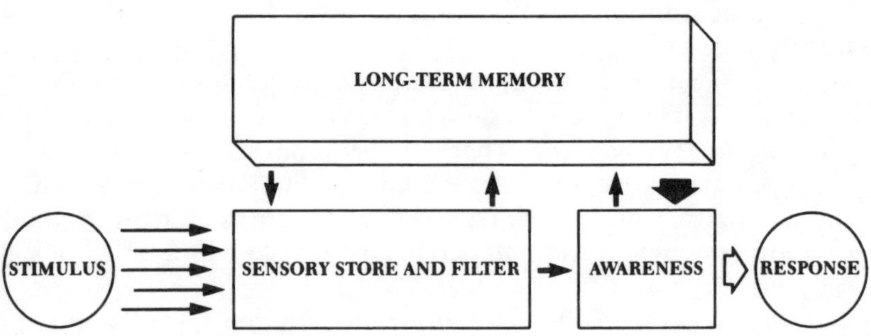

FIGURE 5. A simplified model of the mind, loosely adapted from Donald Norman: Memory screens perception at the earliest stage of information flow, filtering for salience what is allowed through to awareness.

Indeed, contemporary theorists now assume that information passing through the sensory store is subjected to scrutiny and filtered on the basis of its meaning and relevance. "Essentially," sums up Matthew Erdelyi, a cognitive psychologist, "long-term memory itself becomes the filter, deciding what to block from short-term storage (and therefore awareness), thereby determining indirectly what to accept for eventual storage in long-term memory itself."[6]

That means the contents of awareness come to us picked over, sorted through, and pre-packaged. The whole process takes a fraction of a second.

There are compelling reasons for this arrangement in the design of the mind. It is much to our benefit that the raw information that passes from sensory storage to awareness sifts through a smart filter. The region of consciousness would be far too cluttered were it not reached by a vastly reduced information flow. While the information in consciousness seems limited, it also seems to be the case that before getting there, that information—and an even vaster amount left behind, seemingly to evaporate—has gone through a massive amount of analysis.

The more thoroughly information in sensory storage can be sorted out, the more efficiently the next way station—awareness—can operate. If too much gets through, awareness is swamped; as we have seen, one such intrusion is anxiety. It is of critical import that this filter operate at a peak, in order to save us from continuous distraction by a mass of irrelevant information. If the filter were much less thorough we might literally be driven to distraction by distractions, as happens in schizophrenia.

The idea that information passes through an intelligent filter led to what has become the prevailing view of how information flows through the mind. The most commonly pictured flow chart was proposed by Donald Norman in 1968; Figure 5 is a simplified version of his model.[7] In this model what enters through the senses gets a thorough, automatic scan by long-term memory—specifically by "semantic" memory, the repository of meanings and knowledge about the world. For example, every bundle of sounds automatically is directed to an "address" in semantic memory that yields its meaning. If you hear the word "grunt," semantic memory recognizes its meaning; if you hear a grunt, semantic memory also recognizes that that sound is not a word.

All this filtering goes on out of awareness. What gets through to awareness is what messages have pertinence to whatever mental activity is current. If you are looking for restaurants, you will notice signs for them and not for gas stations; if you are skimming through the newspaper, you will notice those items that you care about. What gets through enters awareness, and only what is useful occupies that mental space.

Perception, says Norman, is a matter of degree. In scanning incoming information, semantic memory need not go into every detail; it need only sort out what is and is not relevant to the concern of the moment. Irrelevant information is only partly analyzed, if just to the point of recognizing its irrelevancy. What *is* relevant gets fuller processing. For example, if you casually scan a newspaper page and suddenly see your name, it will seem to "leap out" at you. Presumably the words you saw as you skimmed were partly processed and found irrelevant; your name—which is always relevant—rated full processing.

This model of the mind has several important implications. For one, it posits that information is screened by memory at every stage of its processing, and that memory scans information and filters it for salience. All this processing goes on *before* information enters awareness; only a small portion of the information available at a given moment filters through to consciousness.

That is not to say that attention is entirely passive. We can, after all, decide to scan for something, and so awareness can modify how the filter operates. But awareness does so indirectly, through the services of long-term memory: the activity of the filter is never directly evident to awareness. We can, however, bring information into awareness from long-term memory. There is two-way traffic, then, between awareness and long-term memory, but there is only one-way traffic between the filter and awareness. There is a very real sense in which long-term memory—the sum total of experience one has about life—has a more decisive say in the flow of information than we ordinarily realize.

HOW MUCH CAN WE KEEP IN MIND?

Certain blind people—sightless as the result of stroke or brain injury, rather than damage to the eye—can do a remarkable thing. If an object is put in front of them, they cannot say what or where it is. If they are asked to reach for the object, they will say it is impossible, since they cannot see it. But if they can be persuaded to *try*, they will find it with a sureness that amazes even themselves.

This uncanny ability is called "blindsight." It turns out these people have superb vision, but they don't *know* they can see, according to Anthony Marcel, a psychologist at Cambridge University who has done research on blindsight. Using a high-speed camera, Marcel tracked the precise vectors of the patients' arms, hands, and fingers as they reached for objects they could not consciously see. Their reach, analysis of the film showed, was quite precise.

What could account for this startling performance? The neurological understanding of blindsight is that the brain damage that has rendered these patients blind is confined to neural areas that play a role in awareness, not those areas that have to do with seeing per se. While their vision is fine, what their eye sees is never transmitted to the part of the brain that brings vision into awareness. Blindsight suggests a startling possibility about the mind: that one part may know just what it is doing, while the part that supposedly knows—that is, awareness—remains oblivious.

Other experimental work by Marcel shows that for normal people, too, the mind has the capacity to know *without awareness of what is known*. Marcel inadvertently made this discovery while studying how children read. He would flash words on a screen very rapidly, some so fast that they could not be read. When he asked the children to guess at the words, he was struck by a "clever mistake": some children would guess a word with a closely related meaning, such as "day" for "night."

Intrigued, Marcel began to study the phenomenon more methodically. He would flash words for just a few thousandths of a second—so quickly that people did not even know they had seen a word. Then he would ask his subjects which word in a subsequent pair meant or looked the same as the one that had just flashed by. If, for example, the unseen word was "book," the lookalike would be "look," the related word "read."

Even though his subjects had not the slightest idea what the first word had been, they were right in their guessing about 90 percent of the time—an astounding rate of accuracy for people who did not even know they were reading.

The results of these studies on what Marcel calls "unconscious reading" and on blindsight are inexplicable in terms of how we commonly think about the mind. But contemporary researchers have adopted a rather radical premise: that much or most consequential activity in the mind goes on outside awareness.

The tenability of this proposition hinges on two facts: the channel capacity of awareness—the amount it can hold at one time—and the ability of the mind to carry on its work unconsciously. Current wisdom in cognitive psychology puts the capacity for awareness at "seven, plus or minus two," which is the title of a famous article on the topic by George Miller.[8] Miller, basing his ideas on a detailed review of technical evidence, proposed that seven or so "chunks" of information were about all that could be held in short-term memory at one time. "Chunk" is the term used to describe a single unit of information. For example, in a seven-digit phone number, each digit is a chunk. Phone numbers of much more than that length—say ten or twelve digits—are hard to hold in mind unless they are rechunked, for instance by remembering an area code as a single unit (Manhattan as 212, Los Angeles 213).

A more current estimate, made by Herbert Simon, puts the capacity of short-term memory at five plus or minus two chunks—an even more restricted capacity. If awareness has that small a capacity, and if information must pass through this narrow channel in order to lodge in long-term memory, then this juncture is a massive information bottleneck. The offerings of information at the threshhold in sensory storage are overrich; the transfer from there to the pinched channel of awareness demands a massive filtering out of information.

But not all theorists agree that the mind must discard so much information. Some psychologists—notably Ulric Neisser—take exception to the idea that there is a necessary limit on capacity at all. Some of Neisser's ammunition was provided by Gertrude Stein.[9]

In the 1890s, before she became a literary figure in Paris, Gertrude Stein was a protégée of the psychologist William James at Harvard. Under James's tutelage, Stein, with her fellow student Leon Solomons as a collaborator, put the idea of channel capacity to a test—long before there was such a model in psychology.

Stein and Solomons were intrigued by automatic writing, an occult fad at the turn of the century. The automatic writer holds pencil to paper, and then waits for it to move as though on its own. No conscious effort is made; whatever writing comes forth presumably does so under the guidance of something other than one's conscious mind. If one has a psychological bent, the writing is seen as emanating from the person's unconscious mind. If one has an other-worldly bent, the writing is seen as a message from the spirit world.

Solomons and Stein acted as their own guinea pigs, resolving to teach themselves to write automatically. They began by copying words the other dictated, while simultaneously reading some other material. Solomons, for example, would read a story to himself while at the same time writing words dictated by Stein. Presumably reading a story occupied the conscious mind, leaving the act of writing the dictated words to some part of the mind beyond awareness.

This was a preliminary stage in training. Later they achieved the remarkable ability to play both parts simultaneously: Each would read aloud to the other—two different stories going at the same time—while each also copied down what the other was reading. From here they went on to automatic writing, where each would read a story aloud simply to avoid paying attention to what his or her hand was writing. Rather than taking dictation, the hand was free to write "automatically."*

The methodology of this experiment, done as it was by two undergraduates in the 1890s, was not strict by modern standards. Neisser, intrigued by the possibility that Stein and Solomons had stretched the limits of cognition, persuaded his graduate students Elizabeth Spelke and William Hirst to repeat that experiment some eighty years later. They hired two Cornell undergraduates to spend an hour a day for a semester doing what Stein had done. Each would read to himself short stories while an experimenter dictated words. The study was well controlled, in all the ways Stein's had not been. For example, each student would start a stopwatch when

* What this training may have meant for Ms. Stein's subsequent literary output can only be a matter of conjecture. Ulric Neisser, who reports details of the Stein/Solomons experiment, comments, "It turned out that what is written spontaneously under these conditions is not very interesting; at least it is not interesting to me. Gertrude Stein seems to have liked it."

he began reading the story and click it off when he finished, then take a written test to see how well he had followed the narrative.

At the outset, the students found it impossible to read and write at the same time. Their reading would go in stops and starts, with a halt while they copied each dictated word. The alternative is to read slowly and understand little. Neither worked well. Despite the difficulty at the start, the students mastered the task within six weeks. By the end they could read with good understanding while taking dictation without pause.

On the basis of this and later studies with various permutations of task demands, Neisser concluded that people can do two equally complex mental tasks at the same time. "Such an achievement," he notes, "challenges the traditional view that all complex activity involves a single channel with a limited capacity." At least in this instance, the bounds of attention seem stretchable.

Yes and no. A third view, offered by the cognitive psychologists Donald Norman and Tim Shallice, reconciles the Neisser objection to a limit on capacity with the Miller theory that the limit is fixed.[10] Norman and Shallice propose that the mind can process several *parallel* strands of information simultaneously. A few strands come within the band of awareness; the amount that can be handled there is limited. But an unknown—and large—number of strands operate out of awareness, never entering consciousness.

This view agrees with Miller that there is a fixed limit to the span of awareness. But it also allows for Neisser's contention that there is no fixed limit to the *total* amount of information the mind can handle. The necessary added assumption is simply that much goes on in the mind out of awareness.

Indeed, people perform a vast number of activities simultaneously: we drive while talking to a companion, listening to the radio, munching a hamburger, and reading freeway signs. We can do all these things so long as most of them are habitual, automatic sequences; these can go on outside awareness, since they need no attention allocated to them.

Donald Norman gives an apt description of how the split between conscious and unconscious activity operates:[11]

> As I sit at my typewriter writing these sentences, my conscious resources are devoted to determining the intention: I then watch over the words as they appear on the paper. I do give conscious guidance to the forms of the sentences and to their higher level structures. I sometimes select particular words that capture the concept I wish to express, and then hold those words in consciousness while the sentence builds up on the paper, constructing an ap-

> propriate scaffolding. I am not normally conscious of the actual selection of words, nor of the activity of typing. I listen to my "inner voice" speak the words. . . and I watch them appear on the typing paper.

This arrangement saves us from the petty details of our lives; we need not plan which key to type, where to put a foot for the next step, how much pressure to grasp a doorknob with, what word to say next. The unconscious mind takes care of it all. This frees awareness to make grander plans: *what* to write, *where* to go, *which* door to open, *what* nuance to get across. What the conscious mind decides and intends, the unconscious executes. But the unconscious can also execute its own intentions. To accommodate this fact, our model of the mind needs one more wrinkle. We need to add a pathway for information flow and the execution of response that bypasses awareness altogether.

Much of our life is lived on automatic. More often than not, so long as we are following routine, we don't even have to plan what to do; we do it automatically. We need to plan only when we deviate from routine. Norman gives an example: In deciding to pick up some fish on the way home from work, he says, "I must have 'fish store' active in mind at the time I pass the critical choice point between home and the store . . . Let 'fish store' lapse from memory at the critical junction and I am apt to find myself at home, fishless."

Norman has studied such moments in detail; he collected more than two hundred instances of what can be called "Post-Freudian slips": While cooking a meal, someone puts the salad in the oven and the cake in the refrigerator and leaves them there for several

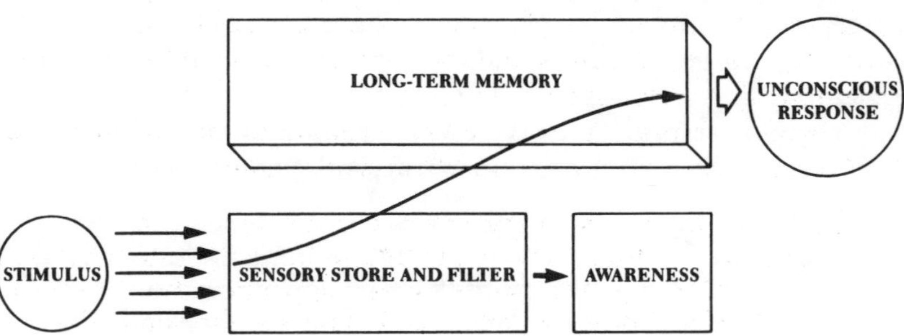

FIGURE 6. Flow of information in an automatic routine: From intake of perceived stimulus through execution of response, the entire sequence is outside awareness.

hours. A jogger comes in for a shower and throws his T-shirt in the toilet instead of the hamper. Someone says, "I want you to be me" instead of "you to be you." The car stops and the driver unbuckles his watchband instead of the seatbelt. Orange juice gets poured into the coffee cup. The sugar lid goes on the coffee cup instead of the sugar bowl.

These mistakes, says Norman, indicate that an automatic sequence has been executed incorrectly. The slip triggers attention to the sequence; it enters awareness for repair work. These mistakes are "post-Freudian" in the sense that they need not be motivated by hidden impulses. They occur by virtue of the errors and slippage that goes on in any complex system. Freud's collection of parapraxes are a subcategory of slips, less innocent and rarer than the errors Norman analyzes.

Learning to do something new requires full attention. It takes continual monitoring to absorb the task's requirement. The point of mastery comes when the task can be done without thinking about it, or with most of it on automatic. Once this information is encoded well in memory, the cues, events, and responses that it entails can go unnoticed as it is done.

Expertise, in this respect, is overlearning. The expert does not have to think about the steps that the novice stumbles over. That's why, when the former world chess champion José Capablanca was asked, "How many possibilities do you see on the board when you ponder a move?" his reply was, "One—the right one."

As long as things go swimmingly, we engage in innumerable mindless trains of activity. But when one of them gives us trouble, it taxes our capacity and we have to stop or slow down most of the others.

Slips demand that attention be reallocated to address the automatic routine that has fouled up. While the repair goes on, the zone of awareness is occupied by what is usually in the parallel unconscious channels. During this repair work, little or no conscious attention is available for allocation to other matters.

The reverse of this invasion of awareness by the automatic channels is the "absent minded professor" phenomenon, in which a person is so absorbed in conscious thought that little attention is available for automatic routines. For example, Einstein's wife, Elsa, used to bundle him up in his overcoat and see him off to the foyer to get on his boots, only to find him there half an hour later, lost in thought. But with most of us, when matters are routine and well-learned, the bounds of attention are quite elastic and the unconscious mind can handle them.

Emmanuel Donchin, a leading researcher in the study of cognitive psychobiology, puts it bluntly: [12] "The notion that information processing is largely pre-conscious or not available to awareness is so clear to me that it seems self-evident.

"There's a huge amount of evidence that when we encounter an event of any sort there's an enormous amount of very fast parallel processing along many multiple channels. These channels are activated in an obligatory fashion, without any conscious control.

"It goes on continually, with incredible rapidness. For example, in our research we find that the mind recognizes a word within the first 150 milliseconds of seeing it. But nothing shows up in awareness for another 100 milliseconds or so, if it shows up at all. Awareness is a limited capacity system. We don't know—and don't need to know—about most of the stuff the mind does. I have no idea how I search memory or how I get grammatically correct sentences out of my mouth. It's hard enough to handle the little you need to keep track of in awareness.

"Figuratively speaking, 99.9 percent of cognition may be unconscious. We'd be in terrible shape if everything were conscious."

In sum, much or most of what we do goes on out of awareness, guided by well-learned sequences. We reserve consciousness for particularly demanding tasks, or leave it as a free space for active attention, for thought and decision-making, or for the reverie that passes for consciousness during much of the waking day. "Consciousness," concludes a text on cognitive psychology,[13] "is the exception, not the rule . . . but by its very nature, conscious thought seems the only sort. It is not the only sort; it is the minority."

The model of mind that follows from these conclusions is almost complete. Still unexplained, though, is the intelligence that guides these unconscious routines, that selects and filters experience and defines the range of awareness. The assemblage of mental systems is rigged together in a machinelike fashion. Yet mental life is rich, pungent, and full. Where are the ghosts that enspirit this machine, that endow it with the qualities of a living mind?

THE PACKETS KNOWLEDGE COMES IN

Around the age of four, I had a vivid fantasy about the construction of reality.

I entertained the benignly paranoid notion that wherever I went and whatever I saw was made of stage sets, rather like Hollywood studio streets which from one side appear to be real and from another stand revealed as false fronts.

The houses, trees, cars, dogs, and people I passed on the street, I was sure, were props placed there just before I came on the scene, which vanished after I left. The rooms I entered likewise came into being and evaporated as I made my way through them.

This Herculean task was accomplished by some group or force outside my ken. I imagined a huge, unseen horde of workers feverishly—but silently—at work constructing these sets as I approached, and just as feverishly dismantling them and storing them away as I left. All this work was guided by hands I never could see directly, and with purpose and motives I never could know.

That childish fantasy, I have since come to realize, is a rather close metaphor for the workings of our minds.

The stuff of experience from moment to moment is concocted for us just beyond the periphery of awareness, in realms of mind which scan, select, and filter the array of information available from the senses and memory.

The pervasive illusion is that we dictate the scope and direction of awareness. The facts seem to be more akin to my childhood fantasy, in which the mind is arranged by unseen forces that operate to present us with a constructed reality, which we apprehend in its final, finished version. It is as though there were invisible stagehands erecting a set—the world around us and in us—in full intricate detail, moment to moment.

Who might be these tinkering presences within the mind, and where do they come from?

They are us—the "us" that accrues from the sum total of our life experience. "Experience is kaleidoscopic; the experience of every moment is unique and unrepeatable," writes James Britton in *Language and Learning*. "Until we can group items in it on the basis of their similarity we can set up no expectations, make no predictions: lacking these we can make nothing of the present moment."

Perception is interactive, constructed. It is not enough for information to flow through the senses; to make sense of the senses requires a context that organizes the information they convey, that lends it the proper meaning.

The packets that organize information and make sense of experience are "schemas," the building blocks of cognition.[14] Schemas embody the rules and categories that order raw experience into coherent meaning. All knowledge and experience is packaged in schemas. Schemas are the ghost in the machine, the intelligence that guides information as it flows through the mind.

Jean Piaget, the pioneer Swiss developmental psychologist, studied how schemas change as children grow. Cognitive development, Piaget saw, is cumulative; understanding grows out of what has been learned already.[15] We have become who we are, learned what we know, by virtue of the schemas we have acquired along the way. Schemas accrue with time; the schemas we have at a given point are the end product of our particular private history.

Piaget used the concepts "assimilation" and "accommodation" to describe how these mental structures are shaped by interaction with the world. As we learn, schemas change. For example, as a child growing up in California, I learned that trees with no leaves were dead. When I saw pictures of spooky-looking trees with no leaves, I took them to be dead. When I moved East, I discovered that trees lost their leaves when winter came, but that they weren't dead. I revised my schema accordingly: a tree is not necessarily dead, I realized, just because it has no leaves.

When someone fails to revise a schema to fit the facts, the resulting perceptions can be bizarre. To make the point Ulric Neisser tells the joke about a man who goes to a psychiatrist with the problem that he thinks he's dead.[16] After several sessions, the psychiatrist sees that the patient is firm in his delusion. So the psychiatrist says to him, "You've heard, of course, that dead men don't bleed."

The patient says, "Yes."

The psychiatrist takes a pin and jabs him in the arm so he bleeds. "What do you say now?" he asks.

The patient says, "Well, what do you know? Dead men *do* bleed."

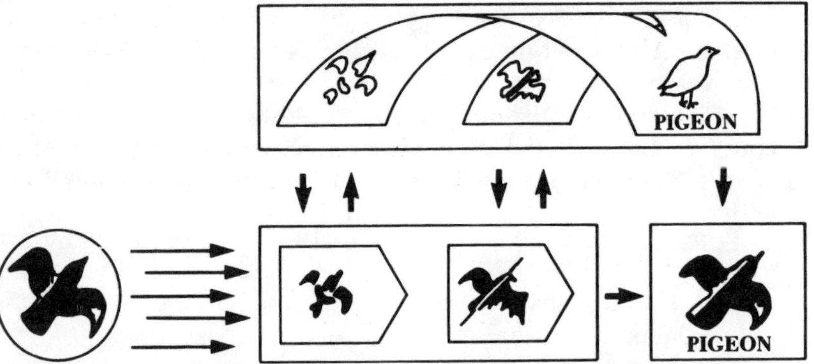

FIGURE 7. When the eye registers an impression, schemas instantly analyze its attributes, such as color and shape, and scan all possible meanings as it passes through the sensory store and filter. The one selected meaning—and appropriate perception—"pops" into awareness.

In a sense, a schema is like a theory, an assumption about experience and how it works. A schema, in the words of the cognitive psychologist David Rumelhart, is "a kind of informal, private, unarticulated theory about the nature of events, objects, or situations which we face. The total set of schemas we have available for interpreting our world in a sense constitutes our private theory of the naturc of reality."[17]

With schemas, we are able to go beyond the data given. If we see a car, we can assume that other attributes go with it—a steering wheel, gas tank, passenger seats, etc.—even though we may not apprehend those aspects directly. Like a theory, a schema embodies assumptions, which we take as givens with complete confidence. This lets us make interpretations that outstrip the immediate evidence from our senses. This cognitive shorthand lets us navigate our way through the ambiguity that is more often than not what we confront in the world.

Like theories, schemas are prone to revision. Our knowledge accrues by revising or adding schemas to our total store. Schemas are theories that test themselves. When an ambiguous situation arises, we adduce schemas to render it clear. Each schema we apply in a puzzling situation is automatically tested for aptness or fit.[18]

Most of the time we have complete confidence in the schemas we use. But when the fit is not quite right—say, when you think a face in the crowd is that of a friend, but aren't quite sure—then the schema's fit is tested against more evidence, just like a theory: could it be she? Would she be here now? As you get closer, does it still look like her? Does she move like her, wear the same kind of clothes? All these questions are small tests of the theory that "it is she."

Stereotypes are simply a variety of schema. The following account by Susan Fiske, a cognitive psychologist, of her stereotype of steel workers says much about the dynamics of schemas in general:[19]

> Since moving to Pittsburgh, I have encountered a new stereotype . . . a "mill hunk," that is, the prototypic steel worker. A mill hunk, so the stereotype runs, can be male or female but is invariably macho and raunchy regardless of gender. A mill hunk always drinks Iron City beer, watches every Steeler game, and wears a T-shirt in all weather. . . . My mill-hunk stereotype is stored as an abstracted generic example, not as a collection of all the steelworkers I have ever known, although the stereotype does contain specific examples too. I am likely to ignore information irrelevant to the stereotype . . . [and] I will tend to recall only consistent information—a mill hunk who reads *Hustler* magazine.

Schemas can deal with domains immense or minute; they act at all levels of experience, all degrees of abstraction. "Just as theories can be about the grand and the small," says Rumelhart,[20] "so schemas can represent knowledge at all levels—from ideologies and cultural truths to knowledge about what constitutes an appropriate sentence in our language to knowledge about the meaning of a particular word to knowledge about what patterns of [sound] are associated with what letters of the alphabet."

The notion of schemas is itself a schema. As such, it is the most promising account we have to explain to ourselves how we explain to ourselves. Schemas are the organizing dynamic of knowledge. To realize how they operate is to understand understanding.

UNDERSTANDING UNDERSTANDING

Schemas are the basic units of experience. Like molecules, they organize lesser elements into a workable whole. Only when experience is organized by schemas is it really useful; embedded in a schema is both an understanding of the experience it organizes, and information about how that knowledge is to be used.

Stephen Palmer, a student of Rumelhart and Norman, demonstrates the point with the hieroglyph below.

These are parts of a whole, but without knowing the context, there is no meaning. The lines suggest interpretations, but do not of themselves conjure a workable one. To understand the context that gives meanings to these parts, turn to page 80.

If you have turned the page to see the context for the lines above, you know them to be parts of a face. The face is immediately recognizable; its parts out of context are not. While the lines might suggest appropriate interpretations (the wiggly line could be a nose), and could eventually lead to you recognize the features of a face, it is much easier when the "face" schema organizes your perception of them.

As Gestalt psychologists have long told us, the whole is greater than its parts—it gives them meaning. Knowing that something is a "face" sets up a vast number of potential uses of that information. A network ties the schema for face to other kinds of information, such as faces of friends, skin care, attractiveness, facial expression,

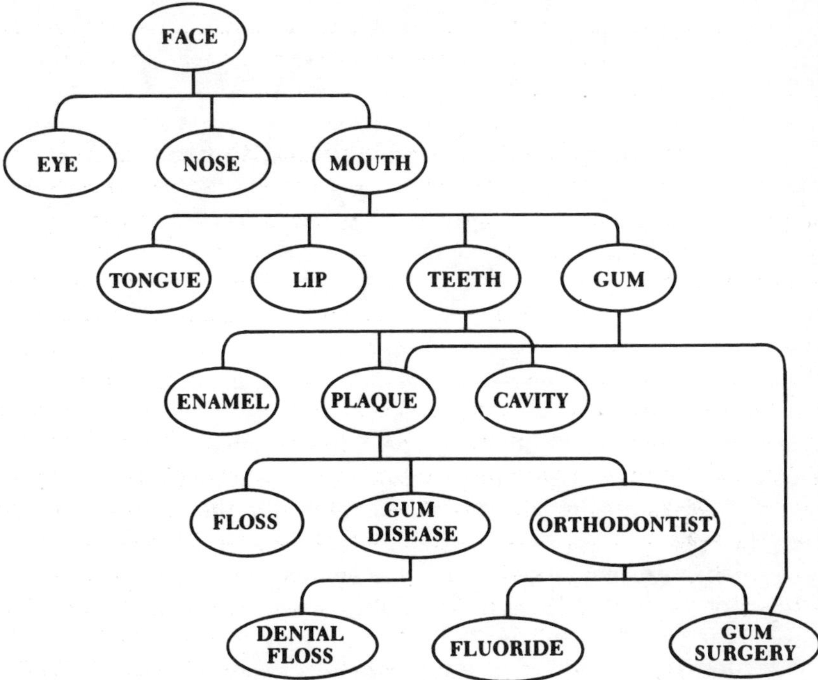

FIGURE 8. The train of thought runs through linked and embedded schemas. "Face," for example, might lead by association to thoughts of a coming dental appointment, linking the schemas shown above.

the colors of eyes. Each of these can, in turn, lead to myriad bits of information; as a schema activates, connected ones more readily activate. "Eye," for example, might tie into schemas such as "the time I first got glasses" "big eyes are sexy," "glaucoma is from pressure within the eyeball," and on and on. Fortunately, schemas attune their connections within the range of focus germane to the moment, neither straying too far afield nor staying too confined.

A schema is the skeleton around which events are interpreted; as events are complex and layered, so schemas are interlocked in rich combinations. A train of association is a roadmap through loosely connected schemas.

Schemas are the structures memories are stored in; the inventory of schemas that a person accumulates makes up the contents of his long-term memory.

Schemas and attention interact in an intricate dance. Active attention arouses relevant schemas; schemas in turn guide the

focus of attention. The vast repertoire of schemas lies dormant in memory, quiescent until activated by attention. Once active, they determine what aspects of the situation attention will track.

This interplay between attention and schemas puts them at the heart of the matter. Schemas not only determine what we will notice: they also determine what we do *not* notice. Consider the question Ulric Neisser poses: "There is always more to see than anyone sees, and more to know than anyone knows. Why don't we see it, why don't we bother to know it?"

The answer given by Freud and Broadbent, implicit in their models of mind, is that we filter experience so we see only what we need to see, know only what we need to know. Neisser's answer, however, is that it is not so much that we filter it out, as that we simply do not pick it up. In terms of our model, information not picked up drops out at the filter.

Our schemas choose this and not that; they determine the scope of attention. Take, for example, the simple act of looking. Do we really see what we look *at?* The best evidence is that we don't; instead, we see what we look *for*. Neisser makes the point with an elegant, straightforward demonstration. He made a videotape of four young men playing basketball. The tape lasts just one minute. About midway, an attractive young woman carrying a large white umbrella saunters through the game. She is on the screen for four full seconds.

Neisser would show the tape to visitors at his lab, who were asked to press a key whenever the ball was passed between players. When Neisser asked afterward if they had seen anything unusual, not one of the visitors mentioned the woman with the white umbrella. They had not noticed her; the schema guiding their viewing held attention on the ball. When Neisser then replayed the tape, they were surprised to see the woman. Neisser's experiment is a visual equivalent of the cocktail party effect. Such selective perception goes on continually. As you read this you are doing it at this very moment; your schemas render the type meaningful. As your focus picks out the words on the page, it ignores what is in your peripheral vision. Just calling this fact to your attention may suddenly make you aware of what surrounds these words in your vision. Otherwise, it is simple to see the effect. Keep your eye fixed on the spot below, but move your attention to the white borders of the page—to the book's edges—and to what surrounds the book itself:

●

While reading, you notice the words, not the margins of the page and what lies beyond. Your attention is channeled like the visitors who watched Neisser's video of the basketball game. You don't notice what is irrelevant until something makes it relevant: your attention is guided by a schema for reading until another one, which directs your attention to the page edge, takes over.

Schemas guide the mind's eye in deciding what to perceive and what to ignore. Here, for example, is an apt description of how schemas operate in directing a man's attention toward women: [21]

> . . . you realize that all your life you have screened women out. Too tall, too short, too fat, too thin, ill-dressed, disturbed. . . . You didn't have to *look*, actually, not to be interested. A hint in the eye's corner kept the eye moving for the fresh face, the springy hair, the youthful waist between firm hips and bust. Negative efficiency. When you're looking for an object, the eye in an instant discards a thousand that are not it.

When emotions stir schemas, they lend a special potency. Emotions and thoughts are part and parcel of the same process.* A thought stirs a feeling; feelings guide thoughts. The intricate connections between thought and feeling can be seen in a depiction

* A debate rages on the exact relationship between cognition and emotion, particularly over whether thought precedes feeling, or feeling thought. No one questions, however, that the two are intimately tied.

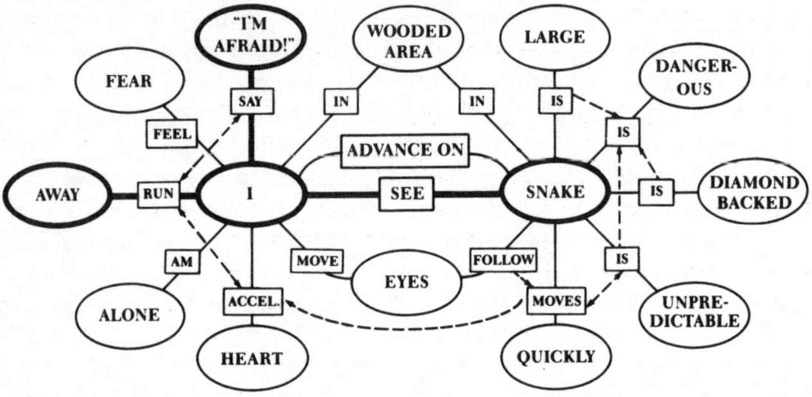

FIGURE 9. Schemas for a person afraid of snakes who comes upon one while walking alone in the woods. Emotions such as fear are strong activators of relevant schemas.

of the schemas in a person fearful of snakes who encounters one in the following scenario.[22]

> A person, walking alone in the woods, sees a large snake moving toward him. The snake has a diamond pattern on its back, and could be dangerous. The snake's quick sinous movement makes his heart race. Snakes are unpredictable, he thinks. He's very frightened. Even though he's alone, he blurts, "God, I'm scared!" and starts to run.

The schemas for his thoughts and his behavioral and emotional reactions are all intricately linked aspects of a single reaction (See Figure 9).

Such emotions as fear hyperactivate schemas, making them compelling centers of attention. Our angers, sorrows, and joys capture attention, sweep us away. The particular case in point, for our purposes, is anxiety. As we saw in Part One, schemas of threat and worry, empowered by anxiety, intrude into awareness. As the varieties of denial demonstrate, attention itself offers antidotes to such intrusions.

In my childhood scenario, unseen hands backstage in awareness constructed reality. The agents of that construction, we have seen, are schemas. Schemas are intelligence in action: they guide the analysis of sensory input in the sensory store, simplifying and organizing it, weeding out what is not salient. They scan information that passes out of the sensory store, and filter it through the priorities and relevancies they embody. Schemas determine which focus attention seeks, and hence what will enter awareness. When

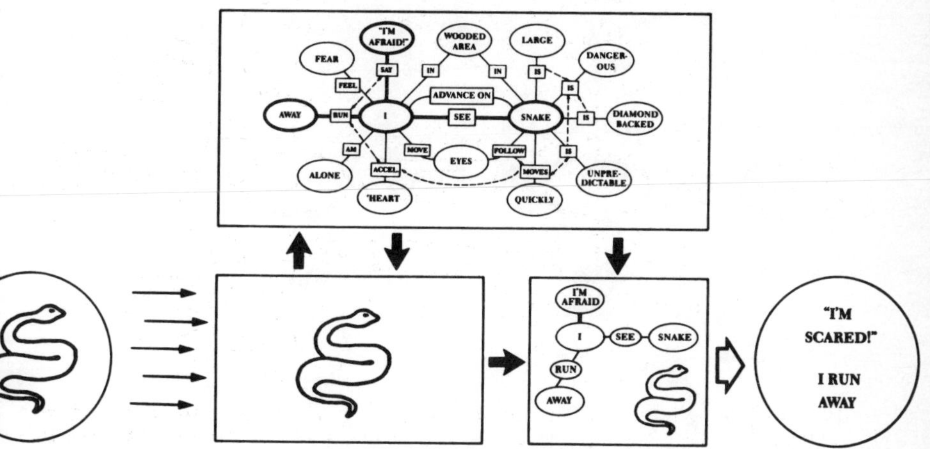

FIGURE 10. Cognitive sequence for someone who sees a snake in the woods, gets scared, and runs away. Activated schemas guide attention, comprehension, and action.

driven by emotions like anxiety, schemas impose themselves with special force.

Another implication of this model is more to the point for now—schemas are the lions at the gate of awareness: they determine not only what enters but what does not.

AWARENESS IS NOT A NECESSARY STOP

If critical information-processing goes on beyond awareness, then much of what we think and do is under the spell of influences we cannot perceive. Freud's sense that this was so led him to posit that there were three zones of consciousness: the unconscious (by far the largest), preconscious, and conscious. George Mandler, a cognitive psychologist, suggests that Freud's model fits well with how schemas act to guide attention.[23] The preconscious is a stage midway between the unconscious and awareness, a sort of backstage area to mental life. Here, says Mandler, there is a pool of schemas at various levels of activation. Which ones are activated varies from moment to moment. The most highly activated schema is the one that reaches consciousness.

An activated schema dominates awareness; it glides from the pool available and guides attention. As you walk down a street, you may not notice a dog approaching, but the relevant schema for dogs would float toward preconsciousness. At the moment you hear a growl, though, the "dog"—or perhaps the "dog bite"—schema becomes most highly activated, and the dog looms into awareness. But while a schema is quiescent in long-term memory, waiting for its moment to come, it is in something very like the unconscious.

For many years, psychologists (other than those with psychoanalytic leanings) doubted that zones beyond awareness existed, or said that if the unconscious existed, its impact on behavior was trivial. This debate broke into public scrutiny when, in the early 1960s, an enterprising advertising man claimed to have boosted sales of Coke and popcorn by flashing subliminal messages during a movie. The psychological community, by and large, hooted.

Subliminal material—that is, stimuli presented so quickly that, no matter how alert and focused you are, you cannot consciously

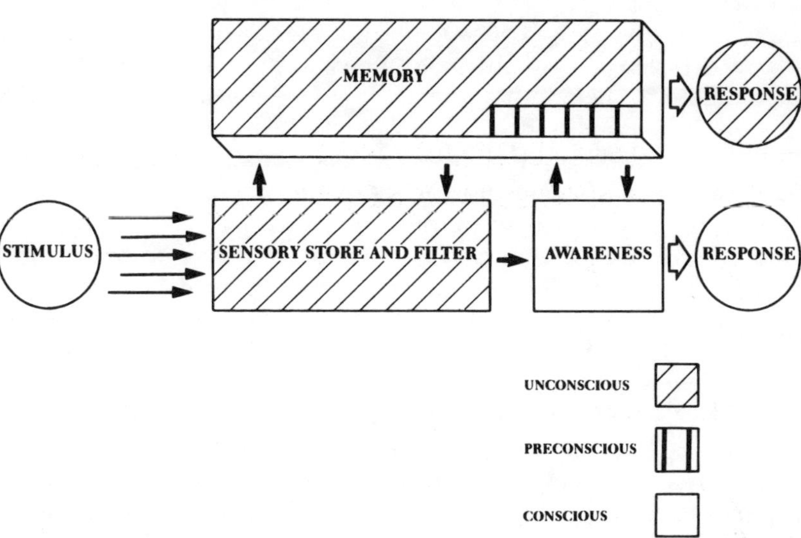

FIGURE 11. Three zones of awareness: The sensory store and filter, and most of long-term memory are unconscious. The preconscious is that part of long-term memory where schemas have been partially activated. Schemas which become activated most fully reach awareness.

see them—was thought to go entirely unperceived. But evidence for unconscious perception was mounting. By 1971, a comprehensive review of research literature concluded that subliminal perception is, indeed, possible.[24] At the same time, a theoretical framework evolved that explains how such perception might be possible. By 1977, although some holdouts remained, many cognitive scientists took unconscious perception for granted. For example, as psychologists discussing the issues noted:[25]

> The basic question of whether people can respond to a stimulus in the absence of the ability to report verbally on its existence would today be answered in the affirmative by many more investigators than would have been the case a decade ago . . . largely because of better experimental methods and convincing theoretical argument that subliminal perception . . . [results] from . . . selective attention and filtering.

In the ensuing years, the weight of evidence for unconscious processing of information has become overwhelming. The case no longer rests on the weight of theoretical arguments, but on strong experimental evidence. For example, in 1980, psychologists published in *Science* data showing that people formed preferences for geometric shapes (a variety of oddly shaped octagons) that they had been exposed to without being consciously aware that they had seen them.[26] The familiar, the data showed, becomes the preferred —even when familiarity is unconscious.

A great deal of other research has made the same point, that information which never reaches awareness nevertheless has a strong influence on how we perceive and act. For example, Howard Shevrin at the University of Michigan measured brain waves while showing student volunteers a series of words and pictures.[27] The presentations were made at a few thousandths of a second, presumably too brief for the volunteers to be consciously aware of their meaning. Meanwhile, the volunteers free-associated aloud.

The flashed messages made an impact on free association. For example, when the volunteers saw a picture of a bee, their free associations strayed to connected words like "bug," "sting," and "honey." Although they had no idea what the word or picture might have been, there was clear evidence that they got the message at a level out of awareness, and their schemas were activated accordingly.

Shevrin's explanation fits well with the working model of the mind we have described:[28]

> At any one time we are aware of only a small percentage of the total stimulation reaching our senses. We actively select what we attend to mainly on the basis of need, interest and perceptual prominence. *The selection process itself, however, is unconscious.* We experience something "popping" into consciousness but a complex and *unconscious* process prepares that "pop." . . . Taken together, subliminal and attention studies show that our brains are humming with cognitive and emotional activity prior to consciousness.

The model of mind we have generated here easily accommodates this version of the mind's operations. Schemas work backstage, in the vicinity we have labeled "long-term memory" (another, more general term might be better—like "the unconscious"). The mind is aware of the meaning of an event before that event and its significance enter awareness. In schema terms, this preawareness means that schemas which are activated but are out of awareness organize experience and filter it before it gets into awareness. Once the most relevant schemas are activated, they "pop into consciousness."

But, as the research results suggest, schemas can guide awareness while remaining out of awareness. We observe only their ef-

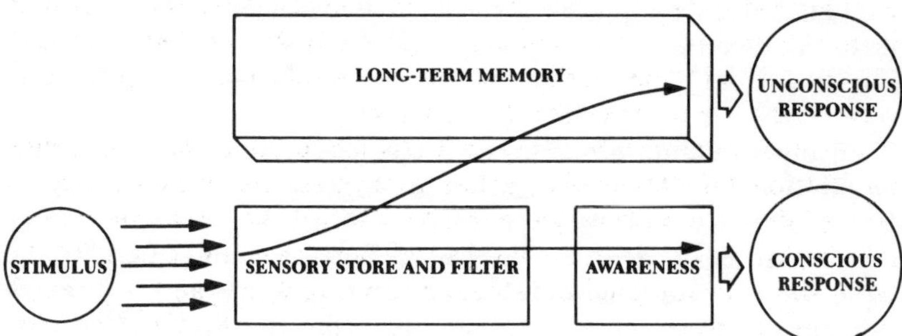

FIGURE 12. In an unconscious response, information flows from the sensory store and filters directly into memory, bypassing awareness altogether. The response is also executed outside awareness. Automatic routines follow this pathway, as do other out-of-awareness phenomena. Note that this allows for parallel channels of perception and action, one in awareness, the other unconscious.

fects, not their identity. As Freud put it, "We learn from observing neurosis that a latent, or unconscious, idea is not necessarily a weak one."

This model can accommodate several diverse phenomena that have long puzzled students of the mind (see figure 12). For instance, Ernest Hilgard, a noted hypnosis researcher at Stanford, tells of a classroom demonstration of hypnosis during which a volunteer was hypnotized and told he would be temporarily deaf. While "deaf," the volunteer did not flinch at loud sounds like a gunshot and blocks being banged together.[29]

One student asked whether "some part" of the subject might be aware of sounds, since his ears were presumably functioning. The instructor then whispered softly to the hypnotized student:[30]

> As you know, there are parts of our nervous system that carry on activities that occur out of awareness, [like] circulation of the blood. . . . There may be intellectual processes also of which we are unaware, such as those that find expression in . . . dreams. Although you are hypnotically deaf, perhaps there is some part of you that is hearing my voice and processing the information. If there is, I should like the index finger of your right hand to rise as a sign that this is the case.

To the instructor's dismay, the finger rose. Immediately afterward, the hypnotized student spontaneously said that he felt his index finger rise, but had no idea why it had done so. He wanted to know why.

The instructor then released the volunteer from hypnotic deafness and asked what he thought had happened. "I remember," said the volunteer, "your telling me that I would be deaf at the count of three, and would have my hearing restored when you placed your hand on my shoulder. Then everything was quiet for a while. It was a little boring just sitting here, so I busied myself with a statistical problem I was working on. I was still doing that when suddenly I felt my finger lift; that is what I want you to explain."

Hilgard's explanation (assuming the volunteer is to be believed) is that there is a capacity of mind that can register and store information outside a person's awareness. Under certain circumstances, that unconscious awareness can be contacted and can communicate, still outside the person's main awareness. That special capacity Hilgard calls the "hidden observer."

Hilgard, since the surprise discovery of this capacity, has performed numerous experiments which confirm the robustness of the hidden observer. For example, in a study of hypnotic analgesia, Hilgard hypnotized a young woman who was able to immerse her hand in a bucket of icy water, but reported she felt no pain. When Hilgard asked one hand to report out of the woman's awareness what was going on, the hand filled out a pain rating scale showing an increasing level of distress, essentially normal pain. Meanwhile, when asked, the young woman was calmly reporting she felt no pain at all.

An even more exotic line of inquiry adds to the weight of evidence for the potency of out-of-awareness cognition: the study of multiple personality. Such cases have long puzzled psychiatry; books and movies about them, like *The Three Faces of Eve* and *Sybil*, have fascinated a large public.

The bizarre puzzle of independent subpersonalities inhabiting the same mind is well captured by this journalistic account of one case:[31]

> The searing pain roused Marianna from sleep. She switched on the bedside light and saw dark red streaks of blood covering her sheets. She counted the fine lines of 30 razor cuts on her arms and legs before she carefully climbed out of bed. On her dresser was a note, written in childish scrawl:
>
> WARNING TO MARIANNA
> *The lies must stop. Put a stop to the child or I'll kill.*
> —THE RIPPER
>
> It was a death threat. But it was also a suicide attempt—for Marianna, the Child and the Ripper all inhabit the

> same body. The Ripper, a violent male personality given to fits of rage, felt angry and threatened because the Child, a youngster of four, had told their therapist the deeply hidden secrets the Ripper had guarded for so many years. His vicious attack was intended to make sure the Child stopped tattling. Never mind that he, the Child and Marianna all share the same body; they do not share the same pain. To the Ripper, they are different people, and he does not realize that death to the Child means death to him, too.

Our model handles both the hidden observer and multiple personality.* Both require that there be faculties of mind that can operate outside awareness. The model allows for this: it shows that awareness is not a necessary stop as information flows through the mind.

A completely different line of research underscores the potency of unconscious information. Surgical wisdom has it that patients under anesthesia can neither hear nor recall what goes on in the operating room. This frees surgeons for banter, sometimes at the patients' expense.

A group of researchers at a rehabilitation hospital in Chicago tested the effects of a message on patients undergoing back surgery.[32] The patients were under total anesthesia at the time; presumably they had no awareness of what was going on in surgery.

The single most common postoperative complication for this sort of surgery is the inability to urinate voluntarily. The medical solution is catheterization. The researchers, however, tried another route. Near the end of surgery, while the patient was still anesthetized, the surgeon addressed the patient by name and said:

> The operation has gone well and we will soon be finishing. You will be flat on your back for the next couple of days. When you are waiting it would be a good idea if you relax the muscles in the pelvic area. This will help you to urinate, so you won't need a catheter.

The results were striking. According to the researchers, not a single patient given this suggestion needed a catheter after surgery. More than half of those in a control group, who heard no such suggestion, needed catheterization.

Another group of medical researchers made the point more

* The multiple personality requires a special adjustment. One must posit subcensors that operate within long-term memory to keep the routines and experiences of each subpersonality separate from the rest. The model can, with some speculative stretching, accommodate this possibility, too, if we assume that when one subidentity occupies awareness, the others are cut off from awareness.

directly.[33] During an operation a tape, played into earphones worn by anesthetized patients, suggested to them that when a researcher came to interview the patient afterward, "it is very important that you pull on your ear so I can know you have heard this."

During the interviews, more than 80 percent of the patients who heard that suggestion tugged at their ears; most did so six times or more.

In summary, perception need not be conscious. The weight of research evidence supports this contention; the prevailing models of mind assume it. Indeed, perhaps the most crucial act of perception is in making the decision as to what will and will not enter awareness. This filtering is carried out before anything reaches awareness; the decision itself is made outside awareness.

The later volitional decision of what to attend to has, as a consequence, a prelimited range. William James suggested that conscious, voluntary attention is the essence of will. The evidence reviewed here, though, suggests will is free only within limits: The array presented to awareness, from which we can choose to note one thing or the other, is preselected. Attention can range freely, but within a delimited domain. We never can know what information our schemas have filtered out, because we cannot attend to the operation of the filter that makes the selection.

The pieces are in place. The model of the mind shows that an intelligence scans, filters, and selects information; schemas embody that intelligence. The whole operation goes on out of awareness. What does this portend for the trade-off between anxiety and attention? Answering that is our task in Part Three.

PART THREE

Secrets from the Self

JOHN DEAN'S MEMORY

"My mind is not a tape recorder, but it certainly receives the message that is being given." The words are John Dean's, from the Watergate hearings in June of 1973. There was to be an ironic twist to Dean's comparing his memory to a tape recording. Soon after his testimony came the revelation that President Nixon had taped conversations in the Oval Office, including many Dean testified about.

Dean's comments were remarkably long and detailed; he submitted a 245-page statement recounting events and conversations over the many months he was involved in the Watergate cover-up. The statement was so specific that Senator Inouye, incredulous, was moved to ask Dean, "Have you always had a facility for recalling the details of conversations which took place many months before?"

That same question moved Ulric Neisser to compare Dean's recall of conversations with what the tapes revealed to find in what ways Dean's memory was accurate, in what ways it was off.[1] The analysis showed that Dean was on target only in recalling the spirit of those encounters. His facts were often scrambled. The nature of that scramble is instructive: it seems to have been dictated to a large extent by what might be called "wishful memory," skewing specifics to make himself look more important.

Take, for example, the events of September 15, 1972. On that day a grand jury indicted the five Watergate burglars, along with Howard Hunt and Gordon Liddy. Dean was exultant, because his chief task had been to contain the Watergate inquiry.

Dean was summoned to the Oval Office that afternoon for a meeting with Nixon and Haldeman that lasted fifty minutes. Here is how his prepared statement describes it:[2]

> The President asked me to sit down. Both men appeared to be in very good spirits and my reception was very warm

> and cordial. The President then told me that Bob—referring to Haldeman—had kept him posted on my handling of the Watergate case. The President told me I had done a good job and he appreciated how difficult a task it had been and the President was pleased that the case had stopped with Liddy. I responded that I could not take credit because others had done much more difficult things than I had done. . . . I told him that all I had been able to do was to contain the case and assist in keeping it out of the White House. I also told him there was a long way to go before this matter would end and that I certainly could make no assurances that the day would not come when this matter would start to unravel.

When asked while testifying to recount that same conversation, Dean gives very much the same story.

How accurate are Dean's written and spoken accounts? Not very. According to Neisser:[3]

> Comparison with the transcript shows that hardly a word of Dean's account is true. Nixon did not say any of the things attributed to him here: he didn't ask Dean to sit down, he didn't say Haldeman had kept him posted, he didn't say Dean had done a good job (at least not in that part of the conversation), he didn't say anything about Liddy or the indictments. Nor had Dean himself said the things he later describes himself as saying: that he couldn't take credit, that the matter might unravel some day, etc. (Indeed, he said just the opposite later on: "Nothing is going to come crashing down.") His account is plausible, but entirely incorrect.

In trying to understand these distortions, Neisser concludes that Dean's testimony really describes not the meeting itself, but his *fantasy* of it: the meeting as it *should* have been. "In Dean's mind," says Neisser,[4] "Nixon *should* have been glad that the indictments stopped with Liddy, Haldeman *should* have told Nixon what a great job Dean was doing; most of all, praising him *should* have been the first order of business. In addition, Dean *should* have told Nixon that the cover-up might unravel, as it eventually did, instead of telling him it was a great success [as Dean actually did]."

The stitching that holds together such pseudomemories is, in this case, wishful thinking. Dean, for example, gives prominence to Nixon's compliments on containing the grand jury investigation. In fact, Dean was putting words in Nixon's mouth. Nixon's compliment never came—at least not as Dean reports it. But it certainly must have been what Dean yearned for. As he wished it to be, so he recalled it.

Neisser's analysis shows that memory, like attention, is vulnerable to skews. The relationship between attention and memory is intimate. Memory is attention in the past tense: what you remember now is what you noticed before. Memory is in double jeopardy, for apart from an initial skew in what is noticed, there can be later biases in what is recalled.

"Are we all like this?" asks Neisser. "Is everyone's memory constructed, staged, self-centered?" A single case history is scarcely basis for a scientific answer to that question. Yet, Neisser conjectures, there is a bit of John Dean in all of us:[5] "His ambition reorganized his recollections: even when he tries to tell the truth, he can't help emphasizing his own role in every event. A different man in the same position might have observed more dispassionately, reflected on his experiences more thoughtfully, and reported them more accurately. Unfortunately, such traits of character are rare."

Dean may have been knowingly twisting the truth, or may have believed his own story and misled himself. Whether his dissembling was knowing or not, his reconstruction of events betrays a selective recall in action.

Another such example was provided by the Darsee affair.

John Darsee, a research fellow at Harvard Medical School, was caught falsifying data on his research. When, as one newspaper account reports, "several young researchers watched in astonishment as Dr. Darsee forged data for an experiment," Darsee blithely admitted that fabrication while denying any others.[6]

After a thorough investigation showed that virtually all his data had been faked for several years, Darsee wrote a letter to federal investigators "in which he stated that although he had no recollection of falsifying any research data, he acknowledged that the inquiry had established both the falsification and his personal role."

Darsee's letter, if it is to be believed, displays the mind's power to stonewall even what it accepts as fact: it seems to have happened, I seem to have done it, but I disavow it—I don't remember doing so. Dean and Darsee offer public examples of a private fact. The ease with which we deny and dissemble—and deny and dissemble to ourselves that we have denied or dissembled—is remarkable. But, as we shall see, the mind's design facilitates such self-deception.

WHO CONTROLS THE PAST CONTROLS THE FUTURE

One's past is a gradually increasing weight," wrote Bertrand Russell. "It is easy to think to oneself that one's emotions used to be more vivid than they are and one's mind more keen. If this is true it should be forgotten, and if it is forgotten, it will probably not be true." Russell's sentiments are given a more sinister twist in a slogan from Orwell's *1984:* "Who controls the past controls the future: who controls the present controls the past." Who, in the realm of mind, *does* control the past?

Memory is autobiography; its author is the "self," an especially potent organization of schemas. Sometimes also called the "self-system" or "self-concept," it is that set of schemas that define what we mean by "I," "me," and "mine," that codify a sense of oneself and one's world.

The self is built up slowly, from childhood on, as perhaps the most basic grouping of schemas the mind holds. Its origins are in the interactions between parent and infant; its development runs along lines carved by the contours of relationships with parents, family, peers—any and all significant people and events in one's life. The self-system sculpts the way a person filters and interprets experience; it invents such self-serving readings of past events as Dean's and Darsee's. In doing so, the self has in its power all the tools—and temptations—of a totalitarian state. The self acts as a censor, selecting and deleting the flow of information.

In an article entitled "The Totalitarian Ego," Anthony Greenwald, a social psychologist, makes the case for the analogue between self and dictator.[7] Greenwald paints a portrait of the self from many areas of research. "The most striking features of the portrait," says he, "are . . . cognitive biases, which correspond disturbingly to thought control and propaganda devices that are . . . defining characteristics of a totalitarian political system." While the self may be a dictator, he adds, there may be good reasons: what seems "undesirable in a political system can nonetheless serve adaptively in a personal organization of knowledge."

As the central observer and recorder of life, the self stands in the role of historian. But impartiality is not one of its virtues; as Greenwald notes—and Dean showed—"The past is remembered as if it were a drama in which self was the leading player." Reviewing extensive research findings, Greenwald concludes that the self "fabricates and revises history, thereby engaging in practices not ordinarily admired in historians."

Greenwald cites experimental results showing how egocentricity pervades mental life. Some examples: Facts are better remembered the more they have to do with oneself. Or, most people in a group feel that they are the center of activity. In international politics, decision-makers perceive the acts of distant nations as being aimed at themselves, when in fact they reflect local conditions. And people see their own acts as accounting for chance events, such as winning a lottery ticket.

People, too, take credit for success, but not for failure, another form of egocentric bias. Language reveals this bias: after a university football team lost a game, students reported "they lost"; after a victory, the report was "we won." Or, from a driver's explanation of an accident to an insurance company: "The telephone pole was approaching. I was attempting to swerve out of its way when it struck my front end." A deliberately tongue-in-cheek example of this variety of egocentricity is Greenwald's own footnote of acknowledgment, which reads in part:

> The author is prepared to take full responsibility only for the good ideas that are to be found in it. I am nonetheless grateful to the following people, who commented on earlier drafts. . . . [There ensues a long list of names.] If this disguise of gratitude is itself seen as inept, then the reader should know that it was the suggestion of Robert B. Zajonc, modified with the help of Robert Trivers.

A telling sign of the self's egocentricity is the failure of schemas to accommodate new information. This bias becomes manifest in science, for example, as the inclination of researchers to disregard results inconsistent with their own theories. People hold to beliefs of all sorts in the face of evidence and arguments to the contrary.

These self-deceptions and biases are so pervasive, Greenwald argues, because they are highly adaptive; they protect the integrity of the self's organization of knowledge. Specifically, they all reflect the self's propensity to encode information around a central organizing principle: what matters to the self. Without such an organizing structure, knowledge and behavior would be linked willy-nilly; with it new information is assimilated in an orderly and useful fashion, indexed in the way that will be easiest to find.

There is, in other words, a structural advantage to having the self as a central framework for memory and action; crucial knowledge can cohere within a single coding scheme. The analogue Greenwald uses is a cataloging system in a library: "Once a commitment is made to a specific cataloging scheme, it may be more efficient to maintain consistency with that scheme than to allocate librarian effort to . . . recataloguing and reshelving the existing collection . . . every time another indexing system comes along." The self holds sway as the Dewey Decimal System of the mind.

In a review of the self-concept, Seymour Epstein remarks on how inaccurate people's views of themselves can be. The inaccuracy is not always in keeping with the positive biases Greenwald describes:[8]

> People who are highly competent sometimes feel deeply inadequate; people who are inferior feel superior; people with an ordinary appearance feel beautiful; and people who are attractive feel ugly. More impressive yet, some people who have lived exemplary lives are torn with severe guilt to the point they no longer wish to live, while others who have committed horrendous crimes suffer not a twinge of conscience.

The basis for these skewed perceptions, says Epstein, is people's self-esteem. A school of thought argues that one's sense of value and worth is embodied by the self-system. A threat to these views of oneself is particularly upsetting; there is an overriding need to preserve the self-system's integrity. Information that fits the self-concept is easily assimilated—Dean was glad to report how important his efforts were considered by the President—but data that challenges the self is hard to take; Dean is oblivious to the fact that the President did not actually say most of the laudatory things Dean recalls.

Information that threatens the self—that does not support the story one tells oneself about oneself—threatens self-esteem. Such threats are a major source of anxiety. For animals, stress is most often in the form of a threat to life or limb. For humans, though, a challenge to self-esteem is enough to brew anxiety.

Aaron Beck, a psychiatrist, describes low self-esteem in operation in one of his patients, a depressed man. Within a period of a half an hour the man reported the following events:[9]

> His wife was upset because the children were slow in getting dressed. He thought, "I'm a poor father because the children are not better disciplined." He noticed that this showed he was a poor husband. While driving to work, he thought, "I must be a poor driver or other cars would not be passing me." As he arrived at work, he noticed some other personnel had already arrived. He thought, "I can't be very dedicated or I would have come earlier." When he noticed folders and papers piled up on his desk, he concluded, "I'm a poor organizer because I have so much work to do."

Such self-defeating trends of thought, Beck observes, are the hallmark of depression, which he sees as the chronic activation of negative self-schemas. In milder depressions, says Beck, a person will have negative thoughts about himself, but retain some objectivity about them. But as the depression worsens, his thinking will become increasingly dominated by negative ideas about himself.

The more such negative self-schemas activate, the more distorted his thinking becomes, and the less able he is to see that his depressing thoughts may be distortions. At its most severe, a depressed person's thoughts about himself are completely dominated by intrusive, preoccupying self-condemnations, completely out of touch with the situation at hand.

Self-schemas in depression, says Beck, finally lead the person "to view his experiences as total deprivations or defeats and as irreversible. Concomitantly, he categorizes himself as a 'loser' and doomed." Beck contrasts the skewed self-perception of a depressed person with the more balanced view of someone who is not in the grips of the disorder: [10]

THE DEPRESSED SELF-SCHEMA	THE HEALTHY SELF-SCHEMA
1. I am fearful	I am moderately fearful, quite generous, and fairly intelligent
2. I am a despicable coward	I am more fearful than most people I know
3. I always have been and always will be a coward	My fears vary from time to time and situation to situation
4. I have a defect in my character	I avoid situations too much and I have many fears
5. Since I am basically weak, there's nothing that can be done	I can learn ways of facing situations and fighting my fears.

Epstein proposes that, within the self-system, schemas (which he calls "postulates") are arranged in a hierarchy. Lower-order self-schemas include specific minor facts: "I am a good tennis player," "People say they like my piano-playing." A higher-order self-schema might be "I am a good athlete," or "People know I am a good musician." A much higher-order self-schema along these lines might be, "I am worthwhile."

Lower-order schemas usually can be challenged by events without much threat to self-esteem: If one loses a tennis game or does not get a compliment for playing piano, not much is at stake. But if a higher-order schema is challenged, the stakes are high. Dean, no doubt, was facing a great challenge to his sense of worth in testifying before the Senate, as was Darsee in defending his falsifications.

Unloving parents, hostile siblings, unfriendly peers can all lower self-esteem; happy experiences with these people in one's life can raise it. Says Epstein:[11]

> People with high self-esteem, in effect, carry within them a loving parent who is proud of their successes and tolerant of their failures. Such people tend to have an optimistic view about life, and to be able to tolerate stress without becoming excessively anxious. Although capable of being disappointed and depressed by specific experiences, people with high self-esteem recover quickly, as do children who are secure in their mother's love.

In contrast, people with low self-esteem carry the psychological burden of a harsh, disapproving parent. They are prone to oversensitivity to failure, are all too ready to feel rejected, and take a long while to get over disappointment. Their view of life is pessimistic, much like a child insecure in his parent's love.

When a threat to the self-concept looms, anxiety can be warded off by a healthy self-schema through an artful maneuver or two. Events can be selectively remembered, reinterpreted, slanted. When the objective facts don't support the self-system, a more subjective recounting can: If I see myself as honest and good, and events don't support that view, then I can preserve self-esteem by skewing my rendering of them.

As we have seen, the wherewithal to do this is entirely outside awareness. The self-system can sanitize its portrayal of events through the filtering that goes on prior to awareness. I need confront only a finished, polished view of myself; the dirty work goes on behind the scenes. Some research suggests that depressed people are less self-serving than the nondepressed, who see life in terms of an "illusory glow" of positivity. Such self-serving reinterpretations of reality go on for most of us some of the time, but we are rarely found out. After all, the dissembling goes on discreetly, behind the screen of the unconscious; we are only its recipients, innocent self-deceivers. A convenient arrangement.

THE SELF-SYSTEM: GOOD-ME, BAD-ME, AND NOT-ME

Schemas change continually through life, as do images of the self. Past self-images leave their trace: no one has just one fully integrated self-image, a single harmonious version of the self. Various points and stages in life accrue overlapping selves, some congruent, others not. A new self-image emerges and becomes dominant: A gangly, isolated adolescent can become a svelte, gregarious thirty-year old, but the svelte self does not completely eradicate traces of the gangly one.

Trauma in later life can activate an earlier self-image. Says Mardi Horowitz:[12]

> If a person has an accident with subsequent loss of his arm, or if he is fired from his work, there may be a rapid shift from a competent self-image to an already existing but previously dormant one as worthless and defective. . . . Suppose that a person has a dominant self-image as competent that is relatively stable and usually serves as the primary organizer of mental processes. Suppose also that this person has a dormant, inactive self-image as an incompetent. . . . ' When that person sustains a loss or insult, the event will be matched against two self-images: competent and incompetent. For a time the incompetent self-image may dominate thought, leading to a temporary reaction of increased vulnerability.

Working from an interpersonal view, the psychiatrist Harry Stack Sullivan came to a parallel notion, one that presents a simple, plausible model of how we learn to trade off diminished attention for lessened anxiety.[13] Sullivan traces the root of this process to the infant learning to pilot his way through the world on a course between tender rewards for being good and punishments for being bad. When the "mothering one" (as Sullivan refers to the key caregiver) shows disapproval, the infant feels anxiety at the loss of tenderness. As in the game of getting hotter or colder, he learns to act in ways that will increase tenderness and avoid disapproval.

Along the way the infant inevitably has some heavy going in, for example, distinguishing crucial boundaries between cleanliness and feces, or food and those things that cannot go in the mouth. An infant who is suddenly the object of his mother's anxious or angry yell—"No, dirty!"—is apt, in Sullivan's words, to be suddenly cast "from a condition of moderate euphoria to one of very severe anxiety," a bit like a sudden blow on the head. The range of the mother's disapproving acts, from mild reprimand to utter anger, produces a matching, graduated range of anxiety in the child. This anxiety gradient more or less directs the course of how the child develops.

The child's history of praise or censure comes to define his experience of himself. Three sorts of experience are key to identity. Sullivan writes, "With rewards, with the anxiety gradient, and with practically obliterative sudden severe anxiety there comes an initial personification of three phases of what presently will be *me*." He calls these three personifications "good-me," "bad-me," and "not-me."

In the "good-me," satisfactions have been enhanced by a reward of tenderness. The good-me emerges as the sense of self we garner from all those times we have felt happy at being a "good" little girl or boy, at being loved; it propels much of behavior all through life. "As it ultimately develops," says Sullivan, the good-me "is the ordinary topic of discussion about 'I'." The good-me is who we like to think we are.

"Bad-me," on the other hand, entails experiences in which varying degrees of disapproval have generated like levels of anxiety in the child. The bad-me is the sense of self connected with the anxiety, guilt, and shame of being naughty. Anxiety of this sort is interpersonal; the naughty child feels love withdrawn, which in turn generates anxiety. The bad-me arises in the mind in tandem with those things we do or have done about which we feel regrets or remorse. For example, a sardonic writer recalls an incident which typifies the bad-me:[14]

> . . . One of the few insufficiently repressed memories of my pathetic grammar-school days involves one Emily Johnson and some Betty turning during a math test and giggling. "Now he's picking his nose," Emily said. "Ick!" was Betty's rejoinder. I looked around, hoping they weren't talking about me, but no. Fear replaced obliviousness in my relations with the opposite sex.

The "not-me" bears on a realm of experience of a different order. Although the bad-me arouses anxiety, its contents—the specifics of what arouse that anxiety—remain in awareness. Not so with the not-me. The not-me evolves from experiences of what Sullivan calls "uncanny emotion"—feelings of terror and dread so powerful that they disrupt the ability to comprehend what is happening. Uncanny emotion overpowers the mind, blasting what caused it out of awareness. As Sullivan describes it, the events that shape the not-me result from "such intense anxiety, and anxiety so suddenly precipitated, that it was impossible for the then-rudimentary person to make any sense of, to develop any true grasp on, the particular circumstances which dictated the experience."

Because such intense anxiety shatters the ability to comprehend what is happening, it registers as inchoate confusion. The schemas that encode the not-me remain out of awareness: something overwhelming happened, but the person can't find words to say just what it was. Such moments, says Sullivan, are filled with a non-specific dread, loathing, and horror. With no content to make sense of these powerful feelings, they can best be described as "uncanny."

These experiences of anxiety alter that organizing principle in awareness, the self-system. To efficiency in organizing information Sullivan adds another principle shaping the self-system: the need to evade anxiety. The self-system, he wrote,[15] "is organized because of the extremely unpalatable, extremely uncomfortable experience of anxiety; and it is organized in such a way as to avoid or minimize existent or foreseen anxiety."

The self-system is both early-warning radar against anxiety and the force that marshals the efforts to ward it off. It is constantly vigilant, noticing, as Sullivan put it, "what one is not going to notice." The self-system performs its mission by operating on experience itself.

It is driven to this strategem, Sullivan suggests, because the world does not always allow the source of anxiety to vanish by virtue of how one *acts*—an observation identical to Richard Lazarus's about options for coping with stress. If the locus of anxiety in the world is immovable, then that leaves room for change only in how one *perceives* the world. The infant, for example, has the very early experience of frustration when he can't always get what he wants: "The infant's discovery of the unobtainable, his discovery of situations in which he is powerless" are both inevitable and anxiety-provoking.

The infant learns to manage this sort of anxiety through what Sullivan calls "security operations," tampering with his own awareness to soothe himself. "Even before the end of infancy," says Sullivan, "it is observable that these unattainable objects come to be treated *as if* they did not exist." If I can't have it, says the infant in effect, I will deny it.

Sullivan, theorizing in the 1940s, spelled out how security operations protect the self from anxiety. (Sullivan, a neo-Freudian, modeled "security operations" on what Freud called defense mechanisms, as we shall see.) Taking his cue from Freud, he observed that these operations go on "quite exterior to anything properly called the content of consciousness, or awareness."

But for Sullivan, as for Freud, theory was inferred from clinical phenomena. Such evidence from the clinic is taken lightly in research circles, since data corroborating the clinician's theory—as data on the "totalitarian self" show—may be due to bias in the clinician rather than the facts as they are.* Sullivan and Freud, in this view, were better as theorizers than as testers of theory. It remained for contemporary information-processing theory to provide the framework, and experimental research to provide the crucial data. That framework and data show, in modern terms, how the self-system protects us against anxiety by skewing attention.

* Indeed, the entire experimental enterprise in science is geared to counteract just such bias.

NOTICING WHAT NOT TO NOTICE

A schema implicitly selects what will be noted and what will not. By directing attention to one pattern of meaning, it ignores others. In this sense, even the most innocuous schema filters experience on the basis of relevancy. This filter of perception becomes a censor when it suppresses available information on the ground that it is not just irrelevant, but forbidden.

I once had the opportunity to ask Ulric Neisser whether there might be schemas that tell you "Do not attend to that." [16] "Yes," said he, "I'm sure there are, at several levels. Often they're not very subtle or interesting. It probably starts from cases like the woman with the umbrella who was unnoticed while people watched the basketball game video. They don't shift their attention from the task at hand. But the mechanism would be much the same when you have a pretty good suspicion of what's over there if you were to look, and you'd rather not deal with it. And you don't look; you don't shift your attention. You have a diversionary schema that keeps you looking at something else instead."

Lester Luborsky showed this mechanism at work in a series of studies in the 1960s.[17] He used a special camera to track the target of people's eye movements while they looked at pictures. The camera monitors a small spot of light reflected from the cornea of the eye to peg the person's exact point of regard; it is relatively unobtrusive and does not interfere with the person's line of sight.

Luborsky had his subjects look at a series of ten pictures and rate which they liked and which they disliked. Three of the pictures were sexual in content. One, for example, shows the outline of a woman's breast, beyond which sits a man reading a newspaper.

Certain people gave a remarkable performance. They were able to avoid letting their gaze stray even once to the more loaded part of the sexy pictures. When they were asked some days later what the pictures were, they remembered little or nothing suggestive about them. Some could not recall seeing them at all.

In order to avoid looking, some element of the mind must have known first what the picture contained, so that it knew what to avoid. The mind somehow grasps what is going on and rushes a protective filter into place, thus steering awareness away from what threatens.

A *New Yorker* cartoon depicts the same effect. A prim, elderly woman is standing in a museum before a huge and graphic painting of the Rape of the Sabine Women. Her gaze is studiously fixed on the artist's signature in the lower corner.

Neisser calls these programs not to notice "diversionary schemas." They are a special sort of schema, what I call "metaschemas": schemas that dictate the operations of other schemas.* In this instance, the diversionary schemas direct attention not to register the forbidden object in awareness.

Our language, unfortunately, does not offer a more congenial term for what we are talking about than "diversionary schema." That being the case, a borrowed one will have to do: I will use the term "lacuna," from the Latin for gap or hole, to refer to the sort of mental apparatus that diversionary schemas represent. A lacuna is, then, the attentional mechanism that creates a defensive gap in awareness. Lacunas, in short, create blind spots.

Lacunas are psychological analogues of the opioids and their antiattention effects. Lacunas are black holes of the mind, diverting attention from select bits of subjective reality—specifically, certain anxiety-evoking information. They operate on attention like a magician misdirecting his audience to look over there, while over here a key prop slips out of sight.

A lacuna was at work, it would seem, in the subjects in Luborsky's experiment whose eyes studiously avoided the breast in the picture. Donald Spence, a psychologist, notes that their gaze systematically skirted the forbidden area of the breast without *once* straying into it. "We are tempted to conclude," Spence comments, "that the avoidance is not random but highly efficient—the person knows just where *not* to look."

Spence, in trying to figure out just how such a trick might be possible, suggests there must be some part of the visual system that

* There are other sorts of metaschemas; for example, the linguistic rules that guide our understanding and use of language. Metaschemas are difficult to detect directly. A linguist can infer the rules of a language after much study, but a speaker of that language is at a complete loss to explain how he puts words together in a sentence or comprehends what he hears. Linguistic metaschemas do it for him, irretrievably out of awareness.

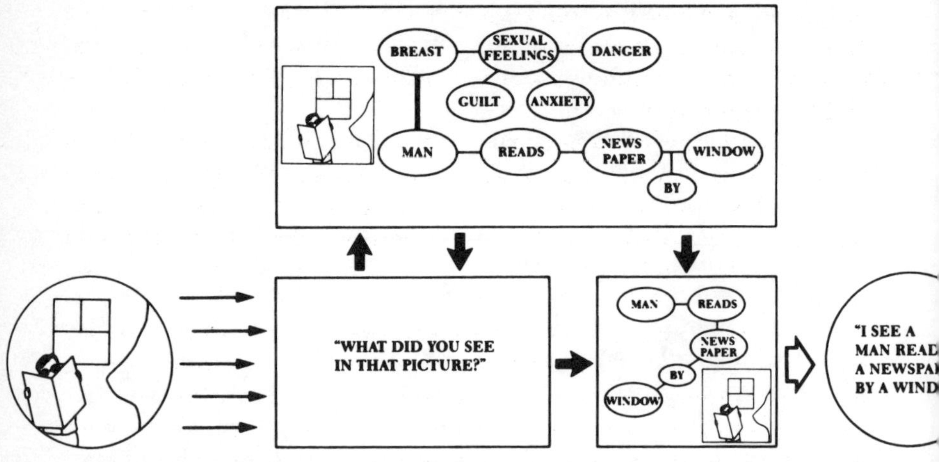

FIGURE 13. The making of a lacuna: When someone looks at the picture showing the breast and the man reading a newspaper and his eye avoids the breast entirely, something like the above flow of information occurs. The sensory store—or some "pre-look"—takes in the whole picture, which the filter then splits into what will be seen (the neutral zones) and what will be avoided (the breast). Only the neutral zones pass into awareness. The response: "I see a man reading a newspaper by a window."

takes a "pre-look," glimpses the naked breast in peripheral vision, marks it as a psychological danger area, and guides the gaze to the safe areas. The whole operation never reaches awareness.

In commenting on this effect, which was once called "perceptual defense," Jerome Bruner, an early researcher on the topic, asked, "How could people *know* that something was potentially threatening unless they could *see* it first? Was something letting a perceiver decide whether to open the portal of perception to let it in?"

Bruner's question is answerable in terms of our model of mind; such a maneuver is easily accomplished, as Figure 13 shows.

An apparent case of another such lacuna is hypnotically induced negative hallucinations. The hypnotist, for example, gives the instruction not to see a chair. When conversation shifts to the chair, the hypnotic subject blanks out: he reports his thoughts madly wander elsewhere, he can't seem to focus on it, he has no perception or memory of it. When a hypnotic subject is directed to forget what happened during the session, posthypnotic amnesia seems to work in the same way.

"I think there's a lot of this kind of repression in everyday life," says Neisser, "lots of limits and avoidance in thinking about or looking at things. An obvious case is when you go to the movies and avert your eyes at the scenes of bloody violence. But the same thing goes on cognitively, in terms of what we turn our minds to—and turn them away from.

"We all do that. There may be some painful experiences in your life which, when you start to think about, you simply decide at some level not to pursue. You're not going to be aware of that painful event. So you avoid using your usual recall strategies. You could probably get pretty skilled at it—at not remembering what's painful."

What *is* painful varies from person to person. Most people, for example, find it easy to recall positive memories, harder to bring back painful ones. For depressed people, though, positive memories come to mind less easily than negative ones. The self-system is, in part, a topographical chart of these painful areas. Where self-esteem is low, where the self-system feels vulnerable, such points of pain are strong. Where these pain nodes lie, I propose, lacunas perform their protective duty, guarding the self-system from anxiety.

Research by a pair of Russian investigators shows this effect.[18] The Russians subliminally flashed a list of words and asked their subjects to guess what they were. Some of the words selected had a special emotional potency; a man accused of thievery, for example, was presented with the word "rob." The Russians found evidence of something like a lacuna at work: the subjects found it especially difficult to report what the loaded words might have been, while at the same time brain measures revealed a markedly stronger brain response to those words. Howard Shevrin, working with patients at the University of Michigan psychology clinic, has obtained similar results.[19]

These evasions are orchestrated by diversionary schemas. Vernon Hamilton offers an analysis of how one such might operate.[20] Take someone who agrees with the statement "I prefer being on my own" on a personality questionnaire. The statement is a postulate about oneself, a schema within the self-system. It might subsume several interlinked schemas, which Hamilton exemplifies with Figure 14.

These schemas reflect a person who is insecure and scornful of crowds, likes to daydream in peace, and feels socially inferior and unloved. The same utterance in another person could betoken quite a different outlook: schemas that suggest self-confidence, independence, and a replete contentedness.

If we could map a person's self-schema, shading in red those that threaten self-esteem or otherwise evoke anxiety, we would be

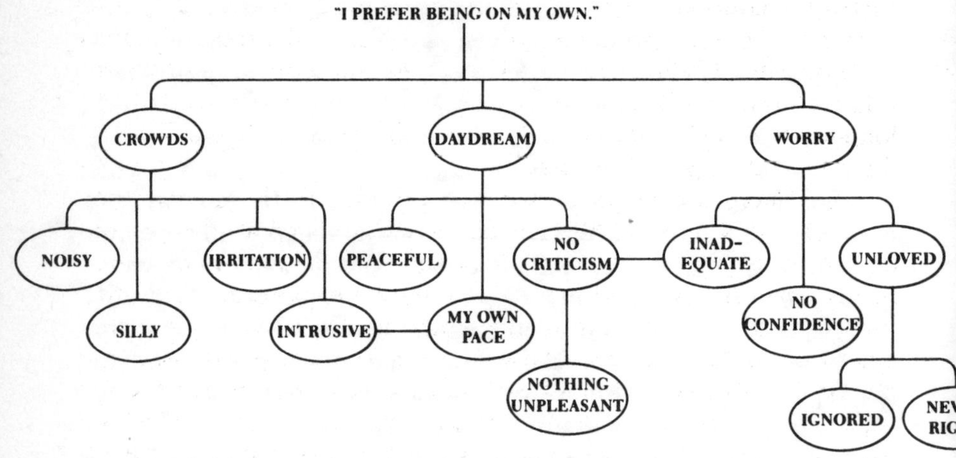

FIGURE 14. Schemas implied by "I prefer being on my own": These are schemas which might be activated by that thought in an insecure, apprehensive person.

able to spot reddened ridges where lacunas most likely occur. In the schemas in Figure 14, for instance, those under "Crowds" might be shaded in mild pink, those under "Daydream" a neutral white. But those under "Worry" would be a hot red.

Should circumstances trigger these disturbing "worry" schemas, one way the mind can deal with the threat of anxiety is via a diversionary schema. Thus, if the thought of "being on my own" leads to thoughts of feeling ignored and unloved, the mind could override these upsetting thoughts by substituting the association "peaceful, my own pace," and "intrusive, irritating crowds." The result is the conscious thought "I like being on my own—it's peaceful, and I can go at my own pace. Besides, crowds are intrusive and irritating." The thought "when I'm alone I feel ignored and unloved" meanwhile remains outside awareness, even though it triggered these substitutes.

Hamilton suggests a similar dynamic for the workings of a lacuna. He gives the hypothetical example of a person who is highly anxious about taking tests and fears failure. If that person is presented with the word "failure" on a tachistoscope so that he registers it out of awareness, and then has to guess what the word was, the following process might unfold.

First, "failure" registers in sensory storage. There it is scanned by the relevant schema held in long-term memory, which activate a program for selective attention. "Failure" is blocked, filtered out.

Instead, cognitions such as "common word," "has an 'f,' " ends with "ure," are passed on to awareness. Meanwhile, such schemas as "I am afraid," "pass exams," "must be quick now," and other related—and worrisome—trains of association are activated in long-term memory. What reaches awareness is: "f . . . ure." What the person guesses is "feature."

The more anxious a person, says Hamilton, the greater the number of his schemas that encode a sense of threat, danger, or aversiveness. The more widespread and well elaborated they are in his cognitive net, the more likely they are to be activated by life's events. And the more such fearful schemas activate, the more a person will come to rely on evasive maneuvers to avoid the anxiety they evoke. His attention will be lacunose, pockmarked with gaps. The greater and more intense the strategies that are used to deny, the more damage they do to awareness. Lacunas take a toll: they make for a deficit in attention as great as that caused by the anxiety they protect against.

The mind has use of many diversionary schemas. The most thorough mapping of their operations is in the work of Freud. Similarly, the most elegant method for detecting and correcting these self-deceptions is psychoanalysis.

SECRETS WE KEEP FROM OURSELVES

In *Notes from Underground,* Fyodor Dostoyevsky wrote: "Every man has reminiscences which he would not tell to everyone but only to his friends. He has other matters in his mind which he would not reveal even to his friends, but only to himself, and that in secret. But there are other things which a man is afraid to tell even to himself, and every decent man has a number of such things stored away in his mind."

Dostoyevsky's observation raises a knotty question: in which category did John Dean's "secret," his distorted reporting of the events of September 15, 1972, belong? Was it of the sort that he would admit only to friends? only to himself? not even to himself? Each type represents a greater remove from conscious control.

If Dean's secret was of the first or second sort, then his telling of the "facts" was a purposeful maneuver. What ended up in the *Congressional Record,* in that case, was a biased report, a lie of sorts. But if it was of the third kind, his report was the best version of truth he was capable of recounting. The skew was in his memory, not in his report of it. It was a secret he kept from himself.

Secrets from oneself are retrievable only under extraordinary circumstances. One technique designed to retrieve such secrets is psychoanalysis; the keeping of those secrets is what Freud called "repression." Repression (in the broad sense of defenses in general) was for Freud the key to his science, "the foundation-stone on which the whole structure of psychoanalysis rests."

In his essay "Repression," Freud gave his basic definition: "the essence of repression lies simply in the function of rejecting and keeping something out of consciousness."[21] While this definition does not say so, the purpose of Freud's writing is to save the term "repression" for the keeping out of awareness of a single class of items—those that evoke psychological pain. The pain can be of many varieties: trauma, "intolerable ideas," unbearable feelings, anxiety, guilt, shame, and so on. Repression is the quintessential lacuna; it lessens mental pain by attenuating awareness, as does its close cousin, denial.

The concept of repression underwent many permutations in Freud's writing and has been further refined by successive generations of his followers.[22] This conceptual evolution culminates in the "mechanisms of defense," the most detailed map to date of the ways in which attention and anxiety interplay in mental life.* The defense mechanisms, as we shall see, are recipes for the ways we keep secrets from ourselves. The defenses are diversionary, activated in tandem with painful information; their function is to buffer that pain by skewing attention.

Repression plays a central role in the drama of psychoanalysis. Painful moments or dangerous urges are repressed in order to ease the burden of mental anguish. But the tactic is only half successful: the pains so defended against skew attention and exert a warp on personality. The task of psychoanalysis is to surmont those defenses, fill in the gaps.

The analytic patient resists the assault. His resistance takes many forms, including the inability to free-associate with full freedom. Whenever his thoughts tend toward a zone of awareness bounded by defenses, a diversionary schema activates and his associations twist away. For this reason, Freud observed, free associations are not truly free. They are governed by both types of Dostoyevskian secrets: some known to the patient but kept from the analyst, others kept even from the patient himself.

Freud conceived of these forbidden zones as having at their center a key memory, usually of a traumatic moment in childhood. The memories are grouped in "themes," a particularly rich set of schemas, like a file of documents. Each theme is arranged like layers of an onion around the core of forbidden information. The nearer to that core one probes, the stronger is the resistance. The deepest schemas encode the most painful memories, and are the hardest to activate. "The most peripheral strata," wrote Freud,[23] "contain the memories [or files] which are easily remembered and have always been clearly conscious. The deeper we go the more difficult it becomes for the emerging memories to be recognized, till near the nucleus we come upon memories which the patient disavows even in reproducing them."

The subtle menace of repression is the silence with which it

* Freud used the notion of defense mechanisms primarily in terms of warding off unconscious sexual or hostile impulses. I am extending the notion somewhat to include anxiety-provoking information in general.

occurs. The passing of pain out of awareness sends out no warning signals: the sound of repression is a thought evaporating. Freud could find it only in retrospect, by reconstructing what must have gone on with his patients at some moment in the past.

Such defenses operate as though behind veils in experience; we are oblivious to them. R. D. Laing observes: [24]

> The operations on experience we are discussing are commonly not experienced themselves. So seldom does one ever catch oneself in the act, that I would have been tempted to regard them as themselves *essentially* not elements of experience, had I not occasionally been able to catch a glimpse of them *in action* myself, and had not others reported the same to me. It is comparatively easy to catch someone else in the act.

This point leads Laing to propose something very like a lacuna, a mental device *"that operates on our experience of operations"* so as to cancel them from experience. This goes on in such a way that we have no awareness either of the operations that extinguish aspects of our experience or of the secondary operations that shut out the first. The whole goes on behind a mental screen, hushed whispers of thoughts disappearing into silence. We can only notice this gap in experience when some later event faces us with it.

The novelist Leslie Epstein captures the dilemma well. He spent a year at the YIVO, an institute for Jewish research, reading about the Holocaust for his book, *King of the Jews*. With some candor, he later recounted: [25]

> Some years ago I wrote a brief account of this period of research and called it a "heart-stopping experience." What rubbish! The most frightening aspect about the year was the way my heart pumped merrily along, essentially undeflected by these stories of endless woe. I think I must have sensed soon after I arrived at the library that if I were to get through such material at all, to say nothing of being able to think about it and shape it, I would have to draw a psychic shutter, thick as iron, between myself and these accounts of the fate of the Jews. Thus I sat through the winter, wrapped in my overcoat—it's not just noisy at YIVO, it's chilly too—calmly and callously reading.

Epstein confesses his secret, that he was untouched by these tales of woe. How could he have come to his casual callousness? He must have sensed the need, he deduces, to draw a protective psychic shutter. There is no report of the moment that iron shutter fell, no record of its clank. Most certainly there is no recall of the moment it fell. The act of repression, it seems, is repressed along with what it represses.

But Epstein's repression was at best a half-successful strategy. Epstein felt guilty for his lack of guilty feelings. As he sat reading callously, he thought, "I'm going to be punished for this. I'm going to have nightmares." But they did not come. Instead there was a curious twist of feeling. One sign was that his book about the Holocaust flowed from his pen in such jaunty tones that it enraged some readers. Another was a muting of feelings in general:[26]

> What I noticed first was a lack of responsiveness not so much to the horrors of the past but to those occurring around me. John Lennon murdered, a Pope and a President wounded: I shrugged it off with at best a flicker of interest in social pathology. The earth quaked, mountains blew up, hostages were taken, and, worse, friends and colleagues suffered the knocks, the vicissitudes, of life. What I did—like the cursed Trigorin in Chekhov's *The Sea Gull*—was take a series of notes. The world was stale, flat . . . it was not only the calamities of the day that rolled off my duck's back like water, it was all manner of pleasures as well.

Epstein realizes that he has played what he calls "an ironical trick" on himself: "It was as if I'd made a pact with my emotions not to feel, not to respond, but had forgotten to set a date at which the arrangement would end." But the unfelt emotions nevertheless insinuated themselves into his writing and were displaced into his other novel. This second manuscript, he realized one day, was full of pain and death, amputations and torture. The horror he had insulated himself against and kept from his book on the Holocaust had moved to a novel set in California. "Instantly I realized," writes Epstein,[27] "that all the horror I had kept from the pages of my Holocaust novel was now returning as if in a reflex of revenge. The thousands of missing corpses were pressing round. . . . one thinks of a compact gone awry, a bargain whose deepest meaning is never grasped by the bargainer, a version of 'The Sorcerer's Apprentice' in which the very powers sought for—to animate, to imagine, to control—become the source, through sheer repetition, of one's own destruction."

"The compact gone awry" is an apt phrase for repression. The trade-off is of a diminished attention in exchange for lessened anxiety—in this case, muted emotions allow a casual contemplation of horrible facts. There is a price, though, for striking such a bargain. What's more, it doesn't work so well: the repressed fear and loathing leak out in disguise, blemishing innocent thoughts.

How did Epstein learn so well to mute emotion? Did repression first come to him in the cold, noisy halls of YIVO? Not if we are to believe Epstein's own inner detective work:[28] "The emotional censorship I practiced at YIVO could not by itself account for this large-scale return of what I believe is called the repressed. When, at what other time, had I purposefully turned my back on my feelings? . . . When my father died, thirty years ago, my brother and I did not go to the funeral." Instead, Epstein and his brother were taken to see *The Lavender Hill Mob* and then to a museum with a full replica of the Spirit of St. Louis. Fun covered over the boys' misery.

According to Freud, the penalty for repression is repetition. Painful experiences not dealt with are, unconsciously, repeated. We do not quite realize that we are repeating ourselves, because the very diversionary schemas we are repeating keep the fact of their repetition from awareness. On the one hand, we forget we have done this before and, on the other, do not quite realize what we are doing again. The self-deception is complete.

FORGETTING AND FORGETTING WE HAVE FORGOTTEN

Epstein's reflections suggest the insights of the analytic session. Indeed, his repression and its handily unlocked secrets can stand as a model of a lacuna. The traumatic center is the day he went to the movies instead of his father's funeral. At some remove from that, but still in the same mental "file" (to use Freud's phrase), is the lighthearted novelistic treatment of the Holocaust. The cocoon that binds these sources of hurt—and probably others from similar moments in his life—is the repression of feeling, the mental cauterizing of pain.

The cauterization, though, is self-defeating. The pain leaks out, the repression is too massive. He loses empathy with the lives around him and the capacity to feel fully his own emotions. His creative side tells him that the pain, though absent from awareness, lurks in concealment: his California novel reads like a Holocaust book.

Notice that Epstein's mental maneuver is not simply to repress a painful memory. He remembers the details, a funeral missed and the movie seen. What is repressed is the *pain* of it; he takes in the facts, but not the feelings that go with them. He brings the same strategem to his readings about the murdered Jews of the Holocaust, whom, he notes elsewhere in his writing, he associates with his dead father. He immerses himself in the details of their agony, but fails to take in the agony himself.

Epstein's attentional tactic is but one of many varieties of repression. As Freud's notion of repression went through refinement, he spelled out several other ways the mind can keep painful thoughts and memories from consciousness. A simple, blanket forgetting was one of numerous twists of mind which could serve.

As Freud and his circle gathered more and more clinical data from psychoanalysis, he described increasing numbers of such lacunas. His case discussions revolved in part around unraveling the intricacies of these maneuvers. For example, in two case histories, the "Rat Man" and "Dr. Schreber," Freud touches on more than a dozen, though not always using the names by which they later came to be recognized.[29]

His general term for these mental maneuvers was "defense," although he also used as a synonym "repression in the broadest sense" because all defensive techniques, in Freud's view, entail some degree of repression. Whatever the specifics of the defenses, they share with repression a single means and purpose: they are all cognitive devices for tampering with reality to avoid pain.

Epstein's repression is unique only in his ability to report it. As Freud points out:[30] "This effortless and regular avoidance . . . of anything that had once been distressing affords us the prototype . . . of *repression*. It is a familiar fact that much of this avoidance of what is distressing—this ostrich policy—is still to be seen in the normal mental life of adults."

The defense mechanisms are, in essence, attentional tricks we play on ourselves to avoid pain. They are the wherewithal for implementing the ostrich policy. These self-deceits are not unique to the psychoanalytic session. Freud's point is well taken: we all use them.

The way a given defense creates its blind spot can be analyzed using the model of mind described in Part Two. Each defensive strategy works in a slightly different way, and taken as a whole they suggest how ingeniously the normal mechanics of mind can be subverted in the service of avoiding anxiety. As Erdelyi points out, this kind of perceptual bias can occur virtually anywhere in the mind's flow, from the very first millisecond brush with a stimulus, to the recall of a distant memory.[31]

There is a potentially endless assortment of specific tactics for creating the bias of perception that leads to a blind spot. As Erdelyi puts it, "bias begins at the beginning and ends only at the very end of information processing," and thus "may be distorted in countless ways for the purpose of defense."

Here follow thumbnail sketches of some of the most common defenses described in psychoanalytic literature, and a tentative analysis of how, interpreted by our model of mind, each might work.

REPRESSION: FORGETTING AND FORGETTING ONE HAS FORGOTTEN.

Freud reserved the term "repression" in its narrow sense for the simple defense of directly keeping a thought, impulse, or memory from awareness. Repression has come to mean the defense wherein one forgets, then forgets one has forgotten. Since all defenses begin with the essential twist on reality that such a blankout provides, repression is the building block of the other defenses. R. D. Laing tells a tale about himself which exemplifies repression in action:[32]

> When I was thirteen, I had a very embarrassing experience. I shall not embarrass you by recounting it. About two minutes after it happened, I caught myself in the process of putting it out of my mind. I had already more than half forgotten it. To be more precise, I was in the process of sealing off the whole operation by forgetting that I had forgotten it. How many times I had done this before I cannot say. . . . I am sure this was not the first time I had done that trick, and not the last, but most of these occasions, so I believe, are still so effectively repressed, that I have still forgotten that I have forgotten them.

Ripe candidates for repression include unacceptable sexual wishes (such as the wish to have sex with one's parent), aggressive

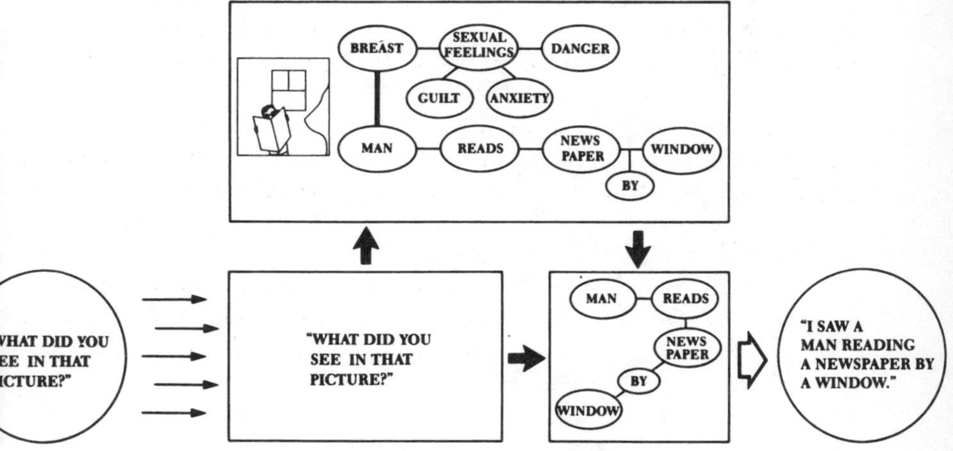

FIGURE 15. Anatomy of repression. The information repressed cannot be recalled from memory, even though the original trajectory of the information may once have passed through awareness.

urges (such as the related wish to kill a parent or sibling), shameful fantasies and dreadful feelings, and, most especially, disturbing memories. The signs of repression include, of course, the paradox that if we *do* repress such items from the mind, there will be no trace that we have done so. The thoughts have seemingly perished.

Using our model of mind as a template, repressed information can be seen to have passed into long-term memory. This passage may have been through awareness. But repression blockades its subsequent path of access to awareness. Although the schemas for that information remain in memory, they cannot be recalled (or cannot be under ordinary circumstances—psychoanalysis, among other tactics, may break the blockade). What's more, once repressed, the fact that information has been repressed is forgotten, and so there is no impetus to *try* to remember it.

Denial and Reversal: What is so is not the case; the opposite is the case.

Denial is the refusal to accept things as they are. While the entire case is not blotted from awareness, as is done in repression, the facts are realigned to obscure the actual case. "I hate you" becomes "I do not hate you." Denial is the common first reaction to devastating loss; patients who are told they have only a few months to live often deny that fact. For the patient with a life-threatening illness the denial typically passes, followed by another reaction such as rage. For the neurotic, though, denial can become a fixture of consciousness, a favored defense.

Reversal carries denial one step further. The fact is denied, then transformed into its opposite: "I hate you" becomes "I love you"; "I am sad" changes to "I am happy." Reversal (sometimes called "reaction formation") is a handy way to sanitize unruly impulses. The urge to be messy is transformed into excessive cleanliness; anger surfaces as smothering nurturance.

In our framework, denial is accomplished by information entering into unconscious memory without first passing into awareness. Once in the unconscious, the denied information undergoes reversal and passes into awareness.

Projection: What is inside is cast outside.

If one's feelings are too much to bear, the mind can handle them at a distance. One way to distance feeling is to act as if it were not one's own. The formula for projection of one's feelings onto someone else includes two parts: denial and displacement. First, an anxiety-provoking feeling, idea, or impulse is denied, blockaded from awareness. Then the person displaces those feelings outward, onto someone else: my anger toward him evaporates, to be mysteriously replaced by his anger toward me. Once cast out onto someone else, the projected part of the self is encountered as though it were a complete stranger—though one that bears an uncanny similarity to the forgotten original. As with reversal, projection transforms data denied and passed into the unconscious. Once altered, it reaches awareness.

ISOLATION: EVENTS WITHOUT FEELINGS.

Isolation is a partial blanking out of experience, a semi-denial. An unpleasant event is not repressed, but the feelings it evokes are. In that way the details can remain in awareness, but cleansed of their aversive tone. Attention fixes on the facts, while blanking out the related feelings. The result is a bland version of experience, in which the facts remain the same but there are no feelings to go with them. This was the tactic Epstein applied in insulating himself from the impact of his father's death, presumably, and accounts for his apparent indifference to the Holocaust.

RATIONALIZATION: I GIVE MYSELF A COVER STORY.

One of the more commonplace strategies, rationalization, allows the denial of one's true motives by covering over unpleasant impulses with a cloak of reasonableness. In a ploy similar to isolation, attention stays with the facts at hand, but blockades the true impulse behind them, replacing it with a counterfeit. Rationalizations are lies so slick we can get away with telling them not only to ourselves, but even to others, without flinching. "It's for your own good" and "This hurts me more than it hurts you" signal rationalization at work, a favored defense among intellectuals, whose psychological talents include inventing convincing excuses and alibis.

SUBLIMATION: REPLACE THE THREATENING WITH THE SAFE.

Through sublimation, one satisfies an unacceptable impulse indirectly by taking an approved object. The formula: a socially objectionable impulse is retained, but takes as its object a socially desirable end. In displacement, a related maneuver, the impulse takes any other object, acceptable or not. Sublimation allows instincts to be channeled rather than repressed, as they are in the more neurotic defenses. Urges are acknowledged, albeit in a modified form. The impulse to steal is reincarnated as a career in banking; the scream masquerades as song; the urge to rape dons the disguise of courtship; the compulsion to maim resurfaces as the surgeon's artistry. Sublimation, Freud argued, is the great civilizer, the force which keeps mankind manageable and makes human progress possible.

The attentional dynamic that underlies projection operates as well in these other defenses—isolation, rationalization, and sublimation. In each, an actual state of affairs is denied—it passes into the unconscious before it reaches awareness. Once in the unconscious, the information can be cosmeticized in a variety of ways. In isolation the negative feelings recede from attention, while the event itself enters awareness. In rationalization it is one's true motives that are split off and more acceptable ones spliced in in their stead. And in sublimation it is the nature of the impulse and its true object that are sanitized. From an attentional perspective, all these defenses share a common procedure with projection. Step one is denial; step two, transformation occurs in the unconscious; step three, the transformed version enters awareness.

As we have seen, Freud's notion that the mind guards against anxiety by deflecting attention is not unique in psychology, nor are the defenses he notes the only such attentional tricks for allaying tension. While defense mechanisms censor memory, security operations distort attention to the present moment. To the list of Freudian defenses, we can add some security operations from Sullivan. Two of them point to yet another way attention can be distorted to defend against anxiety.

SELECTIVE INATTENTION: I DON'T SEE WHAT I DON'T LIKE.

Selective inattention edits from experience those elements that might be unsettling were one to notice them. This is a broad-beamed operation, warding off everyday anxiety—the bill one just happened to misplace, the unpleasant duty forgotten. Selective inattention is an all-purpose response to everyday agonies; it is close to what Neisser described as the simplest instance of a diversionary schema. Through this mini-denial, says Sullivan, "one simply doesn't happen to notice almost an infinite series of more-or-less meaningful details of one's living." The utter simplicity of selective inattention—and its ubiquity in everyday life—qualifies it as a generic defense, perhaps the most common.

AUTOMATISM: I DON'T NOTICE WHAT I DO.

As we saw in Part Two, much of what we do is done automatically, out of awareness. Certain of these automatized activities cover up elements of experience that might make us uncomfortable if we fully realized our motives or objectives. Automatism allows entire sequences of such behavior to go on without our having to notice either that they happened or the troubling urges they might signify. Sullivan[33] cites as an example his walking down the street in Manhattan and noticing that "quite a number of men look at what is called the fly of your pants, and look away hastily. . . . Many of them raise their eyes to yours—apparently . . . to see if they have been noticed. But the point is that some of them, if they encounter your gaze, are as numb and indifferent as if nothing has occurred. . . . Even if it were brought emphatically to the attention of the person who manifested it, his natural inclination would always be to deny that it had occurred."

In both selective inattention and automatism, the main locus of defense is at the filter. In selective inattention a portion of what is perceived is deleted prior to reaching awareness. In automatism, the inattention extends to the response one makes as well.

While defenses operate beneath the surface of awareness, in retrospect we can sometimes realize we have used one, as Epstein's recollections testify. Indeed, when Matthew Erdelyi polled a class of psychology students, he found that virtually all of them said they had at some time used intentional repression to keep painful thoughts or memories from awareness.[34] (The sole exception was one student who, presumably, had repressed having repressed.)

"Most people," reports Erdelyi, "can recall materials they had previously excluded from consciousness in order to avoid psychic pain and can, moreover, recall the specific techniques of defense by which the rejection from consciousness was achieved." In his informal poll, 72 percent recalled using projection, 46 percent realized they had used reversal, 86 percent displacement, and 96 percent rationalization. Each time these defenses were employed, the act went on out of awareness, although in retrospect the students sometimes could see they had used them.

The defenses—our bastions against painful information—operate in a shadow world of consciousness, beyond the fringes of awareness. Most often we are oblivious to their operation and remain the unknowing recipient of the version of reality they admit into our ken. The craft of teasing out and capturing defenses *in vivo* is a tricky endeavor. While people can, perhaps, realize they have at one time or another relied on a defense, without special conditions our self-deceptions are largely impenetrable and unnoticed. The one method tailor-made for pursuing defenses in operation is, of course, psychoanalysis.

THE THERAPIST'S DILEMMA

What can't be seen is hard to change. Both Freud and Sullivan, working from not so very different vantage points, hit on the identical formulation: the person prevails against anxiety by sacrificing his range of attention. This failure to see our self-deceits protects them; Sullivan is struck by "how suavely we simply ignore great bodies of experience, any clearly analyzed instance of which might present us with a very real necessity for change."

The dance-away lover seems doomed to an endless cycle of romances with starry-eyed beginnings and tearful endings. The abrasive manager somehow keeps rubbing up against recalcitrant employees. The compulsive workaholic just can't seem to get his wife to understand his pressing need to bring work home at night. Our defenses insulate us from the vital lie at the heart of our misery.

Sullivan marveled at the "means by which we do not profit from experience which falls within our particular handicap." Freud noted the strange "repetition compulsion" which kept people reliving their worst crises. Not learning the lessons of personal history, we seem doomed to repeat them. Sullivan summed up the dilemma neatly, in terms Freud would most likely have appreciated:[35]

> We don't *have* the experience from which we might profit —that is, although it occurs, we never notice what it must mean: in fact we never notice that a good deal of it has occurred at all. This is what is really troublesome in psychotherapy, I suppose—the wonderfully bland way in which people overlook the most glaring implications of certain acts of their own, or of certain reactions of theirs to other people's acts—that is, what they are apt to report as other people's acts. Much more tragically, they may over-

> look the fact that these things have occurred at all; these things just aren't remembered, even though the person has had them most unpleasantly impressed on him.

One psychoanalyst notes that because these defenses begin very early in life caused by "often well-meaning parents," the internal prohibitions against seeing what has been done are tied up with having to redefine just how "loving" one's parents were—a strong internal taboo. As a result, in later life the individual cannot get to the roots of this repression without help. It is as though "someone had stamped on his back a mark he will never be able to see without a mirror. One of the functions of psychotherapy is to provide the mirror."

It fell to Anna Freud to formulate the classic statement of the therapist's judo in disabling the defense. Her book *The Ego and the Mechanism of Defense* has been in print continuously since 1936, and remains the touchstone for understanding the defenses at work—and what therapy can do to remedy them.

The ego, writes Miss Freud, operates in a delicate balance between pressures from the id—a cauldron of desire and impulse —and the superego—the quality of conscience that inhibits desire. While external dangers are sources of objective anxiety, the id and its impulses spawn *subjective* anxiety, a threat from within. The ego and superego must cap impulse; the defenses are attentional maneuvers for that task.

In tracing the anatomy of defenses, the analyst must do a good deal of detective work. "All the defensive measures of the ego against the id," writes Anna Freud, "are carried out silently and invisibly. The most that we can ever do is to reconstruct them in retrospect: we can never really witness them in operation. . . . The ego knows nothing of it; we are aware of it only subsequently, when it becomes apparent that something is missing."

For example, Miss Freud tells of a young girl who came to be analyzed because of acute anxiety attacks which kept her from going to school. The girl was "friendly and frank" with Miss Freud, save for one exception: she never mentioned her symptom, the anxiety attacks. Whenever Miss Freud would broach the subject, the girl would drop her friendliness and launch a volley of contemptuous and mocking remarks. Miss Freud admits to finding herself at a loss in the face of the girl's ridicule—at least for a while.

Further analysis, though, revealed to Miss Freud the missing component, the defense at work. The girl's outbursts, says Miss Freud, had little to do with the analysis, but rather were triggered "whenever emotions of tenderness, longing, or anxiety were about to emerge" in her feelings. The more powerful the feelings, the stronger the ridicule. As the girl's analyst, Miss Freud was at the receiving end of the outbursts because of her efforts to bring the anxiety into the open.

This mental operation Miss Freud refers to as "defense by means of ridicule and scorn." It began, she deduces from further analysis, with the girl's identification with her dead father, who "used to try to train the girl in self-control by making mocking remarks when she gave way to some emotional outburst."

This single case neatly encapsulates the psychoanalytic attack on ego defenses. One clue to the shape of defenses is an odd blind spot—in this instance, the girl's glossing over the fact of her anxiety attacks. That sensitive topic triggers a strong reaction, aimed at the analyst: the girl lashes out at Miss Freud. The analyst assumes that such reactions are transference, reenactments of early crucial relationships, rather than simple feelings about the therapist. Reading these reactions as further clues, the analyst deduces the structure of the defense: here, a denial of anxiety which is covered over by ridicule.

As Anna Freud puts it, the necessary technique "was to begin with the analysis of the patient's defense against her affects and to go on to the elucidation of her resistance in the transference. Then, and then only, was it possible to proceed to the analysis of her anxiety itself and of its antecedents." In therapy, the analyst watches for responses out of keeping with the business at hand, ones where the analyst is herself the target. These reactions she reads as resistance, clues to ego defenses, with the assumption that she is an innocent bystander to an ancient, childhood drama.

During psychoanalysis the silhouette of defenses stands out in sharpest relief during free association. The patient is invited to speak whatever comes to mind, without censorship—a promise the analyst knows the patient can never keep. The defenses are there to censor whenever threatening material approaches awareness. When such a threat emerges—say, the memory of a childhood molestation, long hidden in a mental attic—"then the ego bestirs itself," in Anna Freud's words, and "by means of one or another of its customary defense mechanisms intervenes in the flow of associations."

The ego stands most exposed when strong feelings are in the air—or about to surface. The ego might ward off, for various reasons, such basic sentiments as "love, longing, jealousy, mortification, pain, and mourning," as well as "hatred, anger, and rage," to name the feelings Miss Freud lists as accompanying, respectively, sexual wishes and aggressive impulses. The ego, in checking such feelings, changes them in some way. Such transformations of feeling are a hallmark of the defenses in action.

The chain of thoughts derails as the threatening material comes near to mind. The result is a sudden silence, or change of topic, or rush of feeling, all of which are suspect responses. Each in its own way signals a lacuna at work, the nature of which is hinted by the particular veer taken. These detours are what the analyst recognizes as "resistance." The resistance is, in one sense, to the fundamental rule of free association—to cease all censorship and speak one's mind freely. In another sense, the resistance is to the material that the defenses guard against.

At this juncture, the analyst's attention switches from the patient's train of thought to the resistance itself—from the content of what is said to the process of what is *not* said. At that moment, says Anna Freud, "the analyst has an opportunity for witnessing, then and there, the putting into operation . . . of one of those defensive measures." Such analytic detective work is of necessity circuitous, a mental analogue of archeological reconstruction. But it is crucial. By studying the shape and flow of the patient's associations and the eddies and crosscurrents that lacunas cause, the analyst can discover—like sensing a rock hidden in a rushing stream—the sort of defense the ego has relied upon.

To tease out the defenses is a piece of what analysts call "ego analysis." It is a crucial step. The next task will be "to undo what has been done by the defense, i.e., to find out and restore to its place that which has been omitted through repression, to rectify displacements, and to bring that which has been isolated back into its true context." The defenses having been pierced, the analyst can then turn to the discovery of *which* impulses necessitated raising these mental barriers in the first place.

In keeping its secrets, the ego reveals to the analyst *how* it keeps those secrets: By the very act of resistance to therapy, the ego bares itself. The essence of analysis, then, is restoring awareness of what we fail to notice—and fail to notice that we fail to notice.

In sum, the ego's task is to control the flow of information in order to deflect anxiety; the architecture of self is shaped, in large degree, by the set of lacunas it favors to censor and guide information flow. As we will see in the next Part, defenses mold personality: the *particular way* we use attention to disarm anxiety indelibly marks us. For example, someone who relies on denial and repression will perceive and act differently from someone who favors reversal and projection. Each will experience—and *fail* to experience—the world differently, and will muddle through troubled events making different sorts of waves.

PART FOUR

Cognition Creates Character

NEUROTIC STYLES

Our favored defenses become habitual mental maneuvers. What has worked well in key moments, keeping anxiety under control with rewarding results, is likely to be tried again. Epstein, the novelist, found as a child that isolation fended off the sorrow of his father's death; that same cutting off of feeling offers itself years later when he confronts the horrors of Holocaust. Anna Freud's patient, whose feelings were damaged by her father's scorn, grows up to be a sarcastic, scornful woman.

Successful defense becomes habit, habit molds style. These familiar tactics become second nature; when psychic pain confronts us, we fall back into their soothing arms. What may have been at first a serendipitous discovery in the battle against anxiety comes to define our mode of perception and response to the world. Becoming adept at such strategies means that we favor some parts of experience while blocking off others. We set bounds on the range of our thoughts and feelings, limit our freedom of perception and action, in order to feel at peace.

Favored tactics of defense become a sort of armor-plating on experience, a gathering around of preferred bulwarks in the battle against unsettling items of information. It was Wilhelm Reich (while still a respected member of Freud's circle) who articulated the notion of defensive armoring most fully.[1] The phrase Reich coined was "character armor," the shielding of the self so it can ward off anxieties as it moves through a threatening world. One's character dons armor in the form of habitual defenses. The armor is in part attentional, for the dangers the self must deflect are in the form of information: threats, dreads, anger, impulse deferred, and the like. "In everyday life," said Reich, "the character plays a role similar to the one it plays as a resistance in the treatment: that of a psychic defense apparatus."

Reich saw that the symptoms patients brought to therapy, whether anorexia or impotence, phobia or depression, were, in a sense, beside the point. The same symptom could bespeak very different underlying dynamics of character structure. Reich advocated that the therapist first attend to the overall *style* of the patient, to the patterning of resistances due to character, not to the presenting symptom.

Defensive style is character armor. In therapy, it leads to a typical mode of resistance, which will arise unmistakably no matter what the specific symptom. The stamp of the armor is on a person's whole mode of being. According to Reich, the resistance stemming from character[2]

> . . . is expressed not in terms of content but . . . in the way one typically behaves, in the manner in which one speaks, walks, and gestures; and in one's characteristic habits (how one smiles or sneers, whether one speaks coherently or incoherently, *how* one is polite and *how* one is aggressive).
>
> It is not what the patient says and does that is indicative of character resistance, but *how* he speaks and acts; not what he reveals in dreams, but *how* he censors, distorts, condenses, etc.

Defenses are, in the main, attentional ploys. But attention is just part of the process. As we have seen, every part of the sequence, from perception through cognition to response, is vulnerable to skews in the service of defense. The person's entire mental apparatus—his mode of being in the world—is shaped in part by his defensive strategy, by his armoring of character.

Character armor is the face the self turns to the world. On it are etched the twists and turns the defenses demand in their struggle to avoid what is unpleasant. By reading character, the defensive structure is revealed, like the skeleton of a cadaver under the anatomist's dissecting knife. That structure maps the special contours of one's experience.

"Character armor," writes Ernest Becker,[3] "really refers to the whole life style that a person assumes, in order to live and act with a certain security. We all have some, because we all need to organize our personality. This organization is a process whereby some things have to be valued more than others, some acts have to be permitted, others forbidden, some lines of conduct have to be closed, some kinds of thought can be entertained, others are taboo—and so on. Each person literally closes off his world, fences himself around, in the *very process of his own growth and organization.*"

Those forbidden acts and thoughts create blind spots. But the patterning of armor, Becker understands, is double-edged. While there are zones outlawed from attention, other parts are highlighted. The areas of ample awareness are zones in which we become particularly adept operators. These regions of expertise are defined by our lacunas: those that block awareness entirely form its margins; those that allow in some information—even if twisting it so as to decontaminate threats—give these zones their inner definition.

Those allowable zones are free of anxiety, or mostly free. We feel at ease there, able to move without constraint. Within those zones we develop our strengths; awareness focuses in them with energy. These zones, Becker proposes, resemble a fetish. "Fetishization," Becker explains, in this sense "means the organization of perception and action, by the personality, around a very striking and compelling—but narrow—theme."

A fetish, as Becker uses the term, is a special range of experience that attracts the flow of attention. Freud used the term "cathexis" to refer to much the same thing. Becker elaborates:[4]

> If everybody has some character armor, everyone is also somewhat of a fetishist. If you are obliged to close yourself to the multiplicity of things, it follows that you will focus somewhat on a restrained area of things; and, if you cannot freely value everything, nor freely weight all things against all other things, then, you must give disproportionate weight to some things *which do not deserve* this weight. You artificially inflate a small area of the world, give it a higher value in the horizon of your perception and action. And you do this because it represents an area that you can *firmly hold on to,* that you can *skillfully manipulate,* that you can *use easily to justify yourself*—your actions, your sense of self, your option in the world.

Let us recapitulate. From the need to soften the impact of threatening information, lacunas arise. They operate on attention, through a variety of tactics, all of which filter the flow of information. These strategies for dealing with the world come to define the shape of responses as well as perception. Their outlines become the frame for character.

David Shapiro, a psychologist on the staff at Austen Riggs Clinic in the 1960s, wrote a series of brilliant papers culminating in a book detailing the crucial role of attention in the patterns of character.[5] Shapiro's special insight was in showing how a specific mode of attending is crucial to an entire way of being; that is, that cognition shapes character.

Shapiro's main interest was in the patterns most often seen in the therapist's office; he called his portraits "neurotic styles." But while these attentional patterns shade into the realm of pathology, for the most part they typify styles within the normal range. Take, for example, the type I call "The Detective."

THE DETECTIVE

The note read: "The supply of game for London is going steadily up. Head-Keeper Hudson, we believe, has been now told to receive all orders for fly-paper and for preservation of your hen-pheasant's life." On reading it, the recipient, a country gentleman, promptly suffered a stroke, from which he never recovered.

That note was to change the course of literature, for indirectly it spawned the genre of mystery novels. It was the beginning of Sherlock Holmes's first case, "The Gloria Scott."[6]

The note is received by the father of one of Holmes's college classmates, and Holmes is soon on the case. Holmes sees at once the letter is a code, which he quickly breaks. Every third word is the real message: "The game is up. Hudson has told all. Fly for your life."

But Holmes's special genius does not stop there. Whoever wrote the code had left some further clues. After the sender wrote the intended message, Holmes reasons, "he had, to fulfill the prearranged cipher, to fill in any two words in each space. He would naturally use the first words which came to his mind, and if there were so many which referred to sport among them, you may be tolerably sure that he is either an ardent shot or interested in breeding."

This bit of reasoning points straight to a man who used to go hunting with the stroke victim every autumn. Holmes, as usual, is well on his way to a solution.

Holmes, though a fictional character, is nevertheless an exemplar of the attentional type we will call "The Detective," in his honor. Consider what we know of Holmes's superb powers of attention and deduction. Where others saw nothing or trivia, Holmes spotted incriminating evidence. He had a special talent for reading the smallest details of a situation. "It has long been an axiom of mine," said he, "that the little things are infinitely the most important."

Holmes's genius was not just in spotting the telling detail. It was also in knowing what to make of it. For example, in *A Study in Scarlet* he spots a flaky cigar ash at the scene of the murder; he recognizes at once that a Trichinopoly cigar had been smoked there. His arcane expertise included bloodstains, footprints, tattoos. Noting a mud spatter, he could say which part of London it had come from. He could distinguish and name forty-two kinds of bicycle-tire impressions and seventy-five brands of perfume. A notch on a tooth would, for Holmes, identify a weaver, while a certain callus on the left thumb would reveal a typesetter.

Holmes represents The Detective at his best. What sets him apart as exemplary for this type is his awareness of the dangers of bias. "I make a point," Holmes once said, "of never having any prejudices and of following docilely wherever fact may lead me."

In this regard, Holmes may have been saved by virtue of his status as a fictional character. In all his cases, by one count, Holmes made at least two hundred seventeen inferences, all of which he blithely presents as facts.[7] He tested his guesses in one way or another in only twenty-eight of these instances. Yet he turned out to have been correct in virtually all of them.

Here Holmes—through Arthur Conan Doyle's design—skirts the pitfall that awaits The Detective in everyday life: the bending of facts to fit a theory. Holmes prided himself on never constructing theories beyond the facts at hand: "Insensibly," he once cautioned Watson, "one begins to twist facts to suit theories instead of theories to suit facts." To the degree that The Detective twists facts to accommodate theory, his character is askew. When carried to its extreme, that bent of mind is diagnosed as paranoia.

The Detective is hyperalert.[8] The sharp acuity of his attention makes him occasionally brilliant in his observation, his catching of the telling detail. He scans with a penetrating gaze. He doesn't simply look; he searches. His attention is unusually acute and active. Nothing out of the ordinary will escape his attention, nor will anything remotely related to his preoccupations of the moment. Shapiro tells of one such patient in therapy who was apprehensive that he would be hypnotized. On his first visit to the therapist's office he "just happened to notice" a book on hypnotherapy and commented on it. The book was on a crowded bookshelf, twelve feet away.

The Detective's alertness is marked by a hypersensitivity. "These people," Shapiro notes,[9] "are exceedingly, nervously sensitive to anything out of the ordinary or unexpected; any such item, however trivial or slight it might seem from the standpoint of the normal person, will trigger their attention in its full, searching intensity. This hyperalertness is . . . not simply a frightened response or a nervous one; it is something more than that. These people seem to want to cover everything, and any new element will also need to be examined according to the dimensions of their suspicious interest and concern."

In other words, The Detective regards anything novel with the kind of apprehensive vigilance that a Manhattanite feels on hearing footsteps from behind on a darkened street at two in the morning. In order for something—a new delivery boy, a surprise phone call from an old friend, an unexpected memo from the boss—to arouse his scrutiny, it need simply be new, surprising, or unexpected. It need not, from an everyday viewpoint, be especially suspicious. For The Detective, though, it is suspicious *because* it is unusual.

Take, for example, a moment from Sherlock Holmes, in which he is discussing with an inspector the disappearance of a race horse. Holmes refers to "the curious incident of the dog in the nighttime."

"The dog," said the inspector, "did nothing in the nighttime."

"That," replies Holmes, "was the curious incident."

The Detective's hyperalertness, says Shapiro, serves a special end: to avoid surprise. Since life is full of surprise, novelty, and change, and since by its very nature one never knows when a surprise will come, his vigilant state is the necessary result of his constant anticipation. As Shapiro observes, "The suspicious person is ready for anything unexpected and immediately becomes aware of it. He must . . . bring it into the orbit of his scheme of things and, in effect, satisfy himself that it is not or at least is no longer surprising."

His purpose is not so much to prove the unexpected innocent of his suspicions. Not at all. He seeks only to satisfy himself that the surprise—the strange noise, the cancelled date—has been scrutinized and categorized. The verdict may be "guilty"—that is, "suspicion justified." But that is as soothing to The Detective as is the other verdict. For it is not to find his suspicion unwarranted that he searches so intently; it is simply to remove the threat of surprise.

What he fears is the unscrutinized novelty, not the existence of danger. His very posture toward the world is that it is full of danger. This assumption justifies his constant suspicions, his ongoing vigilance. In some sense, then, he is reassured by finding his worst fears confirmed. In finding the world full of threats, he reaffirms his basic stance in life.

The Detective's vigilance is, in many situations, a real strength. For one thing, it often shows up as a superior score on tests of achievement or intelligence. Apart from doing well on tests, this type thrives in any calling that benefits from an active and intensely searching attention, such as intelligence or police work, or scholarship of the Talmudic sort, where there is a premium on searching out clues to hidden meanings.

The weakness of The Detective's attentional style is related to its strengths. His search is driven; it is *for something*. Its goal is to confirm a preconceived idea. And here he falls prey to the danger Sherlock Holmes warned against: "One begins to twist facts to suit theories instead of theories to suit facts." When his vigilance is pushed toward its extremes, it twists into a biased search, a search that seeks to prove a notion rather than simply to investigate and let the facts yield up a theory.

This driven search leaves a distinctive distortion in The Detective's perception. He looks so keenly that he does not quite see; he hears so astutely that he fails to listen. In other words, his deficit is not in his attentional powers, which are often brilliantly attuned. His attention is off because it is guided by a lack of interest in the obvious. The surface of things is for him far from the truth of the matter; he seeks to piece through plain facts to the hidden reality. He listens and looks not to gather what is apparent, but what it *signifies*.

Looking so hard for the telling clue to a hidden meaning is like peering into a microscope. The Detective is apt to search so intently that he loses sight of the context that gives meaning to what he sees. That, of course, fits well with his basic stance toward it anyhow: its *seeming* context is the merely apparent, which is for him a false reality. He grasps at a small detail that fits his schema, while ignoring its actual context. The net effect is that he loses a sense of the fact's real significance, replacing it with a special interpretation.

While built upon factual details, such a subjective world can be totally askew in the meaning given those details. And since his conclusions are based on facts, The Detective can agree with you totally as to the details of a case, while having a wholly different sense of their meaning and significance. Such people, notes Shapiro,[10] "do not ignore a piece of data; on the contrary they examine it quite carefully. But they examine it with an extraordinary prejudice, dismissing what is not relevant to their suppositions and seizing on anything that confirms them. . . . They operate from the outset on the assumption that anything that does not confirm their expectation is 'mere appearance.' Thus, they would say that they are interested in penetrating the sham, the pretense, and the superficial; they want to get to the heart of the matter, the underlying truth." That truth, it turns out, is exactly what they expected in the first place.

Shapiro tells, for example, of a man who was convinced his boss "wanted to make him jump through the hoop." The man gathered much evidence to prove the point, some keenly noted, all factual. The boss insisted that the man do things the boss's way, that he be prompt, that he be less removed with customers. The man pointed to a certain edge in his boss's voice, a distinctive attitude of reprimand in the way the boss spoke. All this, the man was sure, amounted to convincing evidence that the boss was, in reality, trying to lord it over the man, "to make him crawl."

But, as Shapiro points out, "These facts did not add up to a particularly unusual boss." He may have done all these things, as most bosses do. They are part of a boss's job. There was work to be done, and the boss was responsible for it. The patient disregarded this context and thus radically altered the significance of these facts.

Shapiro goes on to observe that attention rigidly focused on selective evidence can impose its own conclusions virtually anywhere. Thus, "the suspicious person can be at the same time absolutely right in his perception and absolutely wrong in his judgment."

The Detective's interpretive schema often takes the form of a political or economic view, religious dogma, or grand conspiracy theory. But it can just as well be the mundane conviction that "people are against me," "my boss has it in for me," or "pollution is ruining my health." Of course, any of those propositions could, in a given instance, be true. What sets The Detective apart, though, is the lack of manifest support for his favored scheme of things.

Theodore Millon traces the shaky underpinnings of such a schema:[11] "Little difference exists in their mind between what they have seen and what they have thought. Momentary impressions and hazy memories become fact. Chains of unconnected facts are fitted together. An inexorable course from imagination to supposition to suspicion takes place, and soon a system of invalid and unshakeable belief has been created."

Whether his search to confirm the schema is furtive and apprehensive or arrogant and aggressive, its tone is one and the same: suspicious. His suspiciousness is impressive in its strength. While ordinary suspicions are sparked by some situational cue—a door found ajar, let's say—The Detective needs no such cue. He can be on guard whatever the situation, regardless of its apparent innocence or banality. Where most people would require a door left ajar to enter their home with extra caution, The Detective is predisposed to think, "Watch out—they didn't leave the door ajar this time, but they may be in there."

Trying to talk such a person out of his convictions is particularly frustrating. Rational arguments are of no avail; The Detective will be able to pick out some detail that he takes to confirm his own view. Indeed, the very act of persuasion can become the object of his suspicion. Why, he will challenge, are you so interested in getting me to change my mind? You, too, then come within the purview of his suspicion.

The notion that things are not as they seem can lead to a curious complication. If, after searching every nook and cranny, events fail to confirm his beliefs, The Detective need not let facts upset his preconceptions: the failure to confirm suspicions simply proves how clever and deceitful people can be. Contradictions and disconfirmations are easily dismissed, while trivial or irrelevant data are seized upon.

The dramatic flavor of this nether world of suspicion and imagined intrigue is captured by the spy thriller genre. The works of Robert Ludlum are particularly apt, as the following review of one of his books reflects:[12]

> Do you have clearance to read this article? Are you *absolutely certain* no one followed you home from the newsstand? It's all right; you won't be allowed to finish it anyway—in the world of Robert Ludlum, no one finishes even the most innocent activity before a hulking stranger looms out of the shadows wielding a deadly Graz-Burya automatic. That woman who just got on the bus—wasn't she two carts behind you on the supermarket line? There are conspiracies here so vast that literally *everyone is a part of them.* Secrets so dark that literally *no one knows them.* If you have to ask what's going on, you already know too much.

Not that The Detective is caught up in such a fantasy world of deep intrigue. But Ludlum pushes to its extreme the bent of mind that typifies this sort of cognition. In its garden variety, the same key factors operate: things are not what they seem, a guarded suspiciousness is at work, and a theory of hidden meanings can be confirmed if the proper clues are found. The theory may be utterly mundane—the mailman is withholding my mail, people are talking about me behind my back—but the operations by which it is confirmed are identical to those Ludlum chronicles.

The Detective's sometimes florid view of reality and the attentional maneuvers he uses to validate that view are in themselves the surface signs of deeper mechanisms at work. These traits belie a distinctive set of self-deceits, a particular pattern of psychic barriers erected against the dread of certain threats. Those lacunas give The Detective both his unique talents and his great failings.

THE ANATOMY OF PSYCHIC ARMOR

Threats to his feelings of competence trigger The Detective's defenses. For example, in a passage that reads like the opening of a Franz Kafka short story, Shapiro tells of a well-respected and able man who, nevertheless, was unsure of his competence and defensive about his rank at work. One day he made a mistake.

"It was a mistake of no great consequence," says Shapiro,[13] "easily corrected, and hardly likely to be noticed by anyone else. Nevertheless, for some days afterwards, he was preoccupied with imagining even the most remote possibilities of being discovered and the humiliation that would, according to him, follow from discovery. During that time, when the boss walked by, he 'noticed' an irritable glance and imagined the boss to be thinking, 'This man is the weak link in our organization.' " Shapiro ends the narrative there, but it is easy to imagine a sad tale ensuing, where nonexistent slights and insults concatenate into a grotesque and tragic end.

When The Detective perceives such a threat his defenses mobilize. His attention focuses into a single powerful beam that aims to confirm the suspicion. While he searches the world around him for clues and confirmations, he meanwhile constricts his range of experience so as to cut himself off from his own feelings and impulses. After all, a command headquarters under siege cannot be distracted by such irrelevant stirrings. He handles these unwanted feelings by casting them out—projection.

The formula for projection has two stages. In the first, a disturbing feeling, idea, or impulse raises a tide of insecurity. That, in turn, mobilizes defenses: attention is focused outward, the internal domain—particularly the disturbing aspect—is blockaded. In the second stage the person scans with an intense suspiciousness and seizes on corroborating clues. Those confirmed clues are pieced together to paint a picture of the enemy which bears an uncanny similarity to that original disturbing aspect of the self.

Once cast out, the projected self seems to be a stranger—and a sinister one at that. When he confronts his own projected suspicions and anger in the image he constructs of his enemy, he is unable to recognize any of himself therein.

The Detective's favored intrapsychic posture, then, is a combination of three maneuvers: denial of his own weakness and ill will, the projection of these aspects of himself onto others, and the ongoing effort to confirm the truth of those projections by searching for telltale clues. His denial is fiercer than the garden variety; he not only denies his own inadequacy and hostility, but disowns it by hurling it out onto others. He himself is not malicious, vindictive, or jealous; it is "they"—the others—who harbor these feelings toward him. A simple reversal justifies his resentments while absolving him.

Projection may be mobilized under stress, when the person is on the defensive. But it can also be an active ongoing part of the person's mental organization. In this milder form it most often shows up as peculiar preoccupations with some favorite form of villainy—welfare cheats, say, or the morally impure. It also can come to typify a chronic interpersonal problem, the specific players changing from time to time and place to place.

Projection makes people "difficult." The lives of such people are frequently haunted by a long string of resentful lovers, unfair bosses, or callous landlords. People of this sort often find themselves in stormy relations, particularly when they feel their autonomy is at stake. This puts them at odds with those in positions of authority as well as those whose attachments to them (lovers, spouses, family) threaten to restrict their sense of freedom.

Isolation compounds The Detective's difficulties. Unwilling to trust others and confide his doubts and insecurities, he is bereft of the sympathetic listener—a listener who might offer another perspective more grounded in reality. Without such reality checks, his suspicions continue unrestrained, gathering confirmation of a cockeyed theory. Without closeness or sharing, lacking anyone who can counter his unbridled imagination, he is vulnerable to an increasing inability to see things as others do.

The cognitive patterns that typify The Detective's psychic armoring can be summed up from another angle, in terms of those elements of experience that his blind spots hide and those that they highlight. Those aspects of experience in highlight loom large within The Detective's experience. As Becker would put it, The

Detective "fetishizes" these elements, carving out special talents and finding his unique abilities within that realm. His attentional blind spots, though, leave key aspects of experience hidden in shadow.

A cognitive profile of The Detective's blind spots and highlights:

HIGHLIGHTS	BLIND SPOTS
The telling detail	The obvious
Surprises: anything novel, out of the ordinary or unexpected	Surface meanings, "mere appearance"
Threats or their possibility	The context that lends meaning
Hidden meanings	The real significance of facts
The Clue: The detail that fits his scheme	What is irrelevant to his preconceived schema
An enemy in his own image: angry, weak, etc.	His own hostile feelings, weaknesses, and impulses; how others feel, especially tender feelings
Other people's faults	His own faults

How do such quirks take root in personality? Where does The Detective learn his paranoid stance? In short, how do we take on a diversionary schema? For these answers we have to go back to the early encounters a child has with the world, and the patterns of interaction that mold our most basic schemas.

The paranoid style is a useful case in point simply because it has been so well studied and described in both its benign and extreme forms. But, as we will see, this attentional style exemplifies a universal process of development: We have all learned some ways of alleviating our anxieties by trimming attention, sealing off painful experience.

MICROEVENTS AT THE OK CORRAL

Michael, nine months old, and his mother are having a battle. The object of their fight is a cardboard leaf, one of the pieces of a jigsaw puzzle. Michael's mother offers him the leaf; Michael slowly raises it to his mouth. The battle begins.

"No . . . it's not for eating," says Michael's mother, as she takes the leaf away.

Michael yells, quick and loud.

"Don't you yell at your mother," she says in a feisty tone. But she gives him back the piece. She watches as he again raises it to his mouth, then catches his hand with an emphatic "No!"

"Uh-h-h!" Michael protests.

She lets go, and Michael chews on the leaf with a contented murmur.

"Taste good? It's only cardboard," says his mother, defeated.

This incident is from a videotape recording hours of interactions between Michael and his mother, made by the research psychiatrist Daniel Stern. Dr. Stern has analyzed hundreds of interactions like this, which he calls "microevents," between many other mothers and their infants. Stern calls this particular microevent "The Shoot-out at the OK Corral." He's quite familiar with the interaction. From films of Michael and his mother made over a two-year period, Stern has found sixty-three similar episodes.[14]

Stern sees babies and their mothers as a "couple" of sorts, ongoing partners in life. Michael and his mother have replayed the shoot-out sequence since he was at least four months old, and probably earlier. Its standard routine: Michael puts something in his mouth, his mother tells him to take it out; he gets angry, she relents.

Stern has pieced together a videotape of these sequences, showing it re-enacted with a wooden block, purple shoes, plastic rings from a toy. Michael's mother is there each time, telling him no, that it's yucky. Michael's anger takes several forms: he throws things, shouts, knocks things over.

Through the repeated enactment of this shoot-out, Stern believes, Michael is learning something: if he asserts himself strongly, he gets what he wants. That schema, says Stern, will be reinforced for Michael with progressive variations throughout life.

It is through just this sort of early interaction, say developmental psychologists, that we learn the habits that shape our most basic responses. They encode schemas with far-reaching implications for how we will register and react to life. Many of these early patterns have to do with attention; attentional schemas, as we have seen, shape the deep structure of personality.

Socialization of attention is part of the normal course of growth. But there are some especially telling cognitive patterns—typically inculcated outside the awareness of both the child and parent—that can come to form the attentional armor of the defenses. The child psychologist Selma Fraiberg describes the beginnings of such a pattern in the son of a depressed teenaged mother.[15]

The mother spent much of her time alternating between a depressed sulk and outbursts of rage. Whether depressed or angry, she paid no attention to her son.

Fraiberg made a startling observation. When the son was in a room with strangers, his gaze would rest on their faces but pass over his mother's without a flicker of recognition. He would not look at her, let alone smile at her. When distressed, he would not call out to her. He had learned to avoid his mother, to ignore her presence—a defense that seemed to serve as his bastion against the pain of maternal neglect. He simply visually edited her from his world. What is remarkable is that this happened so early in life: the child was just three months old.

The permutation of that avoidance over the years could easily become articulated in adulthood as a lacuna, the blanking out of pain with one or another form of disattention. Observations of another three-month-old infant and her mother offer details of the kinds of interaction that would lead an infant so young to show the glimmerings of a defense. The observations were made by Stern in his study of microevents; the baby's name was Jenny.[16]

Jenny's mother was an animated woman who on first meeting struck Stern as "intrusive, controlling, and overstimulating by most standards." The mother seemed to need a high level of excitement and "wanted the level she wanted when *she* wanted it." By the time Stern observed Jenny and her mother, they had worked out a dance that went something like this. Whenever their eyes happened to meet, the mother would go into high gear, making faces and boisterous baby talk. It was too much for Jenny: she would look away.

Her mother took this as a cue to up the level of her assault. She would swing around to meet Jenny's averted face head-on, and begin another barrage. Jenny would again turn away, burying her face in the pillow. The mother continued to chase Jenny, moving even closer, burbling even louder, and adding tickling. Stern reports that watching this invasion was "almost physically painful to sit and watch. It engenders feelings of impotent rage and . . . a tightening in the gut or a headache."

Jenny, grimacing, closed her eyes and swung her head to the other side to evade her mother. Her mother followed Jenny over, with new volleys of coos and tickles. After several failures to engage Jenny, the mother picked her up under her arms and held her face-to-face. Jenny looked, but as soon as she was put down, she buried her head in her pillow. As the routine went on, the mother got visibly frustrated, angry, and confused. It ended with Jenny, crying, being put to bed.

Stern found it "inconceivable" that Jenny's mother could be unaware of how obnoxious was her way with Jenny. He suspected "some unconscious maternal hostility" at its root. Still, ever the researcher, he refrained from interfering.

After several weeks of observations, the basic pattern between Jenny and her mother was unchanged. But increasingly each seemed to give up a little on the other. Jenny looked at her mother less and less; her mother tried to engage her less. "I became progressively more concerned," commented Stern, "when a week or so later Jenny's avoidance of eye contact was almost complete . . . her face almost expressionless."

Now Stern was positively alarmed. His alarm stemmed from the knowledge that avoiding eye contact and face-to-face engagement in infancy is one of the earliest symptoms of childhood autism. Was Jenny on her way to schizophrenia?

Happily, no. A month later, worried by the potential seriousness of what his videotapes showed, Stern made a home visit. By then, somehow, they had made peace. Jenny's mother was less dogged in her pursuit of Jenny's attention. And Jenny now seemed better able to take—indeed, to enjoy—her mother's antics. The story does not end there, as Stern notes:[17]

> At each new phase of development, Jenny and her mother have had to replay this basic scenario of overshoot and resolution, but with different sets of behaviors and at higher levels of organization. We do not yet know what strengths and assets or what weaknesses and deficits for the future course of her relatedness Jenny will ultimately

> emerge with. . . . The line between an early coping mechanism and an early defense maneuver is thin.

The mastery of defensive maneuvers as protection against the pains of life is a universal aspect of growing up. Every child learns a variety of attentional tactics; healthy children are flexible about which is used when. Denial has its place, as do each of the other defenses. As Theodore Millon observes:[18]

> These essentially unconscious mechanisms ameliorate the discomfort experienced when children are unable to resolve their problems directly. Any of the classical defense mechanisms—repression, sublimation, rationalization—will serve to relieve the anguish; they are useful also in that they enable the person to maintain equilibrium until a better solution can be mustered. Healthy coping may be characterized, then, both by retreat and self-deception. . . . Only when the person persistently distorts and denies the objective world do these unconscious mechanisms interfere . . .

Trouble typically occurs when the child faces some ongoing, relentless, and repeated threat: a hostile, controlling mother, an abusive father, abandonment. The child comes to expect trouble, and dares not let down his guard. He comes more and more to rely on a favored defense, a habitual mode of keeping his feelings controlled and protected in a heartless world. What once may have been an effective, appropriate maneuver becomes a fixture in his mental economy, expands to vanquish an entire range of experience. In this way, a handy coping tactic becomes neurotic defense.

The popular belief is that defenses and neuroses arise as the result of a single, powerful trauma. Clinical wisdom instead has it that a defensive style is gradually learned, the result of repeated, protracted encounters over a long while. The attentional patterns learned in childhood become self-perpetuating: once a certain expectation of threat is learned, the person becomes predisposed to look for and find it—or look away to avoid it.

When routine strategies for handling difficult times fail a child, says Millon, he will resort to increasingly more distorting and denying maneuvers. The rule of thumb in coping, remember, is that when one can't do anything to change the situation, the other recourse is to change how one *perceives* it. That defensive twist of attention is the job of a diversionary schema. If this works as a temporary tactic for the child, well and good; a balance is restored and he can resume an even keel. But if the threat is too persistent, too unremitting, too severe, the child dares not let down his guard.

In such cases, when exposure to threat and frustration is continual, the child meets life with the expectation that danger is nigh. The attentional armor he adopted for the moment becomes part of his ongoing stance; even when no objective discomfort exists, he keeps his defenses up to ward off a danger that *might* come. "Designed initially to protect against recurrences of the painful past," says Millon, his defensive stance "now distracts and misguides" the child. As a child starts coping with non existent—but anticipated—perils, his cognitive world becomes inflexible: his defense stays prominent, his self-deceptions fixed.

HOW TO RAISE A PARANOID

The Detective's paranoia has roots similar to those described by Dr. Stern. An adult's fully articulated patterns of attention trace back to childhood. In the repetition of microevents the child learns the particular set of schemas—and defensive maneuvers—on which he will come to rely when anxiety threatens.

The case in point is paranoia. One of the most famous paranoids in the annals of psychiatry is Daniel Schreber, a German judge who went mad at the age of forty-two, and whose case was subsequently used by Freud as the basis for his theory of paranoia. Freud's elaborate intrapsychic model of the inner forces that spawn the pathology seems, though, to miss some compelling evidence that the relationship between Schreber and his father was the direct cause of his later paranoia. So immediate was the cause and effect, some suggest, that Freud's elaborate theory of paranoia may be superfluous as an explanation.

The senior Schreber was a sort of nineteenth-century Dr. Spock who wrote a series of books on child-rearing so popular that some went through forty printings and were translated into several languages. The method of child-rearing these books advocate reads like a recipe for inducing the twists of mind and spirit that ripen into paranoia. They seem to have had that result, at any rate, in the case of his son.

Morton Schatzman, in a book called *Soul Murder,* documents in detail the method by which the senior Schreber set the mental stage of his son's later psychosis.[19] These include a nightmarish assortment of devices for physical restraint, ostensibly designed for such purposes as inculcating an erect posture, which the senior Schreber inflicted on his children. When Schreber went mad years later, echoes of these contraptions were evident in his psychotic delusions.*

Parallel to the physical restrictions the senior Schreber inflicted on his son were mental ones. He justified this reign of mental tyranny under the rubric of training the child in self-control, in itself a laudable cause. There is nothing wrong with a parent setting limits and disciplining a child; to do so is quite natural. But the manner in which the senior Schreber went about this task had some unfortunate repercussions in his son's mental condition. For example, Schreber's father wrote:[20]

> Each forbidden desire—whether or not it is to the child's disadvantage—must be consistently and unfailingly opposed by an unconditional refusal. The refusal of a desire alone is not enough though; *one has to see to it that the child receives this refusal calmly,* and, if necessary, *one has to make this calm acceptance a firm habit* by using a stern word or threat. Never make an exception from this. . . . This is the only way to make it easy for the child to attain the salutary and indispensable habit of subordination and control of his will. [emphasis added]

The net effect of such a regime is a double restriction: the child must somehow keep himself from freely expressing his natural impulses and needs, and must also overcome his reaction to their being thwarted. He cannot cry, sulk, or be angry, because the demand is to accept his frustration calmly. A resigned silence is the only approved response. And all this is asked of a child not yet two.

If there is no avenue to express the hurt such a regime must evoke, then another way to meet these demands is to repress that hurt—to stamp out these feelings from one's experience. This is the first step in cultivating a paranoid: train him to deny to himself his feelings of rage and hurt toward his parent.

There are many twists of attention that might result from the double dictum to hide one's feelings and hide the fact that one has hidden them. The paranoid defensive style offers one easy solution. Start with a parent who demands a child suppress his anger at parental abuse. The child can neither let the anger show nor let on that the parent had a hand in arousing it. To shield his parents, the child must somehow keep from blaming them for the feelings they have caused. Attentional tactics work well to hide this essential truth.

What better way to hide it than to deny it to himself? Just to be

* According to Schatzman, Freud seems to have been oblivious to the role this childhood regimen may have played in Judge Schreber's psychosis.

sure, how about displacing it, too? The anger does not evaporate, but it can be made to *seem* to, or to have other causes and objects. If it won't go away entirely, then a disguise will help. One possibility is to turn it against oneself: that way lies a lifelong conviction of worthlessness. Another route is to aim it elsewhere, to find some other target than one's parents. Denial and displacement—either solution is an act of love and devotion: the parents come off blameless, and childhood can be remembered as the happiest of days.

Contrast this child's anxiety-attention trade-off with a child who has not had to deceive himself, who can keep in experience his anger from the pain, wrongs, and ordinary constraints of childhood. Not having had to twist awareness away from these feelings, he knows their natural terrain. He can be openly angry when wounded as an adult. He will not carry with him a burden of rage held back by a dam in awareness.

On the other hand, people who have had to hold in such anger harbor a fear at what might happen should the dam burst. Then the world would turn wildly unpredictable—rage can kill. So they find ways to disguise their rage. Often, they hold back other feelings too; all spontaneity comes to threaten an eruption of feeling beyond control.[21]

A report of children in Denver who were in therapy because they had been abused by their parents portrays just this picture of childhood vanquished.[22] One of the striking features of these children was their somberness. Some never laughed at all; when they played games with the therapist they did so dutifully, without enjoyment. Most saw themselves as "bad" or "stupid" and were hesitant to try anything new lest they do poorly.

Their sense of right and wrong—an obvious legacy from their parents—was extremely rigid and punitive. Their rules for what was good and bad were ironclad. When other children overstepped these bounds, they became furious. But they were unable to display any anger whatever toward adults. The paranoid process, it seems, was at work: they had learned to deny the anger they felt toward their parents (or, as an extension, other adults), and were all too ready to displace it on more amenable targets—other children.

Although they could express no anger toward grown-ups, they were seething with it. Their stories and games were full of brutal aggression:[23]

> Dolls were constantly being beaten, tormented, and killed. Many children repeated their own abuse in their play. One child, whose skull had been broken three times as an infant, always made up stories about people or animals who suffered head injuries. Another child, whose

> mother had attempted to drown her when she was a baby, began the play therapy by drowning a doll baby in the bathtub. . . . The children were almost never able to express their anxieties verbally, yet they harbored intense feelings of rage and a strong desire for revenge, which, however, were accompanied by a great fear of what might happen if these impulses should erupt.

In these tragic children denial and displacement—key mechanisms of the paranoid style—are already in place. These paranoid predispositions need not come from such explosive events as abuse; the same tendencies can be imprinted on the mind by less obvious forms of tyranny. Violence can come in subtler forms—as disapproving looks, silent rebuffs, humiliation, or love withdrawn. The net effect can be the same, provided the implicit injunction is instilled: that the parent is blameless for the feelings of hurt and anger that the child feels.

A child who expects rejection from his parents may become hyperalert to signs of it in his playmates. Such a child is likely to distort innocuous comments, seeing them as hostile. In anticipation of such hostility, the child prepares to counter it by meeting his playmates with a cold, rigid stare and some aggressive words. This in turn evokes the very response it was meant to anticipate—the child becomes the target of his playmates' real, rather than imagined, hostility. His suspiciousness has created what it predicted. The child has found his playmates reject him, just as his parents did, which justifies his becoming even more suspicious and hostile. A vicious cycle is begun, which will end as the full-blown suspiciousness we saw in The Detective.

The basic recipe for shaping attention into this paranoid pattern, in summary:[24]

1. To be hurt as a small child without anyone acknowledging the situation as such;
2. To fail to react to the resulting suffering with anger, denying one's own feelings to oneself;
3. To show gratitude to one's parents for what are supposed to be their good intentions;
4. To forget everything;
5. To displace the stored-up anger onto others in adulthood and fail to notice that what seems to be *their* anger is one's own.

The parent who has suffered a childhood which has hammered his attentional pattern into that of paranoia is quite likely to repeat the same cycle with his own children. The battle once lost as a child to the harsh psychological regime of his parents can be replayed, this time with the child-grown-to-parent as victor.

There are countless variations on this process. We are most familiar with those that end in an attentional extreme like paranoia simply because clinical research has focused on them. The most widely known description of an inculcated style of pathological perception is what Gregory Bateson and his associates described in the early fifties as the "double bind," a pattern of communication between parent and child which culminates in schizophrenia.*

The essence of a double bind is a two-edged message, with the obvious meaning contradicted by a covert one.[25] The overt message is in tandem with a lacuna that shields the contradiction from awareness. The result is befuddlement: it is impossible to comply with both messages at once, but one cannot say why that is so, or even *that* it is so. The covert message commonly is sent nonverbally, by posture, tone of voice, gesture, muscular tightening, and so on. R. D. Laing gives the following example:[26]

> A mother visits her son, who has been recovering from a mental breakdown. As he goes toward her
> a) she opens her arms for him to embrace her, and/or
> b) to embrace him.
> c) As he gets nearer she freezes and stiffens.
> d) He stops irresolutely.
> e) She says, "Don't you want to kiss your mummy?"—and as he still stands irresolutely
> f) she says, "But, dear, you mustn't be afraid of your feelings."
>
> He responds to her invitation to kiss her, but her posture, freezing, and tension simultaneously tell him not to. That she is frightened of a close relationship with him, or for some other reason does not want him actually to do what she invites him to do, cannot be openly admitted by the mother, and remains unsaid by her and the son. He responds to the "unsaid," the unspoken message, "Although I am holding my arms out for you to come and kiss me I am really frightened of your doing so, but can't admit this to myself or to you, so I hope you will be too 'ill' to do so." She conveys, in effect, both "Do not embrace me, or I will punish you," *and* "If you do not do so, I will punish you."

The double-bind theory proposes that the repeated experience of messages such as "Do not submit to my orders"—that is, mes-

* Or so double-bind theory claimed. Schizophrenia research has left double-bind theory behind, by and large. Its lasting impact has been in research and therapy centered on a family's communication patterns, such as Daniel Stern's observations of microevents.

sages which are impossible to comply with—creates a warp in the recipient's habitual mode of perceiving. In this instance, the theory holds, the result is the disordered thinking of schizophrenia. The double-bind theory has inspired the more general view that a family's communication patterns instill in the growing child a characteristic skew in perception.

The pattern of the paranoid is but one of many attentional strategies to allay anxiety. The specifics of what in a child's early experience inculcates a given lifelong attentional style are largely unknown. Researchers have only begun to work out the general parameters of that process for a few extremes—the schizophrenic, the paranoid, the compulsive. But the varieties of attentional style cover a much greater range than those few that are marked as pathological.

Of the attentional strategies within the natural range we know very little; of the specific experiences that shape them we know even less. For now, we can only point to the general forces within a family that make it a unique shaper of attentional habits and thus of personal realities.

Those forces we will explore in the next part. As we shall see, the family stands as the first model we meet in life of how to attend to a shared reality—and how to keep anxiety at bay through tricks of attention. In learning to join in this collective experience, we assume whatever twists that particular attentional pattern contains: self-deceptions operate *among* us as well as *within* us.

We are about to switch gears. Up to this point the topic has been how the attention-anxiety trade-off creates lacunas of various sorts in the individual mind. From here on we will consider how it is that such self-deceptions can come to be shared. To make this transition requires only that we allow the possibility that people can somehow synchronize their schemas to some degree—that is, come to share a common understanding of how to construe events.

That is not such a farfetched assumption. In a sense, all communication is an attempt at such an orchestration. To share a mutual outlook, to have two minds "running on the same track," means that, to some degree, their schemas are at least somewhat similar and operate more or less in tandem.

Conversation is just such a calibration. As John Seely Brown, a cognitive psychologist, put it to me: "When we talk, I'm slowly adjusting your mental model of me, and you're adjusting my model of you. When you ask a question, there's a chance to correct some subtle miscommunications. By asking, you implicitly review your understanding of all kinds of things. That gives me a chance to diagnose the cause of your misunderstanding and fix it. Communication is basically a repair process."

What is being "repaired" is the schemas at hand. When we reach an understanding, I grasp your schemas, you grasp mine. The match may not be perfect, but it's closer than before. In a long-term relationship, schemas can become exquisitely calibrated, so that a single word, gesture, or emphasis can evoke in one's partner a fully understood statement. The more schemas we share, the less need be said.

It is in our ongoing intimate relationships—spouse, lover, friend, colleague—that we most readily come to share defensive schemas in common. Because of the crucial psychological import to us of intimate relationships, there is more opportunity for anxieties, such as the fear of loss, than in casual ties. And where there are such fears, lacunas more readily arise to offer solace.

Thus when both partners in the relationship sense the same touchy areas, they can handle the danger by silently agreeing to veer attention away from these trouble spots. When that attentional skew is mutual and synchronized, a shared lacuna is created. In this way, every relationship, to some degree, is susceptible to a characteristic array of joint delusions. Such efforts, I believe, come automatically to us by virtue of the same sort of microevents that Dr. Stern documented between parent and child.

Lacunas in relationships need not be shared, of course. Ernest Schachtel, a psychoanalyst, describes in one of his patients one such lacuna. The woman, says Dr. Schachtel, complained in therapy that she had "never really looked at her boy friend." Although she could gaze at him, she had the distinct sense that she never really saw him.[27]

In the course of therapy, it developed that the woman's attitude toward her lover was one of trying to please him, and of clinging to him out of fear that she would do something wrong, and so lose him. When she was with him, she was in continual fear that if she looked at him she would see an expression of disapproval on his face. Thus when she did look at him, her attention was highly selective: she saw not his face as it was, but instead scanned for signs of approval or disapproval, love or anger. This lacuna created its blind spot: although she had seen his face many times, she felt it remained unknown to her.

Anxieties such as this woman felt can be shared, or perhaps matched, by different but equally strong fears—and blind spots—in one's partner. To some extent, observes the sociologist Erving Goffman, the bonds of a relationship are strengthened by tacit blind spots. "Thus in well-adjusted marriages," he notes, "we expect that each partner may keep from the other secrets having to do with financial matters, past experiences, current flirtations, indulgences in 'bad' or expensive habits, personal aspirations and worries, actions of children, true opinions held about relatives or mutual friends, etc."[28]

These strategically located points of reticence, says Goffman, make it possible to maintain a desired status quo. Such protective reticence, of course, is all the more secure if we engage in a simple collusion: you don't tell, and I don't ask. And that collusion is possible only if we both know, somehow, what to avoid.

Indeed, Lilly Pincus and Christopher Dare, both family therapists, observe that as they get to know a couple over the course of treatment, they find a sort of unwritten marriage contract. This agreement, they say, is between the unconscious of each, and has to do with the partners' mutual obligations to fulfill certain unspoken longings and soothe unmentioned fears. In its most general form it goes something like this:[29]

"I will attempt to be some of the many important things you want of me, even though they are some of them impossible, contradictory, and crazy, if you will be for me some of the important, impossible, contradictory, and crazy things I want of you. We don't have to let each other know what these things are, but we will be cross, sulk, become depressed or difficult, if we do not keep to the bargain."

Such collusions work best when they operate out of awareness. Thus they are out-of-bounds for attention, marked in awareness only by a protective blind spot. Because it is primal psychological needs that lead to such blind spots, there is a special urgency to this collusion to keep from attention what is actually going on. To pull back the veils on attention is to lay bare sensitive, deeply personal needs. That may explain, in part, why divorces are so ugly.

Each partner in a working couple ignores areas of shared experience that would threaten the partners' shared sense of a secure, comfortable relationship. She doesn't comment on the looks he gives younger women at the beach; he never mentions his suspicion that she fakes orgasms. Over time, these discretions can become converted into lacunas: they do not notice, and do not notice that they do not notice.

But beneath the surface of this uneasy alliance of inattention, there may be a cesspool of anger, resentment, hurt—all unspoken, if not unnoticed. Should the couple separate, the collusion to preserve the status quo at the expense of open attention evaporates.

The ugly feelings emerge in full force once the partners are no longer invested in their mutual pact to disattend.

The unspoken attentional alliances in such relationships can be seen as a prototype for the dynamic that characterizes most any group. My belief is that people in groups by and large come to share a vast number of schemas, most of which are communicated without being spoken of directly. Foremost among these shared, yet unspoken, schemas are those that designate what is worthy of attention, how it is to be attended to—and what we choose to ignore or deny. When that choice—what to ignore or deny—is made in order to damp anxiety, a shared defense is at work.

In the next Part we will explore the means whereby, in learning to see things the same way, people in groups also learn together how *not* to see—how aspects of shared experience can be veiled by self-deceits held in common.

PART FIVE

The Collective Self

THE "WE"

Madness, said Nietzsche, is the exception in individuals, but the rule in groups. Freud agreed. In *Group Psychology and the Analysis of the Ego*, Freud wrote, "A group is impulsive, changeable and irritable." With no little disdain for the ways of the crowd, Freud saw people in groups as regressing to an infantile state as a consequence of membership.

Freud quotes Le Bon, a French commentator on crowd psychology, to the effect that when diverse people get together as a group, they have "a sort of collective mind which makes them feel, think, and act in a manner quite different "from that in which they would act on their own. A group, said Freud, "is led almost exclusively by the unconscious."

Freud continues, after Le Bon:[1]

> A group is extraordinarily credulous and open to influence, it has no critical faculty, and the improbable does not exist for it. It thinks in images, which call one another up by association . . . and whose agreement with reality is never checked by any reasonable agency. The feelings of a group are always very simple and very exaggerated, so that a group knows neither doubt nor uncertainty.

By "group" Freud meant something that bordered on a mob, but also any large organization like the Church or an army, both of which he uses as case examples to illustrate his theory. What separates a "group" from a random crowd is shared schemas: some common understanding, "a common interest in an object, a similar emotional bias in some situation," as Freud put it. The more in common a group shares, and so the higher the degree of "mental homogeneity," "the more striking are the manifestations of group mind."

A hallmark of the person as group member, Freud saw, was the replacement of his self by a group self. The psychology of the group, said Freud, involves "the dwindling of the conscious individual personality, the focusing of thoughts and feelings into a common direction." That translates to the prepotency of shared schema over personal ones.

The group archetype, in Freud's theory, is the "primal horde," a band of primitive "sons" ruled by a strong "father." The particular schemas that constitute the group mind, in this view, would be those dictated by the father, a charismatic, strong leader. The members of such a group, said Freud, relinquish their intellect to the chief; he, however, is autonomous. The group mind, then, is the leader's writ large. In the group mind "the individual gives up his ego ideal and substitutes for it the group ideal as embodied in the leader."

For Freud a primitive family prototype is the model for all groups. In the vast variations of what constitutes a group—fleeting or long-lasting, homogeneous and heterogeneous, natural and artificial, and so on—Freud saw the same dynamic at work: to the extent that there is a common understanding, the members of the group share an outlook—the group's schemas.

In his foreword to Freud's book, the American psychoanalyst Franz Alexander hastens to add that what Freud describes is more true of groups with a single authoritarian leader than of "free, democratic societies, which consist of more independent, self-governing individuals." This caveat changes the dynamic in one crucial detail: for group members to share a schema, they need not take on those of a single strong leader. Rather, an abstract ideal or a set of schemas inherent in the workings of the group can play that role. With or without a clear leader, then, members of a group adhere to some common understanding.

If a group can share schemas, then they can also hold lacunas in common. Erik Erikson points to that likelihood. He reports having once asked Anna Freud if the defense mechanisms she elaborated could be shared. The conclusion was that, indeed, they are "shared . . . [by] individuals and families as well as . . . larger units." Erikson observes that what Freud meant by "ego"—the German *ich*—is more properly translated by "I." Erikson goes on to suggest that when people interact, there can be created a "we" that carries the same weight as the "I"—an organizer of shared experience. In a group, that "we" is the collective self.

A group can be called into being with remarkable spontaneity. At the scene of a traffic accident random passersby become a coordinated band, some helping victims, others calling authorities, others directing traffic, and so on. The assemblage of such a group depends on their sharing schemas for what to do in such situations. More exotic emergencies—say, the escape of an elephant from a zoo, or an unexpected delivery by a pregnant airplane passenger—may not evoke so well coordinated a response. It is the activation of shared schemas that unites the "we"; the more such a common understanding is shared, the more stable the group.

The "shared self" offers a sense of definition and reality to those in the group by virtue of their membership in it. Like an individual's self, the group self entails a set of schemas that define the world as it pertains to the group, that make sense of collective experience, that define what is pertinent and what not.

We slip so easily into group membership, as Freud saw, because we have practiced as children in our families. A group is a pseudofamily: the family models the group; its dynamics are at work in any unified collective, with all the mechanisms of the family self. And the family self, in some ways, recreates the dynamics of the personal self.

As with the individual, the group self is in part retrievable into a shared awareness, and in part consigned to a shared unconscious—a realm of common experience which is never articulated or brought into the open, but which nonetheless exerts its influence on the group as a whole.

The group self has been well described by Wilfred Bion, a psychoanalyst, in terms of a "group mentality," which he sees as the shared pool of members' wishes, opinions, thoughts, and emotions. Any contribution to the group mentality must conform to the contributions made by others—it is only those schemas that are shared which the group self incorporates. The most crucial aspect of this group mentality, says Bion, is those basic assumptions about how to handle anxiety-evoking information—in our terms, the preferred lacunas.

Another expert on groups, Robert Bales, describes the group unconscious in very similar terms. Bales has observed how members of a group come to share a unified fantasy life, so that what one person says has unconscious meaning for the others. In that way there can be a two-tiered communication system, one overt and dealing with the ostensible work of the group, and the other covert, bearing on the unspoken—though commonly understood—anxieties of the group.

A business consultant offers this example of the group unconscious at work among the vice presidents of a company which had recently been taken over by another firm.[2] The vice presidents were worried about losing their jobs or being demoted, and had developed a siege mentality, fearing bad news could come any moment.

As the vice presidents waited for the senior executive to arrive to start the meeting, one started telling about a recent flight in a small plane. The plane had gotten in trouble, and he had been asked to change seats to shift weight. The point of the story was how anxious he had been, and how vulnerable people often feel. Then another vice president joined in, this one with a story of panic among the passengers on a plane that had caught fire just before takeoff. That story led to another of being caught in sniper fire on a trip to Beirut.

The conversation continued in a similar vein until the meeting started. As the consultant interpreted it, the whole conversation had been tacitly understood to refer to the fragility of the vice presidents' own situation and the apprehension they all felt that disaster would strike. That sort of tacit understanding is made possible by the shared schemas of the group self.

In a collective, as with the self, schemas shape the flow of information. In any group the relevant schemas are those that are shared by members, the subset of schemas that are the "we."

The "we," I will argue, is as vulnerable as the self to self-deceptions. The motivating force behind the forming of shared illusions in a group is identical to that in the self: to minimize anxiety.

THE FAMILY SELF

A couple has a bitter fight over who should clean up the children's toys that litter the sidewalk in front of their house. Each accuses the other of not caring what the neighbors think of them, of jeopardizing their relations with neighbors who might trip over the toys. The argument itself reveals the couple's intense preoccupation with the importance of showing a good face to their neighbors, of keeping smooth relationships with them.

The example is offered by David Reiss, a psychiatrist who studies families.[3] He contends that such moments in a couple's or family's life allow a careful observer to detect unspoken shared schemas which define the way they view themselves and their world—what can be called a "family self."

This fight, says Reiss, may spring from an underlying shared assumption such as, "People in this neighborhood get very angry about children's toys on the sidewalk," or "People in this neighborhood are strict and exacting." The complement to that concept is something like "We are very sensitive to the opinion of others." All are schemas at the heart of the family self.

Family selves can be classed along any number of dimensions. For example, the sociologist Robert Merton distinguished between small-town residents who were "locals" and those who were "cosmopolitans."[4] The dichotomy is easily extended to families. A cosmopolitan family, like a cosmopolite, looks toward people, activities, and interests that range far beyond the confines of their neighborhood or town. Their friends, jobs, and schools are scattered; they may move frequently for work or other reasons.

Locals, on the other hand, are rooted. Their family history in the same place may go back generations. Their friends, schools, and jobs are near at hand. Often their work life is not only near home but also dependent on a local network of acquaintances. Locals develop specific, traditional routines and routes for shopping, visiting, recreation. Cosmopolitan families have less well-fixed, more exploratory habits.

The corresponding realities of these families vis-à-vis their surroundings reflect these differences. For locals, the immediate vicinity is sharply defined by ample schemas that encode a rich history: a local store exists for them not only as it is now, but as it has been over the years. For cosmopolitans, the local vicinity is known more sketchily, with large uncharted areas, and so gives rise to fewer schemas. But the map of their world is much larger, with neighborhoods in other cities known as fully as their present one. Each pattern, local and cosmopolitan, has its characteristic blind spots and highlights.

For a decade and a half Reiss and his associates have studied families to determine the nature of their shared outlooks and how these outlooks operate to regulate and define family life. Their findings offer a look at the forces that shape schemas within the family.

In Reiss's theory, families share a group self, which in turn shapes their lives. Shared family experiences, Reiss says, "guide and shape the way families approach specific problems." This shared construing is typically in the background, a buried structure which guides family life. Shared outlooks play the same role for families that schemas do for the person.

The family, when it works as an integrated group, is a sort of consensual mind. In this respect it takes on the same tasks as we have seen in the individual mind: it gathers information, interprets it, distributes it. In this effort shared schemas act to guide, select, and censor information to meet the requirements of the group self.

Dynamics parallel to those at work in the mind are at play in the family. More particularly, there is a trade-off between attention and anxiety: The family as a group selects and ignores information incongruent with its shared self in an effort to protect its integrity and cohesion.

Consider, for example, the family Reiss calls the "Bradys." The family came to Dr. Reiss's center for treatment for Fred, the 27-year-old son, who was suicidally depressed. Fred's father, a successful surgeon, had died twenty years before; Fred's mother was now in her late sixties. Shortly after his death, the father's younger brother—"a timid clerk"—came to live with them in their apartment. The father's belongings were left in place all the while; the trio sometimes referred to him in the present tense. The overriding construct was that it was still a surgeon's family, with stability and prestige. "Clearly," Reiss notes, "they were preserving an important shared illusion about themselves."

The mother was the family specialist in gathering information. She was the only one who watched television and read papers; when home she answered all phone calls. The mother's role was to defend the family against "intruders," which was how all outsiders were seen. She met callers with firm civility, turning them away lest the two men have to engage the world outside. When the doorbell or phone rang, it was she who automatically responded. The mother was, in effect, an attentional border guard. This allowed her to perform the crucial function of selecting what was and was not relevant information and supplying interpretations:[5]

> For example, after many months in the hospital, Fred received a partial discharge, which enabled him to begin his first job as a technician's helper in a hospital laboratory. He never did well in the job, but [the] mother focused exclusively on the medical aspects and presented the job to the family and therapist as evidence that Fred might soon return to college, go to medical school, and become a doctor. Fred and his uncle acquiesced, quite willingly, to [the] mother's highly filtered selection and interpretation of signals. It provided them both with a sense of the family's vigor, prestige, and permanence.

To preserve their sense of self-esteem as a group, the Brady family has to weed out information to protect the treasured family schemas of stability and prestige. Doing so requires ignoring or reinterpreting data that contradicts these schemas. The mother's role as information-gatherer simplifies the task; singly she can efficiently screen out information that might undermine the family self-concept. If all family members were as active as she in collecting data, the risks of disconfirmation would be much greater.

If a family can be seen as a kind of conglomerate mind, in the case of the Bradys that mind is admittedly deficient. Although the odd dynamics of a schizophrenic's family are hardly the best basis for a more general theory, Reiss nonetheless uses it as a jumping-off point for describing the informational world of families in general. The Bradys were one of hundreds of families who have gone through a carefully designed series of tests, each of which assesses an aspect of how that family registers information. It is from these data, as well as from case studies like that of the Bradys, that Reiss offers his theory.

The family's information-processing, says Reiss, follows three interlocked phases. In the first, the family retrieves a subset of information available to it, much as an individual selectively attends. The selection and interpretation of that information, as we have seen with the Bradys, is subject to all the biasing that a shared schema exerts. Finally, the information that has been selectively retrieved and interpreted is distributed throughout the family as the shared schemas are mutually affirmed.

Many families, like the Bradys, have one or two information specialists—typically parents, but not always—whose task is to select and interpret. Alternatively, all or most family members can gather information, then compare notes and interpret it in terms congruent with their shared schemas. Families vary in how well they manage all three of these information missions; the style in which these tasks are done reflects the tone of family life.

To evaluate the shared schemas of more ordinary families, Reiss and his associates used PTAs to recruit 82 middle-class Washington, D.C., families for study. Each family came to Dr. Reiss's center, where they went through a series of tests measuring their perceptual performance. The test battery tapped major phases of joint information-processing. The experiment offered a laboratory analogue for how the families attended to information—or failed to —in normal life.

On one test, for example, the family was given a puzzle in which there were sequences of circles (C), triangles (T), and squares (S). The sequence of these shapes was governed by an underlying pattern, which the entire family tried to guess. A typical sequence was CCCTTT; its underlying pattern could be stated by the rule: "An uninterrupted sequence of circles followed by an uninterrupted sequence of triangles." That rule is a schema of sorts. The experiment allows the observation of how the family forms such a shared schema.

To guess the underlying pattern, the family was asked to make up another sequence that followed the same rule of thumb. Each family member sat at a specially partitioned table where the others could not be seen. Each wrote his or her guess on a slip of paper, passed it to an experimenter, who rated it right or wrong, and then passed it around to all the other members of the family—all in silence. When each member had studied the others' guesses and made a second guess at the underlying pattern, he or she turned on the "finish" light.

Not every family came to a unanimous decision about the underlying rule. Whether or not the decision was a group one, and how the members came to their decisions, were a barometer of the family's overall dynamic. For example, the "Friedkin" family (in another study of families with a disturbed member) duplicated its overall problem in its performance of this simple test.

Mr. Friedkin, a successful businessman, serves as both mother and father to his five teenaged children; Mrs. Friedkin is obese, chronically depressed, and disorganized. Over the course of the trials in the test, Mrs. Friedkin went her own way, paying no discernible regard to either the experimenter's feedback or the guesses of her family; her thinking was chaotic and isolated. The two Friedkin children in the test never quite grasped the underlying pattern, but finally settled on the same guess.

Mr. Friedkin at one point seemed to have hit on the right pattern, but no one else in the family agreed with his guess. He finally ignored the evidence supporting his own correct hunch in favor of the theory his daughters had developed. In settling for their guess, Mr. Friedkin found a unanimity with his children at the sacrifice of accuracy. The final aggregate schema reached this way was a faulty one, but one which served to preserve a sense of unity—an exchange common to groups of all sorts, as we shall see.

Clinical observations of the Friedkin family found the patterns revealed by the test typified their day-to-day interactions. Mrs. Friedkin was split off from family life, a social isolate in her own home. The father and children formed an alliance and built a shared world view on their own. Their need to seem unified was sometimes satisfied at the cost of adopting schemas that did not quite fit a more objective reality.

"Families differ in their shared view of their social world," Reiss writes. "Some, for example, have a persistent, trusting, and confident picture of the world as ordered and masterable; other families see their social world as capricious, unpredictable, and potentially dangerous."

Families' collective outlooks were evident to Reiss in how they construed the experiment itself:[6]

> Our families seemed to have shared constructs of the laboratory setting which they had readied before they came or formed almost instantaneously after they arrived. Some families felt the situation was safe and masterable; others felt it was overwhelming and dangerous. Most families did not seem to recognize the subjectivity of their views. On the contrary, they believed that their concept was objective, factual, based on evidence. Frightened families thought that we, the researchers, were really up to some kind of mischief, and confident families trusted us, though they had no ironclad evidence that we were not, in fact, connivers.

The battery of tests distinguished families along several different dimensions, each of which assays an aspect of the family paradigm. For example:

- *Coordination* is the degree to which a family operates as a unified group. When challenged, high-coordination families cooperate and communicate clearly and often, sharing crucial information. But low-coordination families split apart, share little information, and fail to cooperate.

- *Closure* evaluates how open or closed to new information the family is. Delayed closure allows a family to gather new data and consider alternate solutions when faced with a challenge. Early-closure families shut themselves off from new data, answering a challenge with conclusions imposed hastily without considering other options.

While it is unclear how such family paradigms originate, Reiss's data show that there is a very high correspondence among family members.[7] Although by no means every member of a family holds to all aspects of the family's attentional style, members of the same family resemble each other markedly in how they take in and use information. How do families preserve and pass on these shared schemas?

FAMILY RITUAL AS GROUP MEMORY

The sum total of shared schemas, says Reiss, is a "family paradigm." It resides not only in the minds of each member, but also in the interaction *between* them. The family's regular and recurring patterns are delicately organized to serve as a kind of group memory. Some interactions—holidays, arguments, outings—in which all members participate, are key repositories of the paradigm. But, in a minor way, so are all the routinized, day-to-day interactions of family life. In either event, the family paradigm is embedded in daily activity, an unseen regulator of what goes on.

Reiss calls these paradigm-dictated sequences "pattern regulators." In the shared mind of the family they stand as an analogue to unconscious mechanisms in the individual mind. The family is ordinarily unaware of them, although they play a crucial part in shaping the family's awareness:[8]

> The repository of family paradigms might ordinarily be thought of as the memory of individual members—that is, what each member retains in memory of the family's history, myths, heroes, values, secrets, and assumptions as these are melded together into a coherent paradigm. We might more easily regard interaction patterns in families . . . as expressing rather than conserving the nature of the family's paradigm or, in some sense, carrying out some plan which was shaped or toned by the family paradigm. However, we are asserting . . . the behavior itself is the locus, the medium, the storage place of the paradigm as well as a means of expressing it and carrying out the plan it shapes.

A specimen pattern regulator comes from a study of micro-events captured during family therapy. A typical sequence:[9]

Every time the husband { scratched his ear / rubbed his nose / tapped his left foot }
during an argument with his wife,
one of the children would { ask to go to the bathroom / slap a sibling / begin to cry }
so that the husband-wife dispute was never resolved.

Such patterns serve what is felt as a positive purpose. Children who perceive that their parents are not getting along often fear that the parents will resolve their fight by divorcing, dissolving the family. To ward off that possibility the children can intervene, as in this case, to keep the fight from ever reaching its resolution. In this pattern regulator, the children preserve the family by short-circuiting a parental fight.

Sometimes a family ritual can serve to hide a fear, a part of the family schema that is shared by all but is too threatening to be dealt with openly. Such a covert drama can be seen in the "A" family, a troubled New England family of seven who were observed closely by therapist Eric Bermann.[10] Mr. A suffered from a life-threatening heart disease and was soon to undergo dangerous surgery with an uncertain outcome. The family's ritual for dealing with this fear revolved around Roscoe, the fourth of five children.

Roscoe was the family's scapegoat. He was an "accident"; Mrs. A, after having had three children, was looking forward to some liberation from her duties as mother and housewife, when Roscoe's arrival put an end to her hopes. His birth rearoused an earlier anger in Mrs. A: as a child she had had to organize her life around the care of a younger brother because her own mother worked. Poor Roscoe bore the brunt of her built-up resentments.

Roscoe, though, did not become the family victim until the onset of Mr. A's heart problems. As the family's terror grew, a distinctive pattern of interaction emerged, with Roscoe as villain and his older brother Ricky as accuser. For example:[11]

> Ricky discovered that Roscoe had found a crab in a nearby creek. Before the entire family he accused Roscoe of putting sand in the bucket of water which housed the crab. Everyone accepted both the accuracy of Ricky's report and the truth that sand in a bucket could kill a crab. Mr. A ordered Roscoe to return the crab and ridiculed him by saying he "was supposed to be a nature lover." . . . Similar, but not identical, ceremonials were regularly performed; it was claimed that Roscoe would ruin his new

> shoes, that he would break a terrarium, that he taught the family dog dangerous habits, and so on. Each sequence had similar components. Roscoe became engaged in something which interested him; someone else—often Ricky—accused him of damaging it or threatening it; one parent listened to the accusation and then passed judgment, often forcing some humiliating surrender on Roscoe's part.

The family paradigm can have dual levels, one within the collective awareness, the other outside that awareness, though shared nonetheless. Bermann, observing the family, saw this pattern as a way for the family to deal with the submerged terror of what would happen to them if Mr. A's surgery went badly. Their attacks on Roscoe symbolically were a collective counterattack against a world full of murderous, uncontrollable forces. The incident with the crab, according to this interpretation, is especially telling: a murder and a victim are identified, the murderer is dealt with and the victim is saved. For a brief moment the family averts a death that stands for the father's illness, of which they are in terror. The scapegoating of Roscoe offers the family a symbolic relief from a fear they dare never openly confront.

In sum, the family is a group mind of sorts, with many properties of the individual mind. The experience of growing up in a particular family leaves its imprint on the attentional habits of the child, at times with unfortunate consequences, as we saw with the paranoid style. But that pattern marks an extreme of a process that we all go through as our families socialize us into their world of reality.

The family constructs a reality through the joint schemas members come to share. The family's self-image is one subset of shared schemas; the sum total constitute the family's paradigm. The topography of a family's private universe is implicit in routines and rituals, as well as in how members take in, interpret, and share (or don't share) information. There remains for us to explore the ways in which the family resolves the tension between anxiety and attention and its resulting susceptibility to shared illusions.

THE GAME OF HAPPY FAMILY

Hume Cronyn, the actor, grew up during the early years of this century in a very wealthy Canadian family.[12] The household occupied an Edwardian mansion in London, Ontario, and adhered to the strict proprieties of their station and time. The father was stricken with cerebral sclerosis, hardening of the brain's arteries, which in its early stages made him suffer occasional seizures. In that upper-class milieu, the seizures simply did not fit with social conventions, and so were handled by being ignored.

"So long as I live," Cronyn recalls, "I will never forget that night at the dinner table when my father had a spasm and his hand was involuntarily *slammed* down into his steaming hot plate of golden buck—a dish of egg and cheese. He was rendered unconscious and we all had to keep our places while the butler came over and righted my father, wiped him off carefully and served him a fresh plate.

"After a bit, he regained consciousness. He looked around at all of us, bewildered, and then moved to pick up his silverware as we resumed the conversation exactly where it had broken off. But as he went to grasp the fork he stopped, staring at his hand, which was scalded. He had no idea why."

"I have never come across a family," writes R. D. Laing, "that does not draw a line somewhere as to *what may be put into words,* and *what words it may be put into.*" That is, each family has its signature pattern of what aspects of shared experience can be open, what must be closed and denied. When experience is openly shared, the family also has a sanctioned language for what may be said about it.

The process Laing describes is precisely that of schemas at work: they direct attention *here* and away from *there;* they embody how to construe this and that. We comment on how cheery sister seems today, but we tiptoe around mother when she is depressed and drunk, and say she's "a bit under the weather" today. When father has a seizure, we pretend it did not happen.

These rules can operate in the family's collective mind with the same subliminal effectiveness they have within the individual mind. Laing gives the example:[13]

> A family has a rule that little Johnny should not think filthy thoughts. Little Johnny is a good boy: he does not have to be told not to think filthy thoughts. They never have *taught* him *not* to think filthy thoughts. He never has.
>
> So, according to the family, and even little Johnny, there is no rule against filthy thoughts, because there is no need to have a rule against what never happens. Moreover, we do not talk in the family about a rule against filthy thoughts, because since there are no filthy thoughts, and no rule against them, there is no need to talk about this dreary, abstract, irrelevant or even vaguely filthy subject.

Laing codifies the operation of such invisible rules about rules this way:[14]

Rule A:	Don't.
Rule A.1:	Rule A does not exist.
Rule A.2:	Do not discuss the existence or nonexistence of Rules A, A.1, or A.2.

The family's lacunas are the result of rules for what cannot be noticed, and not noticed that it cannot be noticed. They are for the group what the various defenses are for the individual. While they shape and limit experience, we do not readily see that they do so, because they operate outside awareness.

"If you obey these rules," says Laing, by way of illustration,[15] "you will not know that they exist. There is no rule against talking about putting one's finger into one's own mouth, one's brother's, sister's, mother's, father's, anyone's mouth. . . . But, I may say, I have never put my finger in a number of . . . [unmentionable] places. What places? I can't mention them. Why not? I can't say."

The ultimate familial lacuna is what Laing calls "The Game of Happy Family," a prototype of how groups collude to keep members feeling comfortable. As Laing describes it:[16]

> Denial is demanded by the others; it is part of a transpersonal system of collusion whereby we comply with the others, and they comply with us. For instance, one requires collusion to play "Happy Families." Individually,

I am unhappy. I deny I am to *myself;* I deny I am denying anything to myself and to others. They must do the same. I must collude with their denial and collusion and they must collude with mine.

So we are a happy family and we have no
secrets from one another.
If we are unhappy
we have to keep it a secret
and we are unhappy that we have to keep it a secret
and unhappy that we have to keep secret
the fact
that we have to keep it a secret
and that we *are* keeping all that secret.
But since we are a happy family you can see
this difficulty does not arise.

The more horrid the secrets a family harbors, the more likely it will resort to a strategem like Happy Family to maintain some semblance of stability. Michael Weissberg, a psychiatrist, advises that one symptom of an incestuous family can be that it seems *too* happy.[17] Says Weissberg: "Some of the danger signals include the 'perfect' family that always does everything together but with the mother left out because she is depressed, ill, or otherwise emotionally unavailable." A parallel sign is the too-perfect daughter. Often she has assumed parental duties at an early age. She does well at school, is very polite, and seems eager to please. One victim of incest, Weissberg reports, got straight A's in school and had been preparing her family's evening meals by the time she was ten.

Such charades allow the overt denial of a terrible truth that everyone tacitly knows. Guilt, shame, and fear are the immediate motives for the collusion. The fear of being abandoned by one's mate or parents—no matter how horribly they treat one—leads spouses and children to blithely make alibis for the worst treatment, and to skew their perception of blatant cruelty.

Perhaps the saddest secrets are those in families where abuse, incest, or alcoholism go on amid a collusive fog. Such families often go through a cycle of denial and guilt. The denial is that there is anything the matter, or if so, that it was anything more than a quirk that won't happen again. The guilt can take the form of self-blame by the victim: abused wives and victims of incest, the psychiatric literature amply documents, frequently feel they deserve their victimization.

In these families, strong collective defenses operate. Multiple clues to what is happening abound, but are ignored or explained away. An incest victim, now grown, recalls angrily,[18] "I never actually told her what my father was doing, but my God, the laundry could have! There were bloody panties, semen-stained pajamas, soiled sheets. Everything was right there for her to see. And she chose not to."

The web of denial can reach beyond the family to friends, relatives, even police, physicians, and social workers. Take the case of "Margaret," the wife of a leading political figure in a medium-sized midwestern city who was distressed to learn that her husband was molesting their five-year-old daughter.[19] Over a period of years, she went through a harrowing series of encounters. Her husband denied that his "playing" with their daughter was in any way unusual. Her sister-in-law assured her that "that was just the way it was" in their family, and that Margaret needn't worry about it. Increasingly upset, Margaret was hospitalized for six weeks for a nervous breakdown.

Some years later, the couple's fourteen-year-old son told her he had been forcibly raped by the father while they were on a camping trip. When she turned to a lawyer, he advised that the boy be sent away to a boarding school. When Margaret turned to her husband's aunt and uncle they insisted she was "overreacting" and should deal with the situation "like a civilized person"—that is, do nothing. When she asked for help from the principal of her children's school, he said they did not have counselors who were trained in "that sort of thing." If the children came for counseling, he said, they'd do their best. The children were too ashamed to ask.

When Margaret finally went to the police, the chief was brusque: his succinct advice was "Get yourself a gun and blow the bastard away if he ever comes close to your kids again." He offered no other help. Finally, desperate, Margaret went to a meeting of the deacons of her family's church. When the floor was opened to general concerns, Margaret stood up and told the story. "She was answered by a muffled cough or two, the sound of bodies moving uncomfortably about on wooden chairs, and nothing else."

While the story of Margaret is perhaps overdrawn, it points to the social atmosphere that encourages a family to play happy. That game keeps things comfortable for everyone. Weissberg, who directs emergency psychiatric services at a university hospital, notes that clinicians share the same sensibilities as those who play the game: "They don't want to find situations in their patients that are perceived as frightening, evil, and out of control. Clinicians may subscribe to the mistaken notion that what they don't know, don't find, and don't diagnose will not hurt them."[20]

"This is extremely unfortunate," he adds, "since almost *all* the victims and perpetrators of these behaviors give multiple clues that they are in trouble—as if they want to be found out. For example, over half of the people who commit suicide visit their medical doctor in the month before they kill themselves; 80 percent of those who die of an overdose do so with one prescription that they have recently obtained."

He tells of a physician's daughter whose mother brought her to an orthopedist with a sprained ankle; X rays revealed a fracture. Seven months later, the daughter went to another doctor with another broken bone. Only after a third fracture brought her for medical help was abuse suspected. The mother finally admitted throwing her daughter against the wall to "discipline" her. The family's friends and relatives had known about the injuries, but none had intervened.

A lawyer's wife, similarly, made excuses and invented explanations for bruises and other medical difficulties during her pregnancy. Her obstetrician and her friends, though, overlooked the possibility that her husband was beating her, until she miscarried after he pushed her down the stairs.

Then there was "the precocious thirteen-year-old daughter of an army sergeant" who made repeated visits to the family doctor for urinary tract infections. Her father always accompanied her on these medical visits. Ironically, the doctor would reassure him that the daughter was not sexually active. In fact, the father had been having intercourse with her for years.

A remarkably high incidence of child abuse goes on despite some contact with an authority—teacher, therapist, police officer, case worker—who should have noticed a clue and done something about it. Commonly, a parent bringing a child to an emergency room with bruises and broken bones—the result of a beating—explains the wounds away as the result of an accident and the hospital personnel accept the explanation at face value.

Weissberg gives the following examples of what such parents say to avoid discovery:[21]

SAYS	MEANS
I never have problems with my baby.	I had to leave the house yesterday because I was afraid I would strangle the child.
I have no idea how these bruises occurred. . . . Maybe it was an accident.	I was so upset . . . I hit him.

I had no idea my husband was doing these things.	I am so frightened of being alone and I am afraid he will leave me if I criticize him.

Weissberg observes that these lies and rationalizations are often believed because of the anxiety that acknowledging the truth might bring. Denial is easier. But "denial short-circuits the anxiety that accompanies an observer's recognition of abuse; . . . [it] also protects the observer from deciding what action to take if abuse is acknowledged."

The parallel between the family mind and the individual is complete: the trade-off between anxiety and attention is at work here, too. Self-deception in its Happy Family guise keeps anxiety at bay. The implications of this parallel for understanding group life are great, for, as Freud saw, the family stands as a prototype for the psychology of all groups.

THERE'S NOTHING ROTTEN HERE IN DENMARK

The evidence for the collective defenses and shared illusions at work in groups other than families is nowhere better stated than in Irving Janis's research on "groupthink."[22] Famous cases of groupthink include major fiascos like the Bay of Pigs invasion and Watergate. In these instances a small, cozy group of key decision-makers tacitly conspired to ignore crucial information because it did not fit with the collective view. The result of such biased decisions can be a disaster.

Groupthink is not an argument against groups, but rather a danger signal of collective pathology, a "we" gone awry. Groups are a sensible antidote to the risks of a single person's making decisions that are skewed by personal bias. A person alone is vulnerable to sways of emotion, or to blind spots arising from social prejudices, or to a failure to comprehend the complex consequences of a seemingly simple decision. In a group, issues can be aired, other points of view considered, additional information gathered and weighed. When they work at their best, groups can make better decisions than would any single member. But groupthink skews group thinking.

Consider the sad story of Pitcher, Oklahoma. In 1950 a local mining engineer warned the people of this small mining town to flee. An accident had virtually undermined the town; it might cave in any minute. The next day at the Lion's Club meeting, the town leaders joked about the warning. When one arrived wearing a parachute, they laughed and laughed. The message "it can't happen here" implicit in their hilarity was sadly contradicted within a few days: some of these same men and their families were killed in the cave-in.

Janis offers the story of Pitcher as an introduction to his concept of groupthink. That intentionally Orwellian name denotes the deterioration of a group's mental efficiency, attention, and judgment that results from implicit constraints and pressures.

The subtlety of the mechanics of groupthink makes it hard to spot and counter. As people in a group get cozy and comfortable, their very feelings of ease with each other can harbor a corollary reluctance to voice opinions that might destroy the sense of coziness. As Janis describes it:[23]

> . . . The leader does not deliberately try to get the group to tell him what he wants to hear but is quite sincere in asking for honest opinions. The group members are not transformed into sycophants. They are not afraid to speak their minds. Nevertheless, subtle constraints, which the leader may reinforce inadvertently, prevent a member from fully exercising his critical powers and from openly expressing doubts when most others in the group appear to have reached consensus.

Just as with defenses, the impetus for groupthink is to minimize anxiety and preserve self-esteem. Groupthink describes the operations that the group mind employs to preserve the illusion of Happy Family. Janis observes:[24]

> Each individual in the group feels himself to be under an injunction to avoid making penetrating criticisms that might bring on a clash with fellow members and destroy the unity of the group. . . . Each member avoids interfering with an emerging consensus by assuring himself that the opposing arguments he had in mind must be erroneous or that his misgivings are too unimportant to be worth mentioning.
>
> The various devices to enhance self-esteem require an illusion of unanimity about all important judgments. Without it, the sense of group unity would be lost, gnawing doubts would start to grow, confidence in the group's problem-solving capacity would shrink, and soon the full emotional impact of all the stresses generated by making a difficult decision would be aroused.

The very glue that holds a group together can later be its undoing. A *New Yorker* cartoon makes the point. A king in a medieval castle sits surrounded by knights. He says, "Then we're in agreement. There's nothing rotten here in Denmark. Something is rotten everywhere else."

Anxiety and self-esteem play the same role in the "we" as in the "I"; they encourage the bending of reality to preserve heightened esteem and lessened anxiety. For example, in Japan, a culture that puts great importance on group unity, a meeting—and its incumbent chances for dissent—can be a delicate matter. Arthur Golden, who worked at a Japanese English-language magazine, describes a typical meeting there:[25]

> First, an employee who has been charged with looking into a proposal presents his report. The boss (whose job it is to approve or reject proposals, not come up with them himself) nods and harrumphs. Everyone else stares at the floor. Finally, the boss says, "Well, what do you think?" No one answers. He then asks each individual in turn. Keeping the ideal of group unity in mind, they all answer with something ambiguous like "I think it sounds good." More silence and more nodding.
>
> At last, someone will sigh, scratch his head or make some similar sign indicating that, although it is not perhaps a circumstance he would have chosen for himself, a dissenting opinion has nonetheless presented itself to him, and he feels the need to express it to the group. . . . Once an opinion is accepted it becomes the group's opinion and is no longer associated with its originator. This convention helps keep unity intact by not singling out any one individual on the basis of performance or initiative.

Janis came to formulate the notion of groupthink from his research on groups as diverse as infantry platoons and executives in leadership training. In all the groups he studied, he detected, to some degree, a trade-off between preserving a sense of cozy solidarity and the willingness to face facts and voice views that challenged key shared schemas of the group self. The "we" is prone to the same "totalitarian" skews as the self.

For example, Janis recounts sitting in as a counselor on a group of heavy smokers attending a clinic to help them stop. At the second meeting of the group, the two dominant members proclaimed that it was almost impossible to stop smoking. Most of the others agreed, and ganged up against the one member who took issue with this opinion.

In the middle of the next meeting the same man who had been the lone dissenter announced: "When I joined, I agreed to follow the two main rules required by the clinic—to make a conscientious effort to stop smoking and to attend every meeting." He went on to say that he had learned from the group that you can follow only one of those rules. So, said he, "I have decided that I will continue to attend every meeting but I have gone back to smoking two packs a day." At that, the other members applauded, beaming. He was welcomed back into the fold. But when Janis tried to point out that the goal of the group itself was to stop smoking, the members ignored his comments, reiterating that it was impossible to stop an addiction like smoking.

The group was amiable in the extreme; they sought full concurrence on every topic, with none of the upsetting bickering that could ruin the coziness. But that comfortable consensus was built around an illusion: that everyone in the group had a hopeless addiction to smoking. Yet no one questioned it. The first victim of groupthink is critical thought.

Whether in a therapy group or a meeting of presidential advisers, the dynamics of groupthink are the same. Typically, talk is limited to a few courses of action, while the full range of alternatives is ignored. No attention is paid to the values implicit in this range of alternatives, nor does anyone stop to consider the drawbacks of these initial choices. The ignored alternatives are never brought up, no matter what advantages they might have. No one consults expert information that might offer a sound estimate of losses and gains; facts that challenge the initial choice are brushed aside. The group expects success, and makes no contingency plans to deal with failure.

The forces at work in groupthink are a variety of Happy Family. Instead of hiding a secret or shared distress, the group simply cramps its attention and hobbles its information-seeking to preserve a cozy unanimity. Loyalty to the group requires that members not raise embarrassing questions, attack weak arguments, or counter softheaded thinking with hard facts. Only comfortable shared schemas are allowed full expression. Janis offers a law in summary:[26]

> The more amiable the esprit de corps among the members of a policy-making in-group, the greater is the danger that independent critical thinking will be replaced by groupthink, which is likely to result in irrational . . . actions.

FORMULA FOR FIASCO

It is a bizarre twist of history that John F. Kennedy's worst fiasco—the Bay of Pigs—was the result of a suggestion originally made by Richard M. Nixon, his opponent in the presidential election. Nixon, while vice president to Eisenhower, had proposed that the government train a secret army of Cuban exiles to fight Castro. Eisenhower liked the idea, and directed the CIA to train a Cuban guerrilla army.

By the time Kennedy reached office, the CIA had an elaborate plan for a military invasion of Cuba in the works and was training a clandestine army. Two days after Kennedy took office, Allen Dulles, head of the CIA, briefed him on the plan. Over the next eighty days, a small group of presidential advisers considered the operation. By April the plan went into effect: fourteen hundred Cuban exiles made their assault at the Bay of Pigs.

The attack was a disaster from beginning to end. Not one of four ships with supplies arrived. By the second day, twenty thousand Cuban troops hemmed in the assault brigade. By the third day all the surviving members of the brigade were in prison camps. Yet up to the actual invasion, Kennedy and his advisers were confident the operation would topple Castro.

When the attack failed, Kennedy was stunned. "How," he asked, "could I have been so stupid to let them go ahead?"

Janis offers a detailed answer to that question, based on accounts by members of Kennedy's inner circle recalling what happened during those eighty days of discussion before the brigade set sail. The meetings were attended by Kennedy's half-dozen key advisers—Rusk, McNamara, Bundy, Schlesinger, and Robert Kennedy—and the three military Chiefs of Staff, plus Allen Dulles and Richard Bissel from the CIA.

At the meetings, it was Bissel who presented the invasion plan.

Kennedy had known him for years and respected him highly; because Kennedy seemed so in agreement with Bissel, his advisers played along. The result was a number of crucial miscalculations which led to the consensus that the invasion was a good idea. Each of these miscalculations could have been prevented on the basis of information available to one or another member of the group, had they sought it or brought it up. None did; they were in the grip of groupthink.

For example, the group assumed that the invasion would trigger armed uprisings by an underground throughout Cuba, which would lead to Castro's fall. They knew that victory would depend on such uprisings, since the invasion force itself was too small to tackle the Cuban army on its own (there were 200,000 Cubans to 1,400 invaders). Bissel and Dulles assured them that such an uprising would take place, and the group went along with their assurance.

In fact, the CIA had made no such predictions. Nor did anyone —including Secretary of State Dean Rusk—ask the experts at the Cuban desk of the State Department, who maintained a daily surveillance of Cuban political life, what they thought. No one brought up the results of a careful poll, done the year before, showing that the vast majority of Cubans supported Castro. The poll had been widely circulated in government circles, and most who saw it concluded there was little hope of provoking much internal resistance to Castro. "This evidence," Janis reports, "was either totally forgotten or ignored by the political experts in the group."

Then there was the matter of the Escambray Mountains maneuver. Another assumption underlying the invasion was that if the brigade failed in its first battles, it could retreat to the Escambray Mountains and hold out there. It turned out, though, that the mountains were a useful fallback position only if an earlier landing site, at their foot, was used. The Bay of Pigs, later chosen for the landing site, was eighty miles from the mountains, across a thick tangle of swamps and jungles. "This oversight," Janis notes, "might have been corrected if someone in the advisory group had taken the trouble to look at a map of Cuba, available in any atlas."

How, then, could such a bright and well-informed group have gone along with a such a terribly conceived plan? Janis traces the answer to the evolution of a number of illusory group schemas and the mechanisms the group developed to protect those illusions against disconfirming information. While those schemas were open assumptions, the fact that they were illusions was not part of the group's openly shared awareness. The mechanisms that protected them were not in the group awareness at all.

Although an individual member might be aware of some information that did not support the assumptions, or of the ways information was kept from shared awareness, the group's *collective* awareness was oblivious to these things. In that sense, the zone of information out of their awareness constituted the group equivalent of the unconscious mind. It is in the group unconscious that groupthink operates, just as diversionary schemas act in the individual unconscious.

The Invulnerability Illusion. In studying the forces that led to groupthink in this case, Janis pinpoints several ways Kennedy and his advisers went wrong. For one, they labored under an "illusion of invulnerability," the sense that anything they planned was bound to succeed. Kennedy had just been elected, and luck and fate seemed to be on his side. The mood in the White House, says Schlesinger, was buoyant: "Everyone around [Kennedy] thought he had the Midas touch and could not lose. . . . Euphoria reigned; we thought for a moment that the world was plastic and the future unlimited."

The same rosy schema, says Janis, occurs in most groups as they are first coming together as a group. The newly acquired collective self—what Janis calls a "we-feeling"—lends them a "sense of belonging to a powerful, protective group that in some vague way opens up new potentials for each of them. Often there is boundless admiration for the group leader."

This very sense of invulnerability is a grave flaw in the group's ability to assess information realistically. Members are reluctant to do anything that would break the feeling of euphoria or sense of cohesiveness. Simply criticizing the risks of a group decision—no matter how objective the appraisal—is an attack on the group self. "In group meetings," says Janis, "this groupthink tendency can operate like a low-level noise that prevents warning signals from being heeded. Everyone becomes somewhat biased in the direction of selectively attending to the messages that feed into the members' shared feelings of confidence and optimism, disregarding those that do not."

The Unanimity Illusion. Along with the sense of invulnerability comes the illusion of unanimity. Both stem from group coziness. Once the group adopts a belief or decision, individual members are likely to feel it must be right. After all, the members are such great people—how could they be wrong?

The easy assumption is that there is consensus and unanimity among the group. This illusion is maintained, says Janis, because members "often become inclined, without quite realizing it, to prevent latent disagreements from surfacing when they are about to initiate a risky course of action. The group leader and the members support one another, playing up to areas of convergence in their thinking, at the expense of fully exploring divergencies that might disrupt" the atmosphere of congeniality.

Looking back, Theodore Sorensen remarked, "Our meetings took place in a curious atmosphere of assumed consensus." In the key meetings, no strong opposition was voiced, nor were any alternative plans presented. Yet, he thinks, "had one senior advisor opposed the adventure, I believe that Kennedy would have canceled it. No one spoke against it." By remaining silent, these dissenters tacitly added to the illusion of unanimous consent.

Suppressed Personal Doubts. Why do dissenters keep quiet? One reason seems to be a self-imposed censorship on their misgivings. Sorensen, in a post-mortem, concluded that "doubts were entertained but never pressed, partly out of fear of being labeled 'soft' or undaring in the eyes of their colleagues." The atmosphere of glowing unanimity dampens dissent; to object is to stand apart from the group. Schlesinger, for example, later wrote:[27]

> In the months after the Bay of Pigs I bitterly reproached myself for having kept so silent during those critical discussions in the Cabinet Room, though my feelings of guilt were tempered by the knowledge that a course of objection would have accomplished little save to gain me a name as a nuisance.

Rather than become a pariah of sorts, potential dissenters stay silent. To speak out is to destroy the consensus. But that consensus, we have seen, is an illusion. Self-censorship by dissenters means that criticisms never enter the collective awareness, allowing a shaky shared assumption to thrive, unchallenged.

Mindguards. A "mindguard" is someone who takes it on himself to sanitize information so that it conforms to the current schemas. This typically takes the form of putting social pressure on a member who might express a dissenting view; the effect is to ensure that the group consensus is not challenged. The pressure is often blatant: simply telling the would-be dissenter to be quiet if his opinion doesn't match the going one.

A mindguard is an attentional bodyguard, standing vigilant to protect the group not from physical assault, but from an attack by information. "A mindguard," says Janis, protects the group "from thoughts that might damage their confidence in the soundness of the policies to which they are committed."

In the White House circle, the President's brother, Robert, assumed this role vis-à-vis Schlesinger. Robert Kennedy had heard that Schlesinger had some grave doubts about the invasion plan. He took Schlesinger aside at a party and asked what his reservations were. After listening coldly, Kennedy said, "You may be right or wrong, but the President has made up his mind. Don't push it any further. Now is the time for everyone to help him all they can."

The "help" the mindguard offers the group is of dubious value: it preserves the illusion of unanimity at the price of effective consideration of the data at hand. The mindguard actively colludes to preserve the fictions at the heart of the group self, an act equivalent to the defense mechanism of repression.

Rationalizations. Much of what group members say to each other to justify a shaky course of action is rationalization, a story line they pool their efforts to concoct and believe. Rationalizations serve to build confidence and reassure the group about the morality, safety, wisdom, or other validity of their decisions. The Bay of Pigs decision hinged on a slew of rationalizations appraising as safe what was a foolhardy plan. These rationalizations kept the group from contemplating some devastating information—such as the fact that Castro's army outnumbered the invading force by over 140 to 1.

Ethical Blinders. The group's schema includes an unstated belief in its rightness and morality. This glib assumption allows the members to ignore the moral status and consequences of their decisions. This belief flows from the group credo that "we are wise and good," an aspect of its self-image of invulnerability. And, after all, if we are good, then whatever we do must be good. These ethical blinders help the group avoid feeling ashamed or guilty about what otherwise might be questionable means or goals. Their actions can go on cocooned in a comfortable sense of righteousness. The bland assumption was that when the U.S. Government decrees something is best for a people, that choice must be "moral." That assumption was at play in the Bay of Pigs fiasco as it has been in any number of other foreign policy disasters.

Stereotypes. A stereotype is the grossly misfocused lens through which one group views another. The stereotype can be either positive or negative; it is invariably inaccurate. A stereotype is a schema that, once fixed, is preserved by ignoring disconfirming facts and amplifying any that seem to fit. Stereotypes are self-confirming. In the Bay of Pigs decision, the stereotype of Castro as hysterical and inept allowed the White House group to underestimate his response to the invasion. Stereotypes are tenacious; members will stick to them despite all evidence to the contrary. Images of the "enemy" in any group are always stereotypes: the judgment implied in the term "enemy" is incompatible with our knowing aspects of the others that might make them seem not so very much unlike ourselves.

The self-deceit to which groupthink leads can be prevented. Indeed, President Kennedy, sobered by the Bay of Pigs, purposefully encouraged critical thought and open dissent among his advisers in handling the Cuban missile crisis. Critical thinking and dissent are antidotes to shared illusions, ensuring that group schemas will be more in keeping with reality—or, at worst, honest mistakes rather than the product of groupthink.

GROUPTHINK IN THE CORPORATE FAMILY

Groupthink is an especially dangerous pathology for businesses. In making a marketing or product development decision, for example, a cozy executive group, falling into the grip of groupthink, can make costly mistakes. The bottom line, though, also offers business people a safeguard. Their decisions are likely to get a direct judgment from the marketplace about their soundness. In this respect businesses benefit from the built-in corrective of marketing success and failure, a periodic reality-check that is hard to ignore with even the most vigorous groupthink. Government and other policy planners often do not have such a direct and specific measure of the wisdom of their decisions.

Even so, business is replete with instances of Happy Family and groupthink. One Happy Family game common in corporations is the collusion to deny the incompetence of a longtime employee, often an alcoholic. He is gently shunted aside into a noncritical position, his bumbling discreetly ignored. Such collusions frequently end when a new management takes over. The newcomers, who do not share the sense of "family" that built the collusion, see simply the incompetence.

Harry Levinson, an organizational psychologist and a keen observer of corporate life, points out that we bring to the work place the understandings about groups we learned in our families:[28]

> All organizations recapitulate the basic family structure. . . . Our earliest experiences with our parents are repeated in our subsequent relationships with authority. Early family life determines our assumptions of how power is distributed, and as we grow up we form groups on the same model. . . . If everyone knows what the rules are, things run smoothly. Since a business and a family share similar psychodynamics, you find the same sorts of problems in

business—or any organizations—that you uncover in therapy.

Groupthink, like Happy Family, is a danger inherent in the structure of organizations. The success or failure of an employee depends to a large extent on his immediate superior's evaluation. This makes the junior employee more than happy to support the senior one's opinions, utilizing all the handy devices groupthink offers. Another structural tendency toward groupthink comes from the culture of the workplace, where people who work together day after day form a tight in-group.

Take, for example, the groups, sometimes known as "quality circles," set up among employees to cut through red tape and help workers themselves initiate changes in the way things are done. Organizational psychologists sat in on such groups in a battery assembly plant owned by a large corporation in the South.[29] These work groups were set up to do such things as prepare an annual budget, make job assignments, assess quality control, and evaluate job performance of fellow members. They were also encouraged to solve problems as they came up.

At one meeting of a group in the quality-control laboratory, the issue was a recent complaint that they were taking too long in their inspections. While the quality-control team did their tests for defects, production lines were shut down to avoid scrap; the workers who had to wait were indignant.

The quality-control group quickly came to a consensus: the workers who had complained "expect us to drop everything," and "they don't understand how long the tests take." Group members felt they were in the right, that the complaints were unreasonable and unjustified. The matter was dropped, without taking the complaint seriously or searching for a solution.

In the view of the observing psychologists, that resolution was arrived at using two groupthink tactics: rationalization and shared stereotypes. The rationalization was that there was nothing wrong with their own work, negative information to the contrary. The stereotype was that "stupid production workers" could not be expected to understand the intricacies of quality-control work. The result: the complaint was ignored.

In another meeting, where the manager happened to be present, the problem was a quality lapse in battery casings. At the outset discussion was animated and open, with members speaking freely. After a while, though, the manager spoke up, with "Here's what I think you should do. . . ." and took charge of the remainder of the meeting. Once he took over the members were quiet, but their facial expressions made clear that although they would comply with the manager's advice they did not agree with it.

Here self-censorship led to the illusion of unanimity. Although the members covertly did not go along with the manager, no one spoke up to voice differences. This lack of participation led the manager to believe that there was a consensus backing him up. What was essentially his opinion became the "group" decision.

There is some evidence that strong business leaders inadvertently encourage groupthink.[30] In a simulation of corporate decision-making, volunteers role-played executives of "Modern World Electronics" discussing whether to manufacture a microwave oven. Each group member had valuable information to contribute that was known to him alone.

The pseudoboss in each group, who led the discussions, was rated on how much he was motivated by a desire for power. People high in this motivation do things for the sake of making an impact on others, rather than to meet an inner standard of excellence (the hallmark of the achievement motive) or to enjoy the company of others (the affiliation motive). As leaders, those high in power motivation enjoy exercising authority solely for the taste of power. They have little tolerance for interference and bristle at challenges to their opinions.

High-power leaders respond well to ingratiating subordinates. In a group with such a leader, the axis of cohesiveness shifts toward the vertical from the horizontal: rather than feeling close to their fellow members, people in the group tend to form a bond of loyalty to the leader.

In the simulation, the leaders high in power motivation sought fewer facts from other group members and were offered fewer proposals. Once the leader had expressed his views, members fell in line, deferring to him. It was not so much that the leaders stifled dissent—many seemed to be democratic in how they ran things—but that they subtly reinforced compliance with their own opinions. The groupthink that resulted was a matter of degree: somewhat less initiative by members, a notable lack of opposition to the leader's views, a compliant falling in line behind him.

Anyone in the business world will be able to recognize moments like these, and to add ample examples of his own. Of course, not all groups are victims of groupthink, although from time to time even the healthiest may exhibit symptoms. The more often the symptoms crop up, the worse the resulting illusions, and the poorer the decisions that group will make. The healthy alternative, of course, is a group that balances a sense of unity with an openness to all relevant information—even at the risk of a fracas from time to time.

The point is that the group, like the individual, is susceptible to a trade-off between anxiety and diminished attention. In a group, feelings of cozy unanimity stand at the opposite end of a continuum with anxiety. If that coziness breaks down, things can become very tense indeed. When a group maintains its coziness by erecting barriers against information that might upset it, then a collective defense is at work. This process of guarding the group's self-image is precisely parallel to the ways the personal self skews reality to sustain its self-schema. As within, so without.

PART SIX

The Construction of Social Reality

CONSTRUCTING THE REALITY PAR EXCELLENCE

In the movie *Starting Over*, Jill Clayburgh, a teacher, is the target in a "dunk-the-teacher" booth at a nursery-school carnival. Clayburgh sits prim and proper, holding a parasol, lightheartedly urging the ball-throwers on. Burt Reynolds, Clayburgh's lover (with whom she has had a falling out), comes on the scene. Reynolds takes some balls, determinedly attacks the target, and Clayburgh drops into the water tank. Clayburgh stays calm and collected, until the fourth dunking at Reynolds's hands. Exasperated, she yells "Will you cut that shit out!"

A pall falls over the assembled parents and children. "She said the 'S' word!" a shocked nursery schooler cries.

"She did not!" his mother fires back, as she yanks him away to another carnival booth.

In the social realm, a notion similar to that of schemas is Erving Goffman's concept of "frames."[1] A frame is the shared definition of a situation that organizes and governs social events and our involvement in them. A frame, for example, is the understanding that we are at a play, or that "this is a sales call," or that "we are dating." Each of those definitions of social events determines what is appropriate to the moment and what is not; what is to be noticed and what ignored; what, in short, the going reality involves. When the frame is a nursery school carnival, the "S-word" is off limits.

A frame is the public surface of collective schemas. By sharing the understanding of the concepts "play," "sales," and "date," we can join in the action, enacting our parts in smooth harmony. A frame comes into being when its participants activate shared schemas for it; if someone does not share the going schema, the results can be embarrassing. Goffman gives this example, from a San Francisco gossip column, of an unshared frame:[2]

> . . . This guy is lying face down on Powell St., with traffic backed up for blocks. A Little Old Lady climbs down from a stalled cable car and begins giving him artificial respiration—whereupon he swivels his head and says: "Look lady, I don't know what game you're playing, but I'm trying to fix this cable."

We participate with ease in those social realms for which we have a frame. The newcomer or novice who has not yet mastered the schemas for a given frame, such as young children who do not yet have "good manners," has the same status as a foreign visitor or someone new to a sport. When they enter the action, everyone must accommodate to the ways they slow or undermine the business at hand.

Frames can be broken down into "scripts," the sequences of acts and responses that unfold within each frame. Take for an example the restaurant script:[3]

> Suppose I tell you that I went to a restaurant and ordered lobster and that I paid the check and left. What did I eat? Well, I didn't say anything about eating, but it must have been a lobster. Did the management get any money out of it? Of course, although I didn't say anything about management. Did the waitress give good service? What waitress?
>
> When I talk about restaurants, I bring into your mind all the knowledge you have about ordering and waitresses and menus and tipping. A restaurant script. There can be airline scripts and hotel scripts and classroom scripts.

A script codifies the schemas for a particular event; it directs attention selectively, pointing to what is relevant and ignoring the rest—a crucial factor for programming computers.* A computer program has the capacity to make endless inferences about and responses to a situation, almost all of them absurd. A script allows those inferences to be channeled along paths that make sense for a given event.

Indeed, there are scripts for every frame and a frame for any and all events in which people interact with some degree of shared understanding. Those events can range from the simple act of walking past someone coming toward you (Do you pass to the right or left? Do your eyes meet? If so, for how long? Do you speak?) to a procedure as complex as launching the space shuttle, with countless major and minor routines.

* Researchers in artificial intelligence, in striving to concoct computer programs that will allow a machine to mimic a person, study scripts in great detail.

Goffman's approach has its roots in William James's often-cited chapter on "The Perception of Reality," in his *Principles of Psychology,* in which James posed the question "Under what circumstances do we think things are real?"[4] In his answer, James pointed to the crucial role of selective attention in creating subworlds of reality, each with "its own special and separate style of existence." "Each world," James noted, "*whilst it is attended to,* is real after its own fashion; only the reality lapses with the attention."

What James meant by "world," Goffman says, was "a particular person's current world." When that world is shared, a frame is created. We step into such a world—enter a frame—whenever we adapt to one or another definition of a situation. Two examples are given by the phenomenologist Alfred Schutz:[5]

> . . . the radical change in attitude if, before a painting, we permit our visual field to be limited by what is within the frame as the passage into the pictorial world; our quandary, relaxing into laughter, if, in listening to a joke, we are for a short time ready to accept the fictitious world of the jest as a reality in relation to which the world of our daily life takes on the character of foolishness.

The world of our daily life is of course, in some sense as arbitrary a reality as any of the others we can enter into. It is endowed with a weighty sense of being *the* reality par excellence by virtue of the aggregate tonnage of our collective schemas.

The notion that social reality is the product of shared schemas is new for sociology. But that formulation is not much different from those currently in vogue; it simply offers a concept that is more in keeping with the current understanding of how the individual constructs reality.

This idea is close to that suggested by Peter Berger and Thomas Luckmann in their classic, *The Social Construction of Reality.* Berger and Luckmann agree with William James that while there are multiple realities, "there is one that presents itself as the reality par excellence:" the reality of everyday life. They write:[6]

> The language used in everyday life continuously provides me with the necessary objectifications and posits the order within which these make sense and within which everyday life has meaning for me. I live in a place that is geographically designated; I employ tools, from can openers to sports cars, which are designated in the technical vocabulary of my society; I live within a web of human relation-

> ships, from my chess club to the United States of America, which are also ordered by means of vocabulary. In this manner language marks the co-ordinates of my life in society and fills that life with meaningful objects.

If Berger and Luckmann were to dig deeper, to explore what it is that organizes language, the answer would be: schemas. Languages are schemas made audible; social acts are schemas made visible. If for "language" and its equivalents in the above passage the concept of schemas were used instead, the meaning would be unchanged. The implications, though, would be different.

The reality of everyday life, Berger and Luckmann note, is an "intersubjective world," that is, one that can be shared with others. The medium of that sharing, I suggest, is the mutual activation of commonly held schemas—a frame. It offers a reference point, a shared perspective for the business of the moment.

Frames—the rules embedded in the structure of a situation—are often hard to tease out. They are easier to spot when they are broken. In this sense, acts of social deviance—the psychotic who wanders through a department store taking items from one section and depositing them in another—is uncovering rules by shattering them.

Pirandello uses devices in his plays that do the same; he exploits the frames around a theatrical performance by pointing to them. For example, *Tonight We Improvise* begins with the houselights going dim, the audience quieting itself for the play to begin, and then nothing happening. Excited voices are heard from backstage, seemingly some sort of uproar. The play begins:[7]

> A gentleman from the orchestra: [*looks around and loudly asks*] What's happening up there?
> Another from the balcony: Sounds like a fight.
> A third from a box: Maybe it's all part of the show.

This dialogue itself, of course, is part of the show, and when it was first performed in 1930, the effect was jarring. By now such self-reflexive frame breaks are old hat. Joseph Heller uses them in his play *We Bombed in New Haven*, Genet in *The Blacks*. Books, too, can use frame breaks. *Goedel, Escher, Bach* is a self-reflexive meditation on the theme of self-reflex. John Barth's *Lost in the Fun House* has this passage in mid-novel:[8]

> The reader! You dogged unsuitable, print-oriented bastard, it's you I'm addressing, who else, from inside this monstrous fiction. You've read me this far, then? Even this far? For what discreditable motive? How is it you don't go to a movie, watch TV, stare at a wall . . .

The frame gives the context, telling us how to read what is going on. When lips meet, is it a kiss or mouth-to-mouth resuscitation? A frame provides an official main focus for attention, in accord with the business at hand: if the business is artificial resuscitation, enjoying the feel of skin on skin is out of bounds. The world offers a vast amount more than we might attend to in any given moment. The frame is highly selective; it directs attention away from all the simultaneous activities that are out of frame.

As Neisser's unnoticed woman with the white umbrella in the basketball game demonstrates, what is out of frame can easily go unperceived (at least in awareness—it may be registered in the unconscious). In order to hold an intimate conversation on a busy street, one must focus sharply on the immediate line of activity and ignore all the bustle, the other sights and sounds around. Any frame at all, in fact, defines a narrow focus where the relevant schemas direct attention, and a broad, ignored area of irrelevance.

Goffman makes the point with an extreme case, in this passage from Katherine Hulmes's *A Nun's Story:*[9]

> The first time she saw a novice faint in the chapel, she broke every rule and stared. No nun or novice so much as glanced at the white form that had keeled over from the knees, though the novice fell sideways into their midst and her Little Office shot from her hands as if thrown. . . . Then Gabrielle saw the nun in charge of the health of the community come down the aisle. The nursing nun plucked the sleeve of the nearest sister, who arose at once and helped carry the collapsed novice back down the aisle, past a hundred heads that never turned, past two hundred eyes that never swerved from the altar.

All frames, says Goffman, have such dual tracks: one flow of activity is overt and acknowledged, while a parallel track is ignored, treated as though out of frame. Anything out of frame, by definition, does not deserve attention. Since both tracks go on simultaneously, the minor track must constantly be kept out of focus. Further, the dominant track has to be picked out of the entire assemblage of activity.

Set sequences are often bounded by what Goffman (borrowing from Bateson) calls "brackets," conventions that mark the borders of a frame in time and space. They announce when and where a given framed event goes on, such as the start and finish of a session in therapy. The "disattend" track allows for the propriety of acts which are necessary asides (like a yawn). But they must be muted so as not to intrude into the frame.

These parallel tracks—in frame and out of frame—create a structure in social awareness that duplicates the division within the mind between conscious and unconscious. What is out of frame is also out of consensual awareness, in a sort of collective netherworld. As we shall see, the zone defined by the out-of-frame track can serve as a veil for disturbing social facts, creating a social blind spot.

Indeed, the social world is filled with frames that guide our awareness toward one aspect of experience and away from others. But we are so accustomed to their channeling our awareness that we rarely notice that they do so. Take, for example, the frames for work and for social roles.

THE TYRANNIES AND FREEDOMS OF FRAMES

Frames come and go as a society evolves. Consider the frame for work. We take for granted the workday as it exists now; the eight-hour-day at the office or factory is an ingrained convention. There are minor variations—flex-time, four-day weeks, the electronic cottage—but all these are considered deviations from a well-established norm. That norm, however, is itself a social fabrication, a by-product of the Industrial Revolution.

In traditional societies, work and leisure are integrated. Buyer and seller linger over coffee before beginning to haggle; when friends come by, work can be dropped to socialize. The frame of work as we know it is a peculiarity of modern society. It was the British mill owners of the seventeenth and eighteenth centuries who by and large invented our frame for a workday. Even in the early eighteenth century in Britain work offered a high degree of flexibility and independence: whether farmer or tradesman, most people worked at home. Work rhythms by and large went in cycles of intense labor broken by idle, free time.

The eighteenth century saw a crucial shift in the British economy: where before merchants had merely bought and distributed goods, such as home-loomed cloth, they now began to orchestrate the entire production process. Where before manufacturing had been done by rural families weaving and spinning at their homes, the locus of work began to be centralized. The mill—the prototype of the modern factory—was born.

One historian of work comments on this change:[10]

> The home worker . . . was in many respects his own master. . . . The forces that ruled his fate were in a sense outside his daily life; they did not overshadow and envelop his home, his family, his movements and habits, his hours for work and his hours for food. . . . In the modern world most people have to adapt themselves to some kind of

> discipline, and to observe other people's . . . orders, but we have to remember that the population that was flung into the brutal rhythm of the factory had earned its living in relative freedom, and that the discipline of the early factory was particularly savage.

The factory was the scene of a far-reaching reframing of work. As Shoshana Zuboff observes,[11] work was redefined in terms of "developing rigid guidelines for what the daily experience of working might legitimately consist of, and forcefully imposing this new reality on an entire class of people. . . . The new demands of speed and regularity could not tolerate the uneconomic rhythms of peasant life."

Employers assumed the right to control their employees' moves and use of time during working hours. As Zuboff notes, perhaps even more oppressive for the workers of the day, employers also sought to dictate how workers' "attention was organized and distributed across the working day." For example, one observer notes that[12] "If the worker sees a friend . . . he can't clap him on the shoulder and hale him off to the nearest pub. . . . The factory system and machinery brought the blessings of lighter labor, but also the curse of greater attentiveness over fixed stretches of time. In being paced by machines, work took on a new concentration."

The employer was now defined as the owner of the workers' time and attention during the hours of the workday: he decided the content and rhythm of their activities. The frame of the workday was taking modern shape, and it was the manager who constructed it.

The new frames around time and activity of work took shape through a gradual process. Witness, for example, this early account, circa 1831, of what have since become the lunch hour and coffee break:[13]

> The diminution of the intervals of work has been a gradual encroachment. Formerly an hour was allowed for dinner; but one great manufacturer, pressed by his engagements, wished his workpeople to return five minutes earlier. This arrangement was promptly adopted at other mills. Five minutes led to ten. It was found also that breaking and drinking [afternoon meal] might be taken while the people were at work. Time was thus saved; more work was done; and the manufactured article could be offered at a less price. . . . Thus what was at first partial and temporary has become more general and permanent.

This regulation of workers' time, Zuboff shows, was a tidal switch from centuries before. In the sixteenth century, time was imprecise, seasonal; the notion of measured time was thought cruel. One of Rabelais's characters says, "I will never subject myself to hours. Hours are made for man, not man for hours." Although there were some public clocks, the minute hand was thought unnecessary.

By the late eighteenth century, the frame of work was bounded by minute hands: the market for clocks and watches boomed as the demand for a synchronized work force grew. With the purchase of workers' time, employers also set to managing attention. The desired state was nothing less than diligent, silent attention to the work at hand—an absolute about-face from the casual routines workers were used to.

For this reason, it was not easy to recruit and hold workers. For example, Zuboff describes how in 1830 a mill was built in Nantucket, and women and children flocked to work there at first (the men of the town were whalers). After about a month, though, so many had drifted off that the plant was shut down. Three decades later a plant in Lowell set rules saying the factory gates would be locked during the day. The machinists there were incensed at the idea that they could not come and go as they pleased during the workday; they struck to protest the rule.

The great innovator of the workplace, Henry Ford, used the assembly line to up the ante of control over his workers' pace. The assembly line trivialized a job by breaking it up into a series of single, repeated sequences done at a rate fixed by the needs of the factory to maximize output. This new frame of work met with a new wave of resistance. Even though Ford paid the best wages around, the attrition at his factory was so great that, in 1913, for every 100 additional workers the company wanted, they had to hire 963.

The frame of work in this century has gone through two striking shifts: more discipline in the ordering of the sequence and timing of tasks, and a more fragmented and inflexible work schedule. By now we take that frame for granted. Writes sociologist Harold Wilensky:[14]

> The time clock, the plant rules, the presence of a host of supervisors and other control specialists, the close attention to quantity and quality of output—these add up to a demand for discipline on the job. . . . We half forget the sustained regularity insisted upon in office, store, and factory—we are so used to it.

Our attitude toward the work frame for the most part no longer needs to be imposed by dismissals or overt discipline. As Zuboff notes, "One simply learns it by experiencing the subtle attention-directing forces that shape experience in that organization. One comes already adapted, one adapts, or one leaves. No blood is shed to achieve this kind of discipline. It is a civilized process."

In much the same fashion as work, a social role is a frame of sorts, subtly directing and limiting how—and how much—we attend to the person filling it. The contour of a role's frame can be seen in the boundary of attention deemed appropriate in our notice of the person filling it: the one-dimensionality of people in roles demands that we ignore the "rest" of them.

Sartre describes the obligation of tradespeople to constrain their behavior and attentional range as befits their role:[15]

> Their condition is wholly one of ceremony. The public demands of them that they realize it as a ceremony; there is the dance of the grocer, of the tailor, of the auctioneer, by which they endeavor to persuade their clientele that they are nothing but a grocer, an auctioneer, a tailor. A grocer who dreams is offensive to the buyer, because such a grocer is not wholly a grocer. Society demands that he limit himself to his function as a grocer, just as the soldier at attention makes himself into a soldier-thing with a direct regard which does not see at all, which is no longer meant to see, since it is the rule and not the interest of the moment which determines the point he must fix his eyes on (the sight "fixed at ten paces"). There are indeed many precautions to imprison a man in what he is, as if we lived in perpetual fear that he might escape from it, that he might break away and suddenly elude his condition.

The sustaining of a role demands the mutual restriction of attention by both the role-player and his audience. To support the premise that he is merely a waiter or grocer or gas station attendant, we refrain from drawing attention to more personal aspects of his being: that he seems to be nervous today, or is putting on weight, or is truculent. Like Sartre's "soldier-thing," he, too, figuratively averts his gaze so as to ignore those same aspects about us—or anything else beyond the domain of his role. Small talk is okay, but it must remain small: should it overstep the bounds of the role, it would become impropriety, if not an imposition.

Sartre makes the case that the one-dimensionality of people in social roles is symptomatic of a broader alienation in the modern condition. While there may be some truth in this position, it fails to acknowledge the benefits that accrue from the frame's one-dimensionality.

One gain from this shallowness is internal autonomy. The bubble of privacy that one-dimensionality affords means the person is free to fantasize, reflect, daydream—in short, to turn his remaining attention to private pursuits and pleasures, even in the midst of public life. While a given role makes some demands, these are generally routinized, leaving a large range of freedom in the psychological realm. This inner freedom is most possible in a mundane routine well insulated by attentional buffers. The grocer is free to dream precisely because he need not share his dreams.

This freedom would vanish if playing the role required a fuller, more "authentic" interchange with each person encountered in the course of filling it. The waiter's polite aloofness spares him the invasion of his personal sphere by those he serves, just as it affords his customers the illusion of privacy in public. Schemas for those roles deflect attention so that within the constraints of role there lies a certain liberty.

On the other hand, if we don the mask of role, we are in danger of being hidden by it—or hiding behind it. In either case, the person is buried in the role. The entrapment is largely due to the attentional standards that pertain. The waiter is out of line if he comments on the troubles of a couple he serves, even though he may overhear much of their dialogue. The therapist sabotages his frame if he unburdens his problems to a client, even though they may be very much on his mind.

A frame for what one can and cannot call attention to constitutes a barrier as well. Roles exert their tyrrany when these attentional barriers hide the urgent feelings and intense concerns of those involved. This tyranny is a subtext of the film *My Dinner with André*. André Gregory describes such a barrier: [16]

> . . . I remember a night—it was about two weeks after my mother died, and I was in pretty bad shape, and I went out to dinner with three relatively close friends, two of whom had known my mother quite well, and all three of them have known me for years. And we went through that entire evening without my being able to, for a moment, get anywhere near what—you know, not that I wanted to sit and have a dreary evening in which I was talking about all this pain that I was going through and everything—really not at all. But—but the fact that nobody could say, Gee, what a shame about your mother, or How are you feeling? But it was as if nothing had happened.

The tyranny of role that Sartre notes begins when the frame hides genuine and relevant human concerns. At this point the blinders that a role provides allow the person inside the role to be dehumanized rather than liberated—to be given less due than he deserves. Wally Shawn and André Gregory commiserate: [17]

ANDRÉ: . . . if we allowed ourselves to see what we're doing every day, we might find it just too nauseating. I mean, the way we treat other people—I mean, you know, every day, several times a day, I walk into my apartment building. The doorman calls me Mr. Gregory, and I call him Jimmy. The same transaction probably occurs between you and the guy you buy groceries from every day, in some other way. . . . You see, I think that an act of murder is committed in that moment, when I walk into my building. Because here is a dignified, intelligent man, a man of my own age, and when I call him Jimmy, then he becomes a child, and I'm an adult. . . .

WALLY: Right. That's right. I mean, my God, when I was a Latin teacher, people used to treat *me*—I mean, if I would go to a party of professional or literary people, I mean, I was just treated—uh—in the nicest sense of the word, like a dog. In other words, there was no *question* of my being able to participate on an equal basis in the conversation with people. I mean, I would occasionally *have* conversations with people, but when they asked what I did, which would always happen after about five minutes—uh, you know, their faces—even if they were enjoying the conversation, or they were flirting with me or whatever it was—their faces would just, you know, have that expression like the portcullis crashing down, you know, those medieval gates—

The "portcullis crashing down" is simply the withdrawal of attention. Such snubs have the effect of dehumanizing the recipient, of shifting focus from the person to the role. This keeps things at the surface: the role is not penetrated to the person inside. This failure to penetrate the role, to notice the person, can be in the service of a low-order anxiety-attention trade-off. When we'd rather not see—preferring to ignore rather than confront the person—attending only to the role offers an easy out, if not outright solace. It is, as Zuboff says, a civilized process.

THE WELL-MANNERED GAZE

Frames define the social order. They tell us what is going on, when to do what, and to whom. They direct our attention toward the action in the frame, and away from what is available to awareness but irrelevant.

For example, in the Middle East, people stare. I recall walking down the street in Jerusalem the first day of a visit there. As I would approach someone on the sidewalk, with my peripheral vision I sensed being watched. A cautious glance as we passed and my eyes would be met by a full-on stare.

My first reaction was embarrassment. Was it something about me? Was I so obviously a tourist, an outsider? Did I seem so strange?

I began to stare back. Each time my eyes were met by an approaching set of staring eyes. Then I realized that everyone did it to everyone else. Hasidic Jews in fur caps and long coats matched stares with Coptic priests in white robes. Arab women in veils locked gazes with Israeli women in army fatigues.

It wasn't me; it was the ground rule for attention in public. In the Middle East the convention is for people to stare openly as they approach. In America there is a very different rule for gaze. As two strangers in America approach while walking, each covertly glances at the other to plot a course that will avoid collision. By about eight paces each of them averts his eyes and keeps his gaze elsewhere until they pass.[18]

By following their own rule for gaze, the people of Jerusalem made me acutely aware that something was amiss. We were operating in mismatching frames.

Culture is a basket of frames. To the degree that frames differ from culture to culture, contacts between people from different lands can be sticky. For example, bribery is a normal part of doing business in much of the world, a fact that makes Americans indignant.

But Americans have a style of frank openness that Mexicans may regard as weakness or treachery, that Japanese may see as boorish and crude. In many Asian countries, "no" is used little; "yes" can mean yes, no, or perhaps. (A book for English-speaking managers to help them in their dealings with Japanese is called *Never Take "Yes" for an Answer.*)

In India, people can't bear to bring bad news, so they lie: the train, they say, is "just coming," when in fact it is five hours late. How late is "late" varies drastically from culture to culture: five minutes is late but permissible for a business appointment in the U.S., but thirty minutes is normal in Arab countries. In England five to fifteen minutes is the "correct" lateness for one invited to dinner; an Italian might come two hours late, an Ethiopian still later, a Javanese not at all, having accepted only to prevent his host's losing face. The list of cultural misunderstandings goes on and on.

The averted gaze in our culture cushions life in public. Our encounters are manipulated by attentional frames so deeply embedded in the social fabric that in the main we notice them only when they are violated: a passerby fails to look away as we walk toward him, and his stare stirs in us an uneasy self-consciousness. As we move in and out of relation to each other—browse in a store, walk by a stranger, ride in a crowded elevator—our privacy is protected as though by an invisible scrim that veils us from view.

The frames for public interaction define those junctures where paying overt attention is acceptable. The salesperson's "May I help you?" is one such, as is the well-timed "How are you today?" of a casual acquaintance as we pass by, or the quick glance other passengers give as they make room on an elevator. If in any of these instances we find ourselves observed too intently, we feel discomfort, if not embarrassment. To be the object of someone's scrutiny beyond the appropriate points violates our right to feel invisible—a right protected by the frames governing attention in public.

The well-mannered deployment of attention is a large part of what we call "tact." We all depend on each other to employ tact, so that we can maintain our course unruffled. Goffman, in his book *The Presentation of Self in Everyday Life*, describes the attentional etiquette that governs public life: [19]

> We often find that when interaction must proceed in the presence of outsiders, outsiders tactfully act in an uninterested, uninvolved, unperceiving fashion, so that if physical isolation is not obtained by walls or distance, effective isolation can at least be obtained by convention. Thus

> when two sets of persons find themselves in neighboring booths in a restaurant, it is expected that neither group will avail itself of the opportunities that actually exist for overhearing the other.

Frames not only direct traffic; they dictate how people in various roles are to be regarded. Goffman uses the metaphor of the theater to describe the dynamics of social role. When we are in a role, those we address are our "audience." Here, too, attentional manners are crucial to help us through the performances our roles demand:[20]

> We find that there is an elaborate etiquette by which individuals guide themselves in their capacity as members of the audience. This involves: the giving of a proper amount of attention and interest; a willingness to hold in check one's own performance so as not to introduce too many contradictions, interruptions, or demands for attention; the inhibition of all acts or statements that might create a faux pas; the desire, above all else, to avoid a scene.
>
> When performers make a slip of some kind, clearly exhibit a discrepancy between the fostered impression and a disclosed reality, the audience might tactfully "not see" the slip or readily accept the excuse that is offered for it. And at moments of crisis for the performers, the whole audience may come into tacit collusion with them in order to help them out.

This sort of tacit collusion is nowhere more obvious than in breaches of social order. In *The Catcher in the Rye*, Holden Caulfield creates an uproar in his prep school chapel by farting loudly. The breach is not smoothed over; a giggle triggers gales of laughter. His fart captures the attention of the entire assembly, and so succeeds as an act of rebellion against the repressive frames of the school's social order.

The off-key tone of such disruptions can ruin the semblance of smoothness we conspire to create in dealings with each other, which we can do only by activating similar frames in synchrony. When our frames don't mesh, the public order falters. Goffman offers a list of such challenges to the public order:[21]

> First, a performer may accidentally convey incapacity, impropriety, or disrespect by momentarily losing muscular control of himself. He may trip, stumble, fall; he may belch, yawn, make a slip of the tongue, scratch himself, or be flatulent; he may accidentally impinge upon the body of another participant. . . . He may stutter, forget his lines, appear nervous, or guilty, or self-conscious; he may give

> way to inappropriate outbursts of laughter, anger, or other kinds of affect which momentarily incapacitate him as an interactant; he may show too much serious involvement and interest, or too little. . . . The setting may not have been put in order, or may have become readied for the wrong performance, or may become deranged during the performance; unforeseen contingencies may cause improper timing of the performer's arrival or departure or may cause embarrassing lulls to occur during the interaction.

The major strategy for smoothing over such breaches is to ignore them outright. In lieu of denial, the fallback is to shrug it off, most commonly by laughing at it. Laughter acknowledges the frame break, while showing that it is not serious enough to disrupt proceedings. In either case the ploy is denial: of the seriousness of the breach on the one hand, or that it occurred at all on the other. The social fiction can continue, unperturbed.

What we think of as "good manners" are, in this perspective, frames for smooth relations in public. When people interact who do not share the same schemas for how to act properly in a situation, the result is embarrassment, social friction, or outright anxiety. A newspaper column on "Reacting to Boorish Manners" deals with this dilemma:[22]

> Did you see him? Did you see her? Did you see that? Talking throughout the performance. Barging ahead in the checkout line. Smoking during the meal. Redialing a number with five people waiting to use the telephone. He ought to be ashamed. She ought to be ashamed. Someone should say something!
>
> Sometimes someone does—or perhaps not, for these are the minor transgressions in life. . . . Why do they do what they do, and how should we deal with it?
>
> "You certainly don't say, 'Hey you blankety-blank-blank, I was here first,' " said Dr. Leonard Berkowitz, a psychology professor at the University of Wisconsin. "It's not very constructive, and you could get a very nasty reaction."
>
> "As to those transgressed against," he continued, "most of us are uncertain of societal rules, so we're not sure whether it's right to object to a particular action. At the same time, we don't want to generate friction or trouble."

The schemas that constitute social norms for public behavior —that is, "manners"—are susceptible to violation. We are often unsure as to what the "right" frame for the moment is. That uncertainty supports a minor industry of experts, columns like Dear Abby and Miss Manners. Social schemas are embedded and hidden in the fabric of group life; when pressed to state them we confront their implicit nature. Experts to whom we can turn for advice offer a reassuring source of authority.

The socializing of a child, in these terms, is tantamount to recruiting him into the going frames:[23] "any social system, in order to survive, must socialize new recruits into its attentional patterns (of perception, belief, behavior, and so on). This task requires energy, that is, attention. Thus, one might say that the survival of social systems depends on the balance in the ledger of attention income and expenditure."

In other words, it takes some initial investment of attention to introduce a person to the ins and outs of a frame. The more complex that frame, the more investment required: grooming a new secretary, teaching a child "manners," instructing a novice in the etiquette of a royal court—all take effort.

When that effort is no longer made, a frame that relies on it will wither away. For example, in some social milieus, it was the custom for children to address their teachers with the honorific "sir" or "madam," to stand when speaking in class, and so on. That frame of formality survives in fewer and fewer bastions outside some private and parochial schools.

The robustness of a frame depends entirely on its potency in recruiting new users and in getting those who know it to activate it at the appropriate time. The slow evolution of social custom and proprieties is the history of the rise and fall of frames.

Some of this inculcation of frames is covert, some direct. The latter sort is well described in this passage from Charlotte Selver:[24]

> The other day I visited some friends. Among the guests were a couple with their daughter, a little girl of eight. . . . She came upstairs and sat down, one leg hanging down, the other one on the couch. Mother said, "But Helen, how do you *sit*? Take your leg off the couch. A girl *never* should sit like that!" The little girl took her leg down, on which occasion her skirt flew high above her knees. The mother? "Helen, pull your skirt down! One can see everything." The child blushed, looked down on herself and pulled her skirt down but asked, "Why? What is wrong?" The mother looked at her quite shocked and said, "One doesn't *do* that!"
>
> By this time the atmosphere in the room was completely uncomfortable. The little girl not only had her legs down but had them pressed against each other. Her shoulders had gone up and she held her arms tight against her little body. This went on until she couldn't stand it any

> longer. She suddenly stretched herself and yawned heartily. Again, a storm of indignation from her mother.
>
> What will happen to this child? She will hold her unhappy pose for a few minutes before she shakes it off. The next time her mother will admonish her, she will hold it a few minutes longer, and so on, each time a little longer, until at last . . . The mother will have reached her goal: she will have educated her to be socially acceptable.

This education in the restriction of movement is a perfect analogue of what happens to attention as children learn social frames. Socially acceptable patterns of attention are carefully channeled. It is essential that children learn what sorts of things may be noted, what not. The four-year-old may blithely ask a cripple "Why do you walk like that?" or the obese man "Why are you so fat?" The nine-year-old will have learned not to ask, the teenager to avert his eyes, the adult to pretend not to notice. Social schemas tame attention.

In defining what is and is not pertinent to the moment, frames can be used defensively. When something happens that would provoke anxiety, it is often managed by keeping it out of frame. People mesh with an exquisite precision in evoking this defensive use of frames, fending off anxiety through disattention. We don't need to be told what to pretend is not happening; we all know at once, without anything being said.

Take, for example, an incident on a British train described by Paul Theroux. A car is shared by Theroux, an elderly couple, and some young couples with children, on their way to the country. Suddenly a group of "skinheads," tattooed, with earrings, leather jackets, vicious-looking boots, and heads shaved, barge into the rail car, laughing and shouting, yelling at each other to "fuck off." The proper Britons deftly employ the out-of-frame gambit:[25]

> They were loud—earsplitting—but the picnicking English people across the aisle, and the elderly people, and each young family in its own pew did not hear a thing. The picnickers went on eating in their tidy way, and everyone else became silent and small. . . . "The long-range forecast called for fine weather," one of the Touchmores whispered.

The conspiracy of silence in the face of unseemliness works, in its own meek manner, until a little girl pipes up:

> "Daddy, why are those men saying 'fuck off'?"
>
> "I don't know, darling. Now do please let me read my paper."

> His voice was nervous, as if he had been holding his breath. I had certainly been holding mine. . . .
> "There, Daddy, they just said it again. 'Fucking hell.' "
> "Hush, darling. There's a good girl."
> "And that one said 'fuck,' too."
> "That's enough darling." The man's voice was subdued.
> He did not want anyone to hear . . .
> He probably would not have been heard in any case. The Skinheads were screaming, and running in the aisle . . . one little Skinhead, a boy of about thirteen, also tattooed and shaven, and wearing an earring, was yelling, "You fucking cunt, I'll fucking kill you!"

The invasion of the rail car by the Skinheads is an assault; while they did no physical harm, they effectively smashed the other passengers' frames. Their attack exemplifies attentional vampirism. By intruding on the scene in a manner that can't be ignored, the Skinheads force themselves into everyone else's frame. This same imposition is accomplished by obnoxious children, rowdy drunks, manics, and certain sorts of psychotics. All violate the tacit attentional rules that create order in public places.

What we treat out of frame need not be so threatening; it can also be what we'd rather not notice. For example, a woman in her eighth month of pregnancy wrote a letter-to-the-editor recounting what befell her on a crowded train from New Jersey to Manhattan, in a humid 100-degree heat. As the train pulled up to the platform where she was waiting:[26]

> . . . These well-groomed people around me began their usual frantic shove toward the doors, heaven forbid they not get a seat. I managed to dodge most sly elbows, but one hit me hard. I looked at my assailant and pleaded, "Please don't shove." No response.
> . . . I stood right next to two seated "gentlemen" who put on their blinders immediately so they could avoid acknowledging my "condition" and so they could remain in their sacred seats.
> . . . I guess I'll never understand the total apathy of these apparently well-bred, successful people. Are they so selfishly involved in their own pursuits that others have no place in their mental sets? Would they want their own pregnant wives or mothers to stand as I had to, holding on for dear life?

Consider the Good Samaritan study.[27] At Princeton Theological Seminary forty students waited to give a short practice sermon.

At fifteen-minute intervals the seminarians went one by one to another building to give their talk. On the way over, the students passed a man groaning, slumped over in a doorway. Six of every ten seminarians who passed the groaning man went right by, ignoring him. Half of those seminarians were on their way to talk about the parable of the Good Samaritan, the man who helped a needy stranger by the roadside. They were no more likely to help the groaning man than the others who passed him by.

There are probably times when even the most altruistic among us might not help out—for example, when rushing to catch a plane. Indeed, in the case of the seminarians one of the main factors in whether a student stopped to help was whether he was in a rush: of students who thought they were late to give their talk, only one in ten stopped; of those who thought they had plenty of time, six in ten stopped. That some of them were reflecting on the Good Samaritan parable had no effect.

When it comes to helping out, the frame a person holds can make a large difference. In the famous Kitty Genovese murder the thirty-eight Kew Gardens neighbors who heard her screams but did not call the police each ascribed a frame to the event that precluded their helping: "It was a lover's quarrel," or "Someone else will call," or "It's none of my business."

The man lying face down on the sidewalk of a busy street poses a minor puzzle to the passerby. Is he a wino? Junkie? Sick? Hurt? Is he dangerous—could he have a knife in his pocket? Does he need help? Should I try to help or leave him to the police?

The answers to these questions are implicit in the frames each connotes. If he's a wino, the frame dictates no interference. If he's sick and needs help, that's different. But the interpretation "He needs help" leads to another quandary: What to do? Step in, or leave it to the police?

Prompted by the uproar in the wake of the Genovese tragedy, psychologists have done numerous, elaborate experiments to tease out when a person will help another in need. The Good Samaritan study was one of these. Typically, the studies entail a stooge staging an emergency, such as collapsing on a New York City subway, to see under what circumstances people come to his rescue.

One feature is common to all these stagings: the bystanders are all taken by surprise. They are engaged in some other frame—on their way to some other appointment or otherwise caught up in life's comings and goings. Their encounter with the person suddenly in need confronts them with a challenge to their own ongoing frame. To stop what they are doing to help out requires abandoning for the moment their own frame to enter another.

The frames that keep people from helping include evaluation

of the victim's status (winos get no help, well-dressed men do), or state (drunk or drugged, no; ill, yes), as well as the frame of the would-be helper. Being in a rush, as was the case with the seminarians, lessens the likelihood of helping, as do such factors as being alone or nearly alone (the more people around, the quicker people are to help).

Perhaps the major single factor in whether people help or not is the conglomerate of frames that the sociologist George Simmel called the "urban trance." At the turn of the century Simmel proposed that urbanites were less responsive to people and things around them (and so, by implication, less likely to help someone in need). This lack of responsivity was due, said Simmel, to the urban trance, a self-absorbed state city dwellers fall into as a necessary adaptation to the swirl and bustle around them.*

According to Simmel, the sheer volume of events in the urbanite's surroundings produces a self-protective reserve and indifference. More recently, that view was elaborated by the social psychologist Stanley Milgram in terms of "input overload," that is, an intensity of stimuli too great for the person's attentional capacity. The sights, sounds, and demands of the city, argued Milgram, overwhelm the mind's ability to handle them. The mental adaptation to this overload is an obliviousness to all but the most immediately relevant of events. In other words, you register the taxi careening toward you, but take no notice of the drunk you step over in the gutter.

In terms of the model of mind developed here, that means that for the urbanite the threshhold of awareness is higher: it is not that he does not *register* as much information in the mind, but that the price of admission to his awareness is higher. Fewer of the available schemas justify the expense of occupying space in awareness.*

Frames have the power to steer attention away from compelling events. For the most part such obliviousness is higher in benefits than in cost; the mental space a frame creates gives us the luxury of paying full attention to the business at hand without being distracted by the busy world around us. But as the Bad Samaritans demonstrate, there are social costs to that oblivion.

* There may also be a "rural trance": country folk are certainly capable of the same sort of self-absorption.

* This would account for the bewilderment of country folk on coming to the city: their schemas are not adapted to screen out the high intensity of irrelevant events. Their frames are too wide, they notice too much.

The same could be said, of course, for the city dweller in the country: his schemas are not adapted for that setting, which can result in other kinds of confusions. And all of us go through a similar bewilderment on traveling to a foreign country. It is only after having spent some time there—and built up schemas for what is at first exotic and strange—that we feel the same ease as we do at home.

WHAT YOU DON'T SEE WON'T HURT YOU

If frames are the building blocks of social reality, then what is true for the individual mind can be true of the social order: information that makes us uneasy can be handily denied. As is the case in the family and other groups, when some aspects of the shared reality are troubling, a semblance of cozy calm can be maintained by an unspoken agreement to deny the pertinent facts. When stepping out of frame might bring us face-to-face with information we'd rather not notice, then the frame offers itself as a refuge from painful confrontations. Take as an example white lies.

Lies big and small lubricate social life. It is tacitly understood that civilized interaction requires timely deceit: we send double messages, hide true feelings, make crucial omissions; apart from out-and-out lies, we lie by innuendo and ambiguity. Just as smooth social interaction requires that we do not comment on each lapse in decorum, tact dictates we do not challenge every little bit of insincerity.

Social lies have their uses. For example, white lies, such as those we tell to get out of accepting an unwanted invitation, save the feelings of those they are told to. Other lies preserve our social image—for example, what one researcher calls lies of self-presentation: "attempts to present ourselves as a little more kind, a little more sensitive, a little more intelligent, and a little more altruistic than in fact we are."

We overlook social lies; to call our family, friends, and associates on them is tactless. We tacitly encourage one another's lies by virtue of an unwritten social code that says we will see only what we are supposed to see; the unseeable stays out of frame. Without our mutual agreement to follow such rules, the veneer of consensus in everyday interactions would peel away, leaving, no doubt, some rancor in its stead.

Social lies succeed as a lubricant only when received with tactful inattention. Face-to-face dealings frequently present us with the opportunity to detect such lies—for example, by studying various aspects of a person's demeanor to search for discrepancies in what he is telling us.

The most detailed research on the game of sending and detecting social lies—and its implications for the smooth operation of daily life—has been conducted by a social psychologist at Harvard, Robert Rosenthal and a group of his graduate students. To examine the rules that underlie the telling, detecting, or ignoring of the great and small lies of daily life, they began to study deception in the late 1970s.[28]

Their research took a cue from Freud, who wrote of the nonverbal cues that can give away one's true feelings: "If his lips are silent, he chatters with his fingertips, betrayal oozes out of him at every pore." It is a commonplace that the body yields telling clues. A forced smile belies sadness; a clenched fist betrays anger unspoken. But the Rosenthal group's deception research shows that certain aspects of the body's language are better channels for lying—or clues to deception—than others. The face, for example, is far more effective than the body—or even speech—in telling lies.

It was Paul Ekman, an expert on reading facial expressions, who first suggested why the face is probably the least leaky nonverbal channel—and the best liar. A person's ability to deceive, they proposed, depends on several aspects of the channel (such as tone of voice or facial expression) he uses. In general, the greater that channel's "sending capacity," the more deceptive it can be.

Sending capacity is greater the more clearly different messages a channel can send, the more quickly it can send them, and the more visible or obvious they are. The face, Ekman argues, has maximal sending capacity, and so is especially well equipped to lie. By contrast, the body (including, for example, gestures), is less controllable, slower, and less obvious. While this makes the body a less effective channel for lies, it also makes it more prone to leaks, those nonverbal messages that inadvertently reveal a feeling the person is trying to hide. To get a more complete view of leaks, the Rosenthal group extended the list of leaky channels to include a hierarchy of five: face, body, tone of voice, fleeting expressions, and the discrepancies between them.

Tone of voice might seem to us at first more similar to the face in its capacity for fakery than to the "leaking" body. Like the face, the voice can send many nuances of meaning very easily, and people can readily control their tone of voice. The available evidence, though, suggests otherwise. For one thing, because of the acoustics of the skull, the voice we hear while we are speaking does not sound the same to our listeners. (This may explain the almost universal reactions of dismay from people on first hearing their tape-recorded voices.) In a tape people hear inflections and tonal qualities that leak their feelings, but that are seemingly unnoticed by the speaker while talking. For all these reasons, the Rosenthal group rated the tone of voice as more revealing than the body in the hierarchy of clues to lie detection.

Another category of leaky channels the researchers added includes very brief changes in the body (such as a muted hand movement) and face (such as a fleeting half-smile). Ekman claims such momentary displays are typically unintended and uncontrolled, and so are even leakier than the tone of voice.

Even leakier than these microlapses, though, are discrepancies, such as a smiling face with an angry voice. Such a discrepancy, the Rosenthal group proposed, was the most revealing of leaky cues because it involves two channels, both of which are hard to control, especially simultaneously. Thus a liar might be very careful of how he phrased his lie, might even remember, say, to smile in its support, but might not also be skillful enough to control the anger in his voice. That discrepancy could tip off an alert observer to his lie.

When Rosenthal and his co-researcher Bella DePaulo began to study lies and their detection, they were in for a surprise. A decade of research—much of it done by Rosenthal—had shown overwhelmingly that women are far superior to men at reading nonverbal messages: when asked to say what feeling a tone of voice or gesture reflected, women were found to be right much more often than men. But women's accuracy seemed to lag when they were asked to decode leaks, that category of nonverbal clues which unintentionally expose hidden feelings. The more leaky a tone of voice, or the more incongruent a message, the *less* well women did in interpreting it. Men showed just the opposite pattern: as hidden feelings were revealed by more clues, their accuracy *improved.*

Although women were better than men at reading the face, their advantage decreased steadily as they confronted the more leaky channels. Rosenthal and DePaulo interpreted this effect as fitting with women's greater social civility. In their view, paying attention to a person's slips and leaks is tantamount to rudeness; indeed, noticing leaks is a form of eavesdropping.

Along with being more polite in ignoring leaks, women also are more candid and open in the nonverbal messages they themselves send. Empathy research has shown that women are better at telegraphing their feelings than are men. Women, it seems, allow their nonverbal messages to be more legible than do men.

In Rosenthal and DePaulo's view,[29] women are more "polite" in reading other people's nonverbal messages than are men. They go on to add: "Perhaps women in our culture have learned that there may be social hazards to knowing too much about other people's feelings. This relative avoidance of eavesdropping by women is consistent with the standards of politeness and social smoothing-over that are part of the traditional sex role ascribed to women in our culture, a sex role that is only now beginning to change."

The interpretation that women are more "accommodating" and "polite" by virtue of ignoring leaks irks some other researchers on nonverbal messages. One is Judith Hall, another former graduate student of Rosenthal's, who is an expert on sex differences in nonverbal communication.[30] Hall objects to the social motives that are imputed to women in ignoring leaks.

"The need for accuracy at reading leaks," says Hall, "is relatively rare in daily life. I would argue that instead of men having developed a skill that women have not—which is the idea behind Rosenthal and DePaulo's interpretation—women develop some socially useful skills in preference to others. Maybe women are just doing something that represents an intelligent social strategy. Smooth interaction requires that people not notice or comment on every little lapse in decorum, or every little bit of insincerity. Social life works by ignoring little social lies. Women seem wiser to this than men."

And how is it that we learn to ignore social lies? After all, we are not born with that capacity. As the tale "The Emperor's New Clothes" attests, children can be brutally candid, without guile or self-consciousness. Children are notable not only for their lies, but for the lies they don't tell. If the child is young, such forthrightness is excused. But as children become held accountable for courtesy, such frankness is regarded as embarrassing. At this point, children are taught that social lies are to be condoned. To operate smoothly in the adult world, children must learn when it is socially beneficial to be both a good liar and a poor lie-detector.

The child's world is replete with deceits, both large and small. "Some of the lies told to children," writes DePaulo,[31] "are not less preposterous than fairy tales, cartoons, or television comedies. For example, children are often told that once a year, a fat man on a sled is flown through the air by a fleet of deer. Graver facts are usually described by less colorful lies (Grandpa went on a long vacation) or are dodged, evaded, or cloaked by a veneer of silence. Many advertisements might also be classified as lies designed for children—for example, Wheaties make you big and strong. Other kinds of untruths told to children are often regarded as innocuous or even beneficial: for example, adults sometimes tell children that their scribbled blotch of blue really does look like a grasshopper (and quite a handsome one at that), or that the ball dribbled back to the pitcher was a great hit."

In an article in the Annals of the *New York Academy of Sciences,* DePaulo raises the question, "Are we better off seeing right through a person's true underlying feelings or might we sometimes do better not to see what another person does not want us to know?" In the case of lies or deception that might do us harm, she notes, clearly lie-detection is an asset. And in professions like psychiatry or police work such sensitivity is particularly beneficial. But, says DePaulo, available evidence suggests that most people aren't very good at detection. What's more, in general, as people age they get worse and worse at picking up real feelings that are masked by feigned ones (the sex difference in reading leaks is due more to women getting worse at it as they mature than to men getting better).

"It seems," wrote DePaulo, "that what children are learning as they grow older, probably through socialization, is politely to read what other people want you to read, and not what they really felt." That is, attention is increasingly bound by social schemas. Further, those people who are most "polite" in this sense tend to be more popular and show more social understanding; they also feel better about their relationships.

What all this suggests, in DePaulo's view, "is that at least in some ways, in some situations, it may be better for us to see only what other people want us to see and not what they really feel. This is what children seem to be learning as they grow up. . . . Moreover, for people who do not obey this politeness formulation —a formulation which describes women especially well—there seem to be personal and interpersonal costs."

"The polite mode of decoding," DePaulo adds, "is probably an easier way of dealing with interpersonal information than a mere probing and skeptical style would be. . . . People who begin to doubt external appearances are first of all going to experience more uncertainty; they may also feel guilty about their suspiciousness and lack of trust; and finally, they might find out something about the other person's feelings toward them that they might be much happier not to know."

Tact—in the form of discreet inattention—is a keystone of the social alliance to honor the integrity of the frames we share. To call attention to a leaky channel is to violate the social contract that obligates us to protect one another's public face—to break a frame. In this sense the failure to exhibit attentional tact constitutes an attack. It violates the larger codes that preserve the smooth workings of the social order. Goffman observes:[32]

> When an individual projects a definition of the situation and thereby makes an implicit or explicit claim to be a person of a particular kind, he automatically exerts a moral demand upon the others, obliging them to value and treat him in the manner that persons of his kind have a right to expect. . . . The individual has informed them as to what is and as to what they *ought* to see as the "is."

The unhappiness of those who pay an inordinate amount of attention to leaks, then, may be the social cost they pay for betraying a basic social contract. That seems to account for the paradox that those who see—and say—most clearly what people actually feel can pay a price for their clarity. But such paradox is not unusual within the realm of social deception. There, DePaulo points out, "The rules and regulations and reward systems that usually govern our verbal and nonverbal worlds get turned inside out and upside down. Sources of information such as the face, which are ordinarily extremely informative, can instead be downright misleading, and the kinds of skills that we usually get rewarded for—like the ability to understand what other people are really feeling—can instead function like liabilities. The person who knows when deception is occurring and who knows what other people are really feeling has a more accurate grasp of what the interpersonal world is really like. But in some ways, under some circumstances, maybe being good at understanding social and interpersonal cues is just no good at all."

White lies are an innocent, even well-intended, form of social deceit. They are a way of protecting the frames that guide a harmonious social life. But the same dynamic can operate to hide facts that are not so innocent. What begins as a white lie, an innocent agreement to keep touchy facts out of frame, can shade over into less innocent social uses.

QUESTIONS THAT CAN'T BE ASKED

Frames create social reality by directing attention toward the business at hand and away from the irrelevant; what is out of frame does not exist, for the moment. For the most part, this selective attention is useful, but the capacity to keep information out of frame can fall prey to a collusion that buys social coziness at the expense of important truths. These collusions create lacunas, warping social reality to suppress unpleasant information.

For example, a criminal lawyer of my acquaintance tells me that undercover police officers in his county routinely lie in court, particularly in drug cases. Not that these officers perjure themselves all the time, says he, but many do some of the time, and a few do much of the time. This lawyer says he knows because he used to benefit from their lies—he was at one time an assistant district attorney.

Does the judge know? I asked. He may suspect, according to the lawyer, but the judge sees the police day in and day out; the defendant is around only over the course of the trial. It keeps things running smoothly if the judge acts as though he believes the police. Could innocent people be found guilty as a result? Perhaps.

Contrast such false police testimony with the white lies that smooth over social discomforts. The one has dire consequences, the other benign. But ugly collusions partake of the same dynamic that allows white lies to succeed: the tacit agreement among those concerned to ignore the fact that some crucial information has been neglected. The net result is a sort of collective self-deception.

Shared deceits routinely protect members of professions who are inept. For example, of 760 cases of physician misconduct or impairment reported to a New York state board, only 12 were referred through medical societies. William Farley, a Canadian anesthesiologist who now directs a program for rehabilitating addicted physicians, tells of his years as an addict himself.[33] For almost ten years Farley, in addition to being an alcoholic, was addicted to a hypnotic drug called Dalmane. If he went more than three hours without Dalmane he would go through withdrawal, shaking with tremors so strong he could barely insert an intravenous needle, frightening his patients.

The signs of his addiction were obvious. He dressed sloppily and was irritable and argumentative. His eyes were swollen and red. But, says Farley, one thing protected him: "the conspiracy of silence among my colleagues. They knew something was wrong but no one wanted to blow the whistle."

Taboos, a common social deceit, mark anxiety-provoking zones of silence. In the faculty men's locker room of a women's college near my home, for example, the professors shy away from one topic indigenous to most collegiate male locker rooms: how attractive various female students are. The prospect of a professor-student romance at that prim school is too threatening; the whole topic is taboo.

One of the strongest taboos surrounds the subject of death and dying. Often a dying person will not be told directly that he is expected to die, although signs and clues—eyes averted when reassurance is given, for example—may at least hint at the likelihood. The mutual pretense that all involved should act as though nothing is happening is described by Tolstoy:[34]

> What tormented Ivan Illych was the deception, the lie, which for some reason they all accepted, that he was not dying but was simply ill, and that he only need keep quiet and undergo a treatment and then something very good would result. He however knew that do what they would nothing would come of it, only still more agonizing suffering and death. This deception tortured him—their not wishing to admit what they all knew and what he knew, but wanting to lie to him concerning his terrible condition, and wishing and forcing him to participate in that lie.

The collusion to ignore painful information can easily be used to maintain a political fiction. How various nations prefer to recall the troubled years of the Second World War offers ample instances. Canada, for example, was rocked by a book revealing that from 1933 to 1945 its official, implicitly anti-Semitic policy permitted this underpopulated nation to admit only a trickle of Jews (the same has been said of the U.S.). Likewise, the film *The Boat Is Full* made the same charge about Switzerland; the title comes from the expression the Swiss used as a euphemism to refuse admission to

Jewish refugees fleeing Germany. In both countries the shock came because there had been a tacit denial of these facts of the past.

Such guilty secrets are often covered up in history textbooks as official policy. In Japan there was a furor when the Education Ministry decreed that the passages in history texts regarding the Japanese occupation of Asian countries should be less "negative" in future editions.[35] A mention of the 53,000 Korean casualties inflicted by Japanese soldiers when that country was a colony was amended with the note that the Governor General of Korea estimated that there were only 2,000 casualties—but the text neglects to mention the Governor was a Japanese official. The 20,000 people killed in Japanese-occupied Singapore was changed to "more than 6,000;" the statement that 300,000 people were killed in Nanking in 1937 was changed to say that the Chinese *claimed* that so many had died. All these alterations, the Ministry said, were because of the schools' "social mission" to make Japanese youth proud of their history.

In the same vein, American textbooks rarely portray the occupation of Indian lands by "pioneers" as having even the least tinge of injustice. American invasions of Canada, Russia, and Mexico are glossed over, while in the textbooks of those countries those invasions are major events. Similarly, textbooks in France skew their version of world events to fit an official outlook:[36]

> [One] page in *The World Today* . . . was about the wealth and health and culture of France's old African colonies. Another was about wanton power in North America, and another was about misery in South America. . . . The teacher . . . saw nothing odd in the fact that Francophone Africa resembled a set of Chamber of Commerce postcards, whereas New York City looked as if it had been photographed by a police photographer on a slum homicide case.

The collective mind is as vulnerable to self-deceit as the individual mind. The particular zones of shadow for a given collective are the product of a simple calculus of the schemas shared by its members: The areas of experience blanked out in the most individual minds will be the darkest zones for the group as a whole.

Cultures and nations offer the best examples of this principle writ large. The cynical characterization of mass education as the "transmission of social delusion" is accurate to the degree that what is taught is skewed by lacunas. An index of a culture's uniqueness, I suggest, is its blind spots, the particular elements of reality the cultural "we" represses to ease anxieties.

These blind spots are out of the line of sight of people in the culture, but stand out as quirks to those from cultures that do not share them. I remember, for example, hearing about a study done by John Ogbu, a Nigerian anthropologist, of several cultures, in each of which there seemed to operate a caste system. In some countries the castes were racially distinct, in others they were not. In all of them, the lower caste did the "dirty work"—sweeping, collecting garbage, butchering, and the like. In each country the lower castes did poorly in school.

The scholastic deficit, in Ogbu's view, was the outcome of a subtle difference in how these children were treated in school: in their own cultures, no one expected them to have any but the most menial jobs, and so they were treated as inferiors from the start.

In supporting his hypothesis, Ogbu included observations of a school district in a small California city. His data showed that this bias was at work there, as in other parts of the world, with teachers subtly holding minority children to a lower set of expectations. The hypothesis was intriguing, his data compelling. But the real revelation for me was the discovery that the American school district he studied was the one where I had attended school as a child—Stockton, California.[37]

I was thunderstruck. His data and arguments all rang true to me—*but only in retrospect.* While I was in school, and for all these years thereafter, it never occurred to me that this subtle discrimination was going on.

That is just the point: we do not readily see or remember negative social facts. How are such social blind spots fomented? Consider Ingeborg Day, who was four when the end of the Second World War ended also her father's career in the Austrian SS. While growing up, she learned next to nothing about the dreadful facts of the war:[38]

> . . . in Austria . . . the national consciousness simply shed the whole period between the Anschluss and the arrival of the Red Army. . . . Veterans might discuss memories of the Eastern Front among themselves, but in the family circle references to the Nazi period usually shrank to the level of a glance exchanged between parents over some radio news item, a suggestion that children should mind their own business which seldom needed repeating. Ingeborg's school books had a little sticker on the title page which children were not supposed to pick at. Underneath was a little printed cross with crooked legs. To questions, the teacher replied: "They were the stamps of another government, we now have a new government, we will

now learn the names of the rivers and streams of East Styria."

When Ingeborg went to America as an exchange student at sixteen, she was shocked to learn what the Third Reich had done, and how the rest of the world thought of people like her father, who had been Nazis. On her return to Austria, she confronted her father:

> "What was the war about?"
> "I don't want to talk about it."
> "Did you gas any Jews?"
> "If you care to leave my house, forever, right now, you need only repeat what you just said."

In a similar vein, Bini Reichel, born in 1946 in Germany, describes how, in the postwar years, "amnesia became a contagious national disease, affecting even postwar children. In this new world . . . there was no room for curious children and adolescents. We postponed our questions and finally abandoned them altogether." In her history books, the Nazi years were covered in ten to fifteen pages of careful condemnation.

Reichel, too, recalls how that amnesia was inculcated in her at school:[39]

> I suddenly remember how I had perceived that chapter of Germany's past as a teenager. Our curiosity was so manipulated that we weren't even aware that we never asked questions. My history teacher in high school was Fraulein Schubert, a 65-year-old institution in gray, whose obsessive interest in Johann Gutenberg and other icons of centuries long ago prevented her from ever mentioning the name of Adolf Hitler.

In an attempt to break through this group amnesia, Reichel recently sought out and questioned some of the generation who had fought in the war. One question she asked of a former Nazi was why he had never discussed those years with his own children. His reply: "It was beyond discussion. Besides, they didn't ask."

Questions that can't—or won't—be asked are a sure sign of a lacuna. The creation of blind spots is a key tool of repressive regimes, allowing them to obliterate information that threatens their official line. In doing so they define one frame for events as valid, any others as subversive—and still other events are beyond the permissible bounds for attention. Take the case of Argentina. While the military junta was in control, the unaskable question was, What happened to the seven thousand or so political dissenters who mysteriously disappeared? Once a democratic regime took over from the junta, that same question was the first to be asked. The answer, of course, pointed a finger of guilt straight at the junta itself.

The Soviet Union is continually in the throes of struggles over such forbidden lines of inquiry. During the Stalin years, for example, history was rewritten to hide his outrages. When Khrushchev took power he empowered a commission to investigate Stalin's crimes. What that commission found, though, was too disturbing to reveal openly. Khrushchev admitted it in part in a secret speech in 1956, again in watered-down form at a later party congress, and then locked the report away in party archives.

According to Harrison Salisbury, "Khrushchev himself said that the revelations were so shattering that they could not be published, for fear of a repetition of 1937–38, when it was said that half of Russia was accusing the other half of treason."[40] When Khrushchev left office, the investigation stopped.

Some twenty-eight years later a Russian historian, Anton Antonov-Ovseyenko, managed to get access to some of those archives, or to cover much of the same ground through his own efforts. Among the facts he unearthed were the innocence of the victims of Stalin's purge trials of the 1930s, Stalin's complicity in the deaths of his political opponents, including Lenin's widow and Stalin's own wife, and that the total number of Russian deaths through purges and executions under Stalin's reign may have been more than fifty million. Stalin, in short, committed genocide against his own people.

Antonov-Ovseyenko's retrieval of this part of the Russian past is needed, in his words, "because over the course of a generation substantial, often irreversible, shifts take place in the collective memory. Important facts, events, names, entire historical strata disappear. The new generation enters life with a built-in amnesia, artifically induced and maintained." The book, published in America in 1982, was not published in the Soviet Union.

The need to revise history to fit the official version leaves the Russian past full of holes. David Shipler, an American foreign correspondent there in the early 1970s, observes:[41]

> The synthetic history of the Soviet Union, as offered today, is distinguished mostly by what it omits, rather than what it fabricates. The tactic is now often silence: silence about the early debates and dissent within the then-fledgling Communist Party, silence about the hardships and cruelties of forced collectivization; silence about the purges and executions of party leaders and the best Red Army officers before the war; . . . silence about the . . . 1939 nonaggres-

> sion pact with Nazi Germany . . . ; silence on the Soviet Union's unpreparedness for the German attack; silence on the $15 billion in American and British food and military equipment transported at great risk by convoy to Murmansk . . .

In 1974, the poet Yevgeny Yevtushenko told of his dismay when, around a campfire in Siberia, an eighteen-year-old girl proposed a toast to Stalin. Hadn't she heard how many people were arrested and murdered during his rule? Maybe twenty or thirty, she replied. Says Yevtushenko:[42]

> And then I suddenly understood as never before that the younger generation really does not have any sources nowadays for learning the tragic truth about that time, because they cannot read about it in books or in textbooks. Even when articles are published about heroes of our Revolution who died in the time of the Stalinist repressions, the papers fall silent about the cause of their deaths . . . The truth is replaced by silence, and the silence is a lie.

THE FLOW OF INFORMATION IN A FREE SOCIETY

Ideas lead to acts. To the degree that a society limits the range of attention through authoritarian frames, it restricts the choices available to its members. Lacunas can bury "dangerous" ideas. That insight was the idea behind Newspeak, the language in Orwell's *1984* which spawned terms like "doublethink" and "unperson" and gave rise to slogans like "Ignorance Is Strength." Newspeak embodied the attempt to shrink the schemas available to citizens and so control their range of action.

In his Appendix on "The Principles of Newspeak," Orwell makes the principle explicit:[43]

> A person growing up with Newspeak as his sole language would no more know that *equal* had once had the secondary meaning of "politically equal," or that *free* had once meant "intellectually free," than, for instance, a person who had never heard of chess would be aware of the secondary meanings attached to *queen* and *rook*. There would be many crimes and errors which it would be beyond his power to commit, simply because they were nameless and therefore unimaginable.

As time went on and the vocabulary of Newspeak became progressively sparse and its meanings more rigid, people's choices for action would be ever narrower—or so Orwell proposed.

There is a parallel principle at work in attempts to regulate the political and social world through controlling the flow of information in a society. A society handles information in ways that often parallel the workings of the mind. The mark of democracy is that information flows freely; it is appropriate that the constitutional amendment guaranteeing free speech was the first.

A totalitarian state, like the totalitarian self, finds its official version of reality too fragile to withstand an unbridled flow of ideas. For a totalitarian authority to assert control, it must choke off alternative views and facts. Censorship—an essential tool of political control—is the social equivalent of a defense mechanism.

The authoritarian regime, though, represents the extreme of a continuum interconnecting all societies, including the most democratic. The vested interests and vying constituencies that make a democracy healthy also represent biased viewpoints, each with its own blind spots.

Such biases are inevitable: the social self is prone to them for the same reasons the individual one is. The nature of schemas is to guide attention toward what is salient and away from what is not. By establishing a notion of what *is* salient, and how to construe it, the schema is biased from the start.

Contrast the structure of publishing in America with that in authoritarian states. In the latter, state-operated publishing houses, with a very few key decision-makers, control all publishing. In America, books are published by about a thousand independent firms. Although about two hundred firms do 85 percent of the business, there is nothing here like the singleminded vision produced by a state monopoly.*

Even so, there is a noticeable tension within American government between the principle of free information flow and the practices of politicians. A case in point is the Reagan administration's obsession at one point with what one expert on constitutional law calls "the risks of information":[44]

> . . . fearful of both its unpredictability and its potential for leading the public to the "wrong" conclusions . . . its actions are rooted in a view . . . that not only focuses on security but also equates security with secrecy, and treats information as if it were a potentially disabling contagious disease that must be controlled, quarantined and ultimately cured.

In the service of this view, the Reagan administration proposed a remarkable device: a contract to be signed by all officials with access to classified information that would require them to submit their writings to government review for the rest of their lives. The device is remarkable on two counts. For one, as noted in a warning by the American Society of Newspaper Editors, it is "peacetime censorship of a scope unparalleled in this country since the adop-

* Still, some biases in publishing and the press may be less than innocent. See, for example, Herbert Gans, *Deciding What's News* (New York: Pantheon, 1978) and Ben Bagdikian, *The Media Monopoly* (Boston: Beacon Press, 1981).

tion of the Bill of Rights in 1791." For another, it represents the political equivalent of a neurotic repression.

Such a contract would allow the government in power to censor views and opinions out of line with its own. "The effect of the directive is this," notes Floyd Abrams, an expert on constitutional law. "Those people most knowledgeable about subjects of overriding national concern will be least able to comment without the approval of those they wish to criticize."

This way of attempting to muzzle critics—particularly well-informed critics—is rather clumsy compared to those methods already at work by virtue of the unspoken, built-in biases inherent in any collective sensibility, from the smallest group to an entire culture or nation.

For example, in Soviet political life (it is easier to use a case at a distance) a certain class of political dissenters is categorized as suffering from "sluggish schizophrenia" and sent away to psychiatric hospitals. The signs that seem to lead to this diagnosis boil down to the fact that the person is dissenting and is therefore deviant.

When Soviet officials and KGB officers confront a political dissident, one theory holds, they are "struck by a sense of strangeness, a sense that is compounded when the dissidents start lecturing them about their rights under the Soviet constitution." Normal people just don't act that way. The suspicion is that they may be mentally unbalanced; a psychiatrist is called in.

Walter Reich, a psychiatrist who has studied the Soviet system, argues that:[45]

> The Soviet psychiatrists who are called upon to render their diagnostic judgments are themselves Soviet citizens. They grow up in the same culture, are affected by the same political realities and develop the same social perceptions.
>
> And since the way a psychiatrist goes about determining whether a person is ill depends to a great extent on the psychiatrist's assumptions about what is usual and expected in his society, he may, upon coming into contact with the dissident, have the same sense of strangeness felt by the KGB agent—and may go on to suspect that the defendant may be ill.

In short, the Soviet psychiatrist shares the collective schemas that equate dissidence with deviance. Encountering a dissident is startling, even jarring. The feelings evoked are similar to what one feels in encounters with psychotics of all stripes. It is a short step for a doctor to apply a handy psychiatric label. This explanation of how Soviet psychiatry comes to be used to handle dissent is charitable, to say the least: it removes the onus of complicity in political repression from the psychiatrists if they really believe (as well they may) the dissidents are ill.*

This view from afar of a blind spot in the Soviet system suggests something about societies in general. Points of view or versions of reality that don't fit into the consensual view can be dismissed as eccentricity or aberration. In the politics of experience, the ease with which a society can dismiss deviant views—in fact, bury them—suggests that the mechanism for doing so is the aggregate weight of its citizens' shared lacunas. We do not see what we prefer not to, and do not see that we do not see.

* Indeed, the view that psychiatry is a tool to suppress social deviancy has been taken toward Western psychiatry, too, by antipsychiatrists such as Thomas Szasz. In some sense, of course, all psychotics are dissidents from the prevailing social order, to the degree that they deviate in thought and deed from commonly shared schemas.

Conclusion

AN ANCIENT MALADY AND ITS CURE

The dynamic of information flow within and among us points to a particularly human malady: to avoid anxiety, we close off crucial portions of awareness, creating blind spots. That diagnosis applies both to self-deceptions and shared illusions. The malady is by no means new: Buddhaghosa, a monk who wrote a fifth-century Indian text on psychology, describes precisely the same twist of mind as *moha,* "delusion."[1]

Buddhagosa defines "delusion" as "the cloudiness of mind that leads to misperception of the object of awareness," a characterization quite in keeping with the data of modern cognitive psychology. Delusion, in his view, conceals the true essence of things. An "unwise attention," delusion leads to false views, to misinterpreting what one encounters. It is, he said, the root of all "unwholesome" states of mind.

What is fascinating about Buddhaghosa's assessment of the human predicatment is not only its compatibility with the modern view, but its prescription for an antidote. The cure for delusion, says Buddhagosa, is *panna,* or insight—seeing things just as they are.* In terms of our model of the mind, that means a comprehension that is undistorted by the defensive urge to avoid anxiety.

The forms of insight are many; the particulars of that prescription depend on the variety of delusion it aims to cure. Freud, for example, was explicit in commending insight as the cure to neurotic twists of mind. The specific cognitive strategy he recommended makes perfect sense in terms of the model of mind outlined here. The cure of an attention gone askew, said he, begins with an unclouded awareness. In a 1912 lecture to physicians in-

* The Greek philosophers, of course, had much the same sense of the nature and function of insight. Plato defined the philosopher's task as *melete thanatou*—mindfulness of death—a task that requires an unflinching awareness of life.

terested in applying psychoanalysis, he proposed that an analyst should open his own unconscious to the patient's, free of any selection and distortion:[2]

> The technique . . . consists simply in not directing one's notice to anything in particular and in maintaining the same "evenly-suspended attention" . . . in the face of all that one hears. In this way . . . we avoid a danger which is inseparable from the exercise of deliberate attention. For as soon as anyone deliberately concentrates his attention to a certain degree, he begins to select from the material before him; one point will be fixed in his mind with particular clearness and some other will be correspondingly disregarded, and in making this selection he will be following his expectations or inclinations. This, however, is precisely what must not be done. In making the selection, if he follows his expectations he is in danger of never finding anything but what he already knows; and if he follows his inclinations, he will certainly falsify what he may perceive.

In other words, to comprehend the patient's schemas, the therapist must put aside his own for the time being. The attitude Freud commends is, in effect, the purest form of listening. The therapist, in bracketing his own schemas, becomes receptive to the most accurate rendition of the patient's. In the ideal, this means the therapist does not impose his own organization and selection as he attends.*

In some sense, all therapies amount to schema repair. The "insight" therapies—psychoanalysis foremost among them—attempt to shed light on the dark corners of the mind created by defenses. Family therapies take on the same task, trying to regroove the destructive patterns embedded in a family's shared schemas. Even behavior therapies—whose theory ignores all cognition—can be seen as a retraining of self-defeating schemas.

The therapist is able to offer such service because he does not collude with the patient's need to deny anxiety-provoking information: he is willing to make the patient uncomfortable and insecure by having him confront information he has resisted, in order to achieve a healthier security—one that can assimilate such threatening information.

What the therapist does for the patient, a lone voice can do for the group—if he is willing to break the hold of the group's blind

* In actuality, this idea demands retooling the therapist's attentional stance, a task Freud did not leave any further specific suggestions for, other than recommending that an analyst should himself be analyzed.

spots. In his suggestions for countering groupthink, Irving Janis suggests that a group designate one member as a deviant—that is, as a critical evaluator of what goes on, raising objections and doubts. The devil's advocate can save the group from itself, making sure it faces uncomfortable facts and considers unpopular views, any of which could be crucial for a sound decision.

This willingness to rock the boat is the essential quality of all those who would remedy delusion. It is the stance of the investigative reporter, the ombudsman, the grand jury, and the therapist alike. To accomplish their task, they each must bring into the open those facts that have been hidden in the service of keeping things comfortable. All must have the same impartiality; lacking it they are in danger of replacing one bias with another.

That same insight has come from other quarters. The sociologist Georg Simmel, for example, observed the importance of the stranger, or outsider, to the group. The stranger's position, said Simmel, is defined by the fact that he has not belonged to the group from the start, and that he brings a point of view to it that is foreign. He is both inside and outside. Therein lies his particular value: his strangeness brings with it a special objectivity about the group itself.

The stranger as characterized by Simmel describes not only a social role, but also a psychological stance. The stranger, in the psychological sense, is not committed to the unique vision the group shares—he knows its core schemas, but is not invested in them. Thus, while he may understand the gloss on reality that the shared lens imparts, he is not bound by it.

His objectivity is not simple detachment, but a combination of indifference and involvement, intimacy and distance. In his objectivity the stranger has a certain freedom: he has no obligations to the group that might skew his perception or prejudice his understanding. The stranger, as Simmel puts it, "is freer, practically and theoretically; he surveys conditions with less prejudice; his criteria for them are more general and more objective ideals; he is not tied down in his action by habit, piety, and precedent."

While he may have blind spots, they are not likely to be those of the group, and so he can see what the group vision misses. In that state of affairs lies both his great value and his threat. As Janis has observed, these attitudes allow a group member to broach views that can save the group from its illusions. The value of that stance was recognized, for example, in the old practice of Italian cities of seeking judges from other places, since no native was free of local entanglements.

The impulse to obscure dark facts, we have seen, comes from

the need to preserve the integrity of the self, whether individual or shared. A group may implicitly demand of its members that they sacrifice the truth to preserve an illusion. Thus the stranger stands as a potential threat to the members of a group, even though he may threaten them only with the truth. For if that truth is of the sort that undermines shared illusions, then to speak it is to betray the group.

Still, the truth-teller may fill the quintessential modern need. We live in an age when information has taken on an import unparalleled in history; sound information has become the most prized of commodities. In the realm of information, truth is the best of goods. Illusions, on the other hand, are a tarnished coin of sorts.

There is something curative in insight. At its best, the scientific community functions as a powerful system of this sort in its business of gathering information, with self-correcting mechanisms built in to guard against bias. David Hamburg, when he was president of the American Association for the Advancement of Science, proposed the scientific community as a model for dealing with what is inarguably the greatest world threat, the nuclear arms buildup:[3]

> The scientific community is the closest approximation our species has so far constructed of a single, interdependent, mutually respectful worldwide family. It does not solve problems by blaming others but rather by undertaking objective analysis. . . . The spirit of science must be brought to bear on [the] crucial problem of nuclear conflict.*

That, of course, is more easily said than done.

* However, we should not idealize the objectivity of scientists. They too are sometimes susceptible to the social forces that warp perception.

THE VIRTUES OF SELF-DECEPTION

My thesis has been that we are piloted in part by an ingenious capacity to deceive ourselves, whereby we sink into obliviousness rather than face threatening facts. This tendency toward self-deception and mutual pretense pervades the structure of our psychological and social life. Its very pervasiveness suggests that self-deception may have proven its utility in evolution. A modicum of delusion may, somehow, benefit the species in the long run, although its costs for the individual can be great.

Consciousness, we have seen, runs along parallel, interlinked tracks, most of them outside awareness; awareness is the last stop —and not always an essential one—in the flow of information through the mind. Crucial decisions as to what should and should not enter awareness are made in the unconscious mind. Thus that essentially human ability, self-awareness, brings with it the capacity for self-deception.

It is a simple step for the unconscious mind to act as a trickster, submitting to awareness a biased array of facts intended to persuade the aware part of mind to go along with a given course of action. The unconscious, in other words, can manipulate the conscious mind like a puppeteer his marionettes. Why should the mind be so arranged?

Some sociobiologists hypothesize that self-deception has played a large—and largely positive—role in human evolution. For example, in one argument, the male who is the most successful genetically—that is, who has the most progeny and so contributes more to the gene pool—is the one who impregnates the most women. The best strategy for doing so is to convince each one that he will be loyal to her, helping raise the children of their union. That is a lie, since his intent is to love her and leave her. But he will be most likely to succeed, the argument goes, if he is earnest in his assurances of loyalty. His best chance for that is to believe his own lies—that is, to first deceive himself.

There are many variants of this argument for the evolutionary virtues of self-deception. In another, two hypothetical prehistoric hunters and gatherers are out in barren terrain, searching for berries or some small animal. One convinces the other that he would fare better on a distant hill, when in fact the best chances are where they stand. This lie, although unethical, has great genetic value, since if two people are searching for food in a place where there is barely enough for one of them alone, either one might raise his own chance for survival by persuading the other to search elsewhere.

Grant, for the moment, the usefulness of such lies, and the further usefulness of believing them oneself becomes evident. As one sociobiologist puts it, "it is not difficult to be biologically selfish and still appear to be sincere if one is sufficiently ignorant of one's own motives." In other words, to lie well one must first believe one's own lies—a maxim whose truth should not be lost on any modern salesman or politician.

That is not to say that self-deception in evolution need always have been in the service of putting others at a disadvantage; it can strengthen social bonds as well as manipulate them. Indeed, in a study of parent-infant interactions, Kenneth Kaye, a developmental psychologist, concludes that "a baby is more organism than person, has neither a mind nor a self until late in the first year, but . . . adults are tricked into treating babies as communicating partners."

The mother who talks to her baby as though he understood her may be fooling herself. But by interacting with him that way—meeting his eyes, gesturing, speaking with expression and giving special intonation to her words—the mother gives him the experiences he needs to gradually learn to understand all those things. If she did not act as though he understood, she might deprive him of those crucial experiences. Better for evolution to have erred on the positive side, tricking parents into being the tutors of an infant whom they treat as though he knows more than in fact he does. That way, argues Kaye, he is surer to get the lessons he needs.

Self-deception can lead to all sorts of virtuous deeds. For example, consider the heroism of one Spicer Lung on Pan Am flight 925 from Miami to Houston. According to newspaper reports, Mr. Lung broke up an attempt to hijack the plane to Cuba.

About twenty minutes after the flight departed, there was a disturbance on board. A man claiming to have a gun demanded that the plane head for Cuba. Mr. Lung, one of 121 passengers on board, sprang into action.

"You're taking this plane over my dead body," he told the hijacker. With the help of his fifteen-year-old son, Mr. Lung subdued the man. The hijacker, it turned out, had no gun.

"I don't consider myself a hero and I don't want to be called a hero," Mr. Lung said later. "I'm just an ordinary person."

Mr. Lung, a Nicaraguan living in the United States, added, "I didn't want to go to Cuba. I just had to do something to stop him. I wasn't sure whether he was armed, but I'm not scared of a weapon."

In moments of heroism such as this, where a rational weighing of odds would argue against doing anything, bravery may well depend on the variety of self-deception summed up in the words "I'm not scared of a weapon." A mundane form of the same positive self-deception is seen in the tennis player who assumes a more confident manner after winning a point against a better opponent, or the salesman who gives himself a pep talk before making a tough sales call, when a rational weighing of odds would be discouraging.

Throughout human evolution, such self-deception may have fostered acts of bravery and courage, bonding and sharing, or competitive striving, all of which in the long run accrued to the benefit of the species. The remnant of that capacity may still be a boon, as in those moments when our intuition "knows more than we do" and directs us toward a correct decision.

Every act of perception, we have seen, is an act of selection. In evolution, our survival as a species may have hinged in part on our ability to select shrewdly, and to deceive ourselves just as shrewdly. But the capacity of the unconscious mind to pilot the conscious can backfire. When this faculty for self-deception is mobilized to protect us from anxiety, the trouble begins: we fall prey to blind spots, remaining ignorant of zones of information we might be better off knowing, even if that knowledge brings some pain.

VITAL LIES AND SIMPLE TRUTHS

There is an almost gravitational pull toward putting out of mind unpleasant facts. And our collective ability to face painful facts is no greater than our personal one. We tune out, we turn away, we avoid. Finally we forget, and forget we have forgotten. A lacuna hides the harsh truth.

Elie Wiesel, who survived Auschwitz and Buchenwald, says "Memory is our shield, our only shield." For him, only the bringing into awareness of the painful past can innoculate against its repetition. But such memories come at us like the Ancient Mariner, detaining us to tell us tales harsher than we might otherwise choose to hear.

The tellers of such tales, though, offer an essential corrective to the easy forgetting of disturbing truths. Whistle-blowers, like Frank Serpico, whose testimony disclosed layers of corruption in the New York City police force, offer an insider's revelation of things gone wrong. Watchdogs, like Nader's Raiders, do the same from an outsider's vantage point. And insiders-becoming-outsiders, such as Dwight Eisenhower when he warned against the military-industrial complex at the end of his presidency, are suddenly willing to tell how things have gone wrong *because* they are no longer insiders.

These times have seen the emergence of a new American breed, the truth-teller as hero. The best example of the genre is the whistle-blower, usually a very ordinary person who somehow marshals the courage to tell the truth about some abuse. In doing so, he violates the shared lacunas that had both kept him silent and tied him to the group whose blind spots he lay bare. The price he pays is the martyrdom groups have always dealt their betrayers.

Bill Bush, for example, is an Alabama aerospace engineer who chose to file a lawsuit against his employer, the National Aeronautics and Space Administration. The suit charged that there was an arbitrary and secret policy to put older engineers—like himself—in unfamiliar jobs in order to demoralize them so they would retire early. A federal ruling finally vindicated his charges, but only after Bush was demoted and threatened with dismissal.

Since then, Bush has become the hub for a support network of others who are contemplating similar action. Would-be whistle-blowers phone and write him from all over. "I'm very careful what I tell people," Bush told a reporter. "They should be prepared to suffer, and know that it could be disastrous to their family and friends. I tell them plain and simple that it's very dangerous to tell the truth."

It is easier to go along with the silent agreements that keep unpleasant facts quiet and make it hard to rock the boat. But societies can be sunk by the weight of buried ugliness. The beauty of whistle-blowers and watchdogs is that they act as a counterbalance to the inertial pull of collective denial.

Even so, a note of caution. My assumption is that, to some extent, the muting of awareness to avoid anxiety has been largely helpful, even necessary, in the development of our species and of civilization. But like any natural pattern, this one operates within the dynamic balance of a larger whole. "There is always an optimal value," as Gregory Bateson told me, "beyond which anything is toxic, no matter what: oxygen, sleep, psychotherapy, philosophy. Biological variables always need equilibrium."

There may be some optimal equilibrium between denial and truth.

Should all truths be told? Probably not. For example, Theodore Lidz tells of a patient of his, a fifteen-year-old girl who idealized her mother as a model of glamour and efficiency.[4] The mother had a flourishing insurance business, which more than compensated for the father's meager earnings as an artist. The mother was able to buy the daughter the finest clothes and winter vacations in sunny places.

But then the girl noticed that "the mother's business was not what it seemed to be." Her mother's sole insurance client was a wealthy industrialist. On vacations south, it just so happened that the industrialist was staying in the same hotel. Finally, the girl realized that the "business trips" that kept her mother away from home one or two nights each week were trysts with the industrialist. While many other people in their small community were aware of the arrangement, the father was managing not to notice. When the girl's images of her parents were shattered, her reaction was a promiscuous binge; when she was brought for psychiatric help the case came to Lidz's attention.

When an adolescent's search for flaws in her parents leads to the discovery of a disillusioning reality like this, says Lidz, the result is a pyrrhic victory: "The young person in adolescence needs tangible models to follow into adulthood. The adolescent does not really want to demolish her parents; her self-esteem is linked to theirs. By destroying that ideal, the teenager does herself damage."

Such family secrets and pretenses have a pivotal role in many of Ibsen's plays. Ibsen said of these desperate fictions: "Deprive the average man of his vital lie, and you've robbed him of happiness as well." Yet clinging to vital lies can be equally tragic, as with Willie Loman in *Death of a Salesman*.

The mood of many therapists in the early seventies was one that fostered a belief that total confrontation was curative. Will Schutz, at Esalen, directed couples in his workshops to tell each other three secrets as an antidote to stale marriages. The new breed of family therapists was carried along on the credo of Virginia Satir, "There is great healing power in being straight." They sought to unveil family ghosts, skeletons in the closets, secrets, as the path to a cure. They looked with scorn at more traditional therapies, where patients revealed their dark sides only to the therapist, in confidence.

The cultural climate encouraged raw self-revelation. Americans were reacting against secrets in high places—rigged quiz shows, covert war in Southeast Asia, Watergate. Group therapists held out the promise that a cure lay in self-disclosure.

The current view is more sober. The recognition that "truth" can be yet another volley in people's psychological wars, a neurotic strategy rather than a catharsis, is more widely accepted among therapists. In family therapy, for example, there is a growing move not to challenge the family's equilibrium head-on, but to use the judo of paradox and small changes to ease people toward improvement. The answers, it is clear, lie neither in smug self-delusion nor in blatant self-exposure.

While it may well be true, as Franz Boas said, that "all that man can do for humanity is to further the truth, whether it be sweet or bitter," delivering that truth artfully is a delicate matter. When truth is likely to draw open the veils that keep out painful information, the dangers can be great.

Our discussion began with the body's pain system, a neurological model for the trade-off between pain and attention—an exchange we have traced at every other level of behavioral organization. Consider the lessons to be learned from surgery for pain.

When a patient suffers from chronic, intractable pain, when nothing else will help, the physician may recommend surgery. Sometimes it works well. Sometimes it make things worse. While neurological understanding of the pain system has increased dramatically in the last decade or two, much more remains to be learned about the vagaries of that system. The surgeon has that most dangerous of things, a little knowledge.

Thus, certain surgical attempts to stop intractable pain have not had such happy results. Surgery that entails a lesion in any part of the pain system, from the spinal cord and brainstem to the thalamus and cortex, can lead to a sorry condition known as "central pain," an ache different from any its victims have felt before. This kind of pain has uniquely unpleasant qualities: "spontaneous aching and shooting pain, numbness, cold, heaviness, burning, and other unsettling sensations that even the most articulate patients find difficult to describe."[5]

When central pain occurs, it usually develops some time after the surgery has relieved the original pain. The irony, of course, is that it results from surgery intended to *alleviate* pain. The trouble is that neural mechanisms which register and react to pain are intricate, complex, and subtly balanced. The lesson here is cautionary: tampering, even when well intentioned, can make things worse.

That lesson applies to the delicacies of painful realities in general. For example, in diplomacy such realities are often handled by an artful ambiguity. Thus the "normalization" of American and Chinese ties begun by Richard Nixon rested on the haziness of American links with Nationalist China. As an editorial later noted,[6] "Both sides have understood that the pressure of real issues and events would ultimately force them to shed successive veils of ambiguity. Their hope was that by the time each test came, visible advantages of continued relations would offset the pain of unpleasant truths."

The balance between shedding veils and shielding painful truths is a subtle one. Thus, when Janis proposes that a devil's advocate can offset groupthink, he hastens to caution against the threat to group cohesiveness that such advocacy can represent. The dissenter can destroy the consensus that allows the group to function.

It gets trickier still. Since Janis wrote his book in 1971, the idea of designating a devil's advocate has spread, to the point that it is sometimes a hollow ritual:[7]

> For example, President Johnson and other leading members of his Tuesday Lunch Group claimed that they had devil's advocates in their midst each time they decided to intensify the war against North Vietnam. But those devils were not very devilish . . . [They] quickly became domesticated and were allowed by the President to speak their

piece only as long as they remained within the bounds of what he and other leading members of the group considered acceptable dissent.

"Acceptable dissent," of course, is not really dissent at all. It is guided by shared schemas, and challenges no shared illusions.

There is still another complication, this one observed by Gregory Bateson. During a conversation with me, Bateson recounted something that Robert Oppenheimer had told him in 1947:

> The world is moving in the direction of hell, at a high velocity and with perhaps a positive acceleration and a positive rate of change of acceleration; and the only condition under which it might not reach its destination is that we and the Russians be willing to let it go there.

"Every move we make in fear of the next war," Bateson elaborated, "in fact hastens it. We arm up to control the Russians, they do the same. Anxiety, in fact, brings about the thing it fears, creates its own disaster."

Then should we simply stand back and do nothing? "Well, be bloody careful about the politics you play to control it. You don't know the total pattern; for all you know, you could create the next horror by trying to fix up a present one."

What, then, are we to do?

We must act, despite Bateson's caution. To let ourselves be guided by a sensibility riven with blind spots, one twisted by the anxious need to avoid truths, is to increase the rate of our acceleration toward disaster. Truths must be told if we are to find our way out. Indeed, the clear and strong voices of the lucid among us may be our last and best hope. We cannot let caution paralyze action, stay us from trying to see and say things just as they are. We need counsel that flows from insight; insight is curative.

There is, to be sure, a fundamental difference between those blind spots that spring from benign self-protection and those that spring from ugly collusions. When the truth threatens to bring down a conspiracy of silence that protects moral ugliness, the choice is straightforward: speak the truth or join the conspiracy.

But some blind spots, as we have seen, help us survive in the face of painful truths; they are an essential part of the human condition. When the blind spots in questions may be benign in effect —even positive—the course of action is not so clearly marked. Then again, the human predicament is typically so complex that it is not altogether clear which lies are vital and what truths beg for discovery. In *Death of a Salesman*, as Willie Loman drifts toward catastrophe, deluded by lies he cannot sort out, the anguished cry is: "Attention must be paid!"

But how? and to what? Given the delicate balances at risk, how are we to proceed?

Consider Allen Wheelis's 1966 parable, *The Illusionless Man.*[8] The story begins:

> Once upon a time there was a man who had no illusions about anything. While still in the crib he had learned that his mother was not always kind; at two he had given up fairies; witches and hobgoblins disappeared from his world at three; at four he knew that rabbits lay no eggs; and at five, on a cold night in December, with a bitter little smile, he said good-by to Santa Claus. At six when he started school illusions flew from his life like feathers in a windstorm: he discovered that his father was not always brave or even honest, that presidents are little men, that the Queen of England goes to the bathroom like everybody else, and that his first grade teacher, a pretty round-faced young woman with dimples, did not know everything, as he had thought, but thought only of men and did not know much of anything. . . . As a young man he realized that the most generous act is self-serving, the most disinterested inquiry serves interest, that lies are told by printed words. Of all those people who lose illusions he lost more than anyone else, taboo and prescription alike; and as everything became permitted nothing was left worthwhile.

Wheelis's hero marries a woman who is full of illusion. As they are to be wed, he tells her:

> God won't be there, honey; the women will be weeping for their own lost youth and innocence, the men wanting to have you in bed; and the priest standing slightly above us will be looking down your cleavage as his mouth goes dry . . .

By the tale's end, Henry—the illusionless man—and his wife, Lorabelle, are elderly. By then Henry has seen that illusion lends both comfort and meaning to life.

> . . . he could see himself striving toward a condition of beauty or truth or goodness or love that did not exist, but whereas earlier in his life he had always said, "It's an illusion," and turned away, now he said "There isn't anything else," and stayed with it. . . . And when it came time to die Lorabelle said, "Now we'll never be parted," and Henry smiled and kissed her and said to himself, "There isn't anything else," and they died.

Then again, there is the point made by this (no doubt apocryphal) story told about the Dalai Lama:

In Lhasa, it was the custom for monks to gather to discuss theological issues on the steps of the main monastery. One by one they would take a turn at answering a religious riddle. The questions, though, were set long ago, and the answers were always the same, memorized from ancient times.

To his distress, the Dalai Lama was expected to stand before the assembled monks once each year and go through the ritual of the question. His tutors would select a monk to ask him a question they had chosen, for which the answer was well rehearsed. Though the question and its answer were a charade, the assembled monks would gasp with amazement at his answer.

In his thirteenth year, as the question ritual was approaching, the Dalai Lama finally decided he had had enough. He dreaded the masquerade of spontaneity and the gasp of amazement that would predictably follow his rehearsed response—a rote reply that no one really understood.

That year's question: "How do the rivers answer a bird when it rains?"

The answer: "By turning to snow."

The Dalai Lama ardently wished for an original answer, one that would silence forever that false gasp, piercing the veil of ritual courtesy.

The more he searched for a profound response, the more sunken his eyes and wrinkled his brow became. Night after night he sat a restless vigil, day after day he struggled for just the right answer. He seemed to age from a young boy to an old man in a few weeks. Finally, he fell into a deep melancholy.

On the appointed day, he called for his regent, who was astonished at the decrepit aspect of the young lama. The Dalai Lama now looked like a gnarled, dessicated shell.

"There will be no more ritual questions," the Dalai Lama rasped. "I want a fresh question simply put. Something that won't amaze me, but will make us aware of things as they actually are on this earth. And I absolutely forbid anyone to gasp at my answer."

When the shriveled Dalai Lama appeared before his assembled monks, they all gasped silently at what they saw, but managed to stay outwardly composed. But not a single monk could think of a new question. No one had anything suitable to ask.

They sat together, silent, through the day and long into the crystal black night.

At last one of the younger monks asked, in a timid voice, "Aren't you cold, Your Holiness?"

"Yes, I am," was the reply. "Aren't we all?"

"Yes, Your Holiness, we are," the monks replied.

"Then," said the Dalai Lama, "let us go inside."

As the monks reassembled in the assembly hall, with butter lamps burning warmly, the Dalai Lama ascended his throne looking healthy and young once again.

And as he said, "That's just the kind of question and answer we should have," he was once again the boy they knew, smiling the broadest of smiles.

Somewhere between the two poles—living a life of vital lies and speaking simple truths—there lies a skillful mean, a path to sanity and survival.

NOTES

Introduction

1.
Michael Weissberg, *Dangerous Secrets* (New York: W.W. Norton, 1983).
2.
Ibid., 27.
3.
Jesse Jackson, "Playboy Interview," *Playboy,* May 1981, 70.
4.
Samuel G. Freedman, "From South Africa, A Tale Told in Black and White," *The New York Times,* February 19, 1984, H7.
5.
These examples are from Robert Jervis, *Perception and Misperception in International Politics* (Princeton, New Jersey: Princeton University Press, 1976).
6.
Lois Cunniff, "Soviet Photojournalism," *Columbia Journalism Review,* May/June 1983, 45.
7.
John Updike, "Reflections: Kafka's Short Stories," *The New Yorker,* May 9, 1983, 121.
8.
That conversation was reported, in part, in "Breaking Out of the Double Bind," *Psychology Today,* August 1978.

Part One

1.
David Livingstone, *Missionary Travels,* 1857, as quoted in Dennis D. Kelly, "Somatic Sensory System IV: Central Representations of Pain and Analgesia," in Eric Kandel and James Schwartz, eds., *Principles of Neural Science* (New York: Elsevier North Holland, 1981), 211.
2. Dennis D. Kelly, in Kandel and Schwartz, op. cit. The description of the pain system in this chapter is largely based on his account.

3.
Hans Selye, *The Stress of Life* (New York: McGraw-Hill, 1956).
4.
Samuel C. Risch et al., "Co-release of ACTH and Beta-Endorphin Immunoreactivity in Human Subjects in Response to Central Cholinergic Stimulation," *Science* 222 (October 7, 1983), 77.
5.
Brendan Maher, "The Language of Schizophrenia: A Review and Interpretation," *British Journal of Psychiatry* 120 (1970), 3–17.
6.
Buchsbaum's data and arguments are in a series of papers: Glenn C. Davis, Monte Buchsbaum et al., "Analgesia to Pain Stimuli in Schizophrenics and Its Reversal by Naltrexone," *Psychiatry Research*, 1 (1979), 61–69; Glenn C. Davis, Monte Buchsbaum and William E. Bunney, Jr., "Alterations of Evoked Potentials Link Research in Attention Dysfunction to Peptide Response Symptoms of Schizophrenia," in *Neural Peptides and Neuronal Communications*, E. Costa and M. Trabucci, eds., (New York: Raven Press, 1980). Monte S. Buchsbaum et al., "Evoked Potential Measures of Attention and Psychopathology," *Advances in Biological Psychiatry* 6 (1981), 186–194. Monte S. Buchsbaum et al., "Role of Opioid Peptides in Disorders of Attention in Psychopathology," *Proceedings of the New York Academy of Science*, 1982, 352–365. Glenn C. Davis, Monte S. Buchsbaum et al., "Altered Pain Perception and Cerebrospinal Endorphins in Psychiatric Illness," *Proceedings of the New York Academy of Science*, 1983, 366–373.
7.
Floyd Bloom, Salk Institute, in personal communication with author.
8.
Y. Shavit et al., "Endogenous Opioids May Mediate the Effects of Stress on Tumor Growth and Immune Function," *Proceedings of the Western Pharmacology Society* 26 (1983), 53–56.
9.
The intricate relationship between attention and stress centers is described in David M. Warburton, "Physiological Aspects of Information Processing and Stress," in Vernon Hamilton and David M. Warburton, *Human Stress and Cognition: An Information Processing Approach* (New York: John Wiley and Sons, 1979).
10.
Karl H. Pribram and Dianne McGuinnes, "Brain Systems Involved in Attention-Related Processing: A Summary Review," presented at The Symposium on the Neurophysiology of Attention, Houston, July 1982.
11.
Warburton, op. cit.
12.
G. Weltman, J. E. Smith, and G. H. Egstrom, "Perceptual Narrowing During Simulated Pressure-Chamber Exposure," *Human Factors* 13 (1971), 79–107.

13.
Mardi Horowitz, "Psychological Response to Serious Life Events," in Shlomo Breznitz, ed., *The Denial of Stress* (New York: International Universities Press, 1983).
14.
The list of intrusions is paraphrased from Horowitz, ibid., 136.
15.
David Alpren, *The New York Times*, Section 10, 1, September 27, 1981.
16.
Richard Lazarus, "The Stress and Coping Paradigm," paper given at conference on The Critical Evaluation of Behavioral Paradigms for Psychiatric Science, Gleneden Beach, Oregon, November 1978.
17.
C. H. Folkins, "Temporal Factors and the Cognitive Mediators of Stress Reaction," *Journal of Personality and Social Psychology* 14 (1970), 173–184.
18.
Aaron Beck, *Cognitive Therapy and the Emotional Disorders* (New York: International Universities Press, 1976), 14.
19.
Michael Wood, "In the Museum of Strangeness," *The New York Review of Books,* March 19, 1981, 44.
20.
Robert Jay Lifton, *Death in Life* (New York: Basic Books, 1967), 10.
21.
Horowitz, op. cit., paraphrased from 134.
22.
"Positive Denial: The Case for Not Facing Reality," *Psychology Today,* November 1979, 57.

Part Two

1.
Sigmund Freud, *The Interpretation of Dreams* (New York: Basic Books, first published 1900).
2.
Ibid., 540.
3.
The best review of this saga and the issues dealt with in modeling the mind is in Matthew Hugh Erdelyi, "A New Look at the New Look: Perceptual Defense and Vigilance," *Psychological Review* 81 (1974), 1–25. Also recommended: Colin Martindale, *Cognition and Consciousness* (Homewood, Illinois: Dorsey Press, 1981).
4.
R. N. Haber, "Nature of the Effect of Set on Perception," *Psychological Review* 73 (1966), 335–351.

5.
Donald E. Broadbent, *Perception and Communication* (London: Pergomon Press, 1958).
6.
Erdelyi, op. cit., 19.
7.
Donald A. Norman, "Toward a Theory of Memory and Attention," *Psychological Review* 75 (1968), 522–536.
8.
George Miller, "The Magical Number Seven, Plus or Minus Two; Some Limits on Our Capacity for Processing Information," *Psychological Review* 63 (1956), 81–97. Also, Herbert A. Simon, "How Big Is a Chunk?" *Science* 183 (1974), 482–488
9.
Ulric Neisser, "The Limits of Cognition," in Peter Jusczyk and Raymond Klein, eds., *The Nature of Thought* (Hillsdale, New Jersey: Lawrence Erlbaum Associates, 1980).
10.
Donald A. Norman and Tim Shallice, "Attention to Action: Willed and Automatic Control of Behavior," Center for Human Information Processing, December 1980. It was Michael Posner who proposed that Neisser's expandable capacity is not on the limits of conscious awareness, but on unconscious channels, at a panel on "Psychoanalysis and Cognitive Psychology," during the annual meeting of the American Psychological Association, August 1983.
11.
Donald Norman, "Slips of the Mind and a Theory of Action," Center for Human Information Processing, University of California at San Diego, unpublished manuscript, February 22, 1979, 8.
12.
Emmanuel Donchin, personal communication with author. Donchin is head of the Laboratory for Cognitive Psychobiology at the University of Illinois, Champaign-Urbana.
13.
Roy Lachman, Janet Lachman and Earl Butterfield, *Cognitive Psychology and Information Processing* (Hillsdale, New Jersey: Lawrence Erlbaum Associates, 1979).
14.
A thorough account of schemas is given in David Rumelhart, *Schemata: The Building Blocks of Cognition,* Center for Human Information Processing, University of California at San Diego, December 1978.
15.
Jean Piaget, *The Construction of Reality in the Child* (New York: Basic Books, 1971). A more inviting introduction to Piaget's work is Dorothy G. Singer and Tracey A. Revenson, *A Piaget Primer* (New York: New American Library, 1979).

16.
Unless otherwise indicated, Ulric Neisser's comments in this chapter are from a conversation we had at Cornell in November 1982.
17.
Rumelhart, op. cit., 13.
18.
Emanuel Donchin, "Surprise! . . . Surprise!" *Psychophysiology* 18 (1981), 493–513.
19.
Susan Fiske, "Schema-Triggered Affect: Applications to Social Perception," in M. S. Clark and F. T. Fiske, eds., *Affect and Cognition* (Hillsdale, New Jersey: Lawrence Erlbaum Associates, 1982), 55–77.
20.
Rumelhart, op. cit., 14.
21.
Charles Simmons, "The Age of Maturity," *The New York Times Magazine*, December 11, 1983, 114.
22.
Peter Lang, "Cognition in Emotion; Concept and Action," in Carroll Izard, Jerome Kagan and Robert Zajonc, eds., *Emotion, Cognition, and Behavior* (Boston: Cambridge University Press, 1984).
23.
George Mandler, "Consciousness: Its Function and Construction," Center for Human Information Processing, University of California at San Diego, June 1983. Some of Mandler's ideas presented here are from his Presidential Address to the Division of General Psychology, American Psychological Association, August 1983, and other presentations there.
24.
Norman Dixon, *Preconscious Processing* (New York: John Wiley and Sons, 1981).
25.
Richard Nisbett and T. Wilson, "Telling More Than We Can Know: Verbal Reports on Mental Processes," *Psychological Review* 84 (1977), 231–259. The debate within psychology over the existence of the unconscious is reviewed in Howard Shevrin and Scott Dickman, "The Psychological Unconscious: A Necessary Assumption for All Psychological Theory?" in *American Psychologist* 35 (1980), 421–434.
26.
William Kunst-Wilson and R. B. Zajonc, "Affective Discrimination of Stimuli That Cannot be Recognized," *Science* 207 (1980), 557–558.
27.
Howard Shevrin, "Some Assumptions of Psychoanalytic Communication: Implications of Subliminal Research for Psychoanalytic Method and Technique," in Norbert Freedman and Stanley Grand, eds., *Communicative Structures and Psychic Structures* (New York: Plenum, 1977).
28.
Howard Shevrin, "The Unconscious Is Alive and Well," unpublished manuscript, December 1979.

29.
Ernest Hilgard, *Divided Consciousness* (New York: John Wiley and Sons, 1977).
30.
Ibid., 186. There is a controversy about the validity of the hidden observer. See, for example, Jean-Roch Laurence, Campbell Perry, and John Kihlstrom, " 'Hidden Observer' Phenomena in Hypnosis: An Experimental Creation?" *Journal of Personality and Social Psychology* 44 (1983), 163–169.
31.
Ellen Hale, "Inside the Divided Mind," *The New York Times Magazine*, April 17, 1983, 100.
32.
Willard Mainord, Barry Rath, and Frank Barnett, "Anesthesia and Suggestion," presented at the annual meeting of the American Psychological Association, August 1983.
33.
Henry Bennett, Hamilton Davis, and Jeffrey Giannini, "Posthypnotic Suggestions During General Anesthesia and Subsequent Dissociated Behavior," paper presented to the Society for Clinical and Experimental Hypnosis, October 1981.

Part Three

1.
Ulric Neisser, "John Dean's Memory: A Case Study," *Cognition* 9 (1981), 1–22.
2.
Hearings Before the Select Committee on Presidential Campaign Activities of the United States Senate, Ninety-third Congress, First Session, 1973, 957.
3.
Neisser, op. cit., 9.
4.
Ibid., 10.
5.
Ibid., 19.
6.
The New York Times, February 16, 1983, 23.
7.
Anthony Greenwald, "The Totalitarian Ego," *American Psychologist* 35 (1980), 603–618.
8.
Seymour Epstein, "The Self-Concept: A Review and the Proposal of an Integrated Theory of Personality," in Ervin Staub, *Personality: Basic Aspects and Current Research* (Englewood Cliffs, New Jersey: Prentice-Hall, 1980), 84.

9.
Aaron Beck, *Depression: Clinical, Experimental and Theoretical Aspects* (New York: Hoeber, 1967), 135.
10.
Aaron Beck et. al., *Cognitive Therapy of Depression* (New York: Guilford, 1979), 13–15.
11.
Epstein, op. cit., 104.
12.
Mardi Horowitz, "Psychological Response to Serious Life Events," in Shlomo Breznitz, ed., *The Denial of Stress* (New York: International Universities Press, 1983), 139.
13.
The dynamics of the self-system are most cogently presented in Harry Stack Sullivan, *The Interpersonal Theory of Psychiatry* (New York: W. W. Norton, 1953).
14.
Mark Jacobson, "How Summer Camp Saved My Life," *Rolling Stone,* July 21, 1983, 48.
15.
Sullivan, op. cit., 190.
16.
I visited with Ulric Neisser at Cornell in November 1982.
17.
Lester Luborsky, Barton Blinder, and Jean Schimek, "Looking, Recalling, and GSR as a Function of Defense," *Journal of Abnormal Psychology* 70 (1965), 270–280.
18.
The account of the Russian research is in Howard Shevrin, E. Kostandov, and Y. Arzumanov, "Averaged Cortical Evoked Potentials to Recognized and Nonrecognized Verbal Stimuli," *Acta Neurobiologiae Experimentalis* 37 (1977), 321–324. Howard Shevrin told me of the experimental details.
19.
Shevrin reported his research at the annual meeting of the American Psychological Association, August 1983.
20.
Vernon Hamilton, "Information-Processing Aspects of Denial: Some Tentative Formulations," in Shlomo Breznitz ed., *The Denial of Stress* (New York: International Universities Press, 1983).
21.
Sigmund Freud, "Repression," in J. Strachey, ed., *The Standard Edition of the Complete Psychological Works of Sigmund Freud* vol. 15 (London: Hogarth Press, 1957; originally published 1915).
22.
Matthew Erdelyi and Benjamin Goldberg, "Let's Not Sweep Repression Under the Rug: Toward a Cognitive Psychology of Repression," in John Kihlstrom and Frederick Evans, *Functional Disorders of Memory* (Hillsdale, New Jersey: Lawrence Erlbaum Associates, 1979). Erdelyi has done

seminal work in understanding Freud as a cognitive psychologist. I owe much to his thinking on the role of repression, both from the article cited here and from personal conversation.

23.
Freud, op. cit.

24.
R. D. Laing, *The Politics of the Family* (Toronto: CBC Publications, 1969), 27–28.

25.
Leslie Epstein, "Round Up the Usual Suspects," *The New York Times Book Review,* October 10, 1982, 9, 27–29.

26.
Ibid., 28.

27.
Ibid.

28.
Ibid.

29.
Erdelyi and Goldberg, op. cit.

30.
Sigmund Freud, *The Interpretation of Dreams,* J. Strachey (translator and ed.), *Standard Edition,* vols. 4 and 5) (London: Hogarth Press, 1953; originally published 1900), 600.

31.
Matthew Erdelyi and Benjamin Goldberg, op. cit. See also Morton Reiser, *Mind, Brain, Body* (New York: Basic Books, 1984).

32.
R. D. Laing, Politics of the Family (Toronto: CBC Publications, 1969), 28.

33.
Harry Stack Sullivan, *The Interpersonal Theory of Psychiatry* (New York: W. W. Norton, 1963), 321.

34.
Erdelyi, op. cit.

35.
Sullivan, op. cit., 319.

Part Four

1.
Wilhelm Reich, *Character Analysis* (New York: Farrar, Straus & Giroux, 1972).

2.
Reich, as quoted in Daniel Goleman and Kathleen Speeth, eds., *The Essential Psychotherapies* (New York: New American Library, 1982), 71.

3.
Ernest Becker, *Angel in Armor* (New York: Free Press, 1975), 83.

4.
Ibid., 85.
5.
David Shapiro, *Neurotic Styles* (New York: Basic Books, 1965). Additional clinical detail comes from Theodore Millon, *Disorders of Personality* (New York: John Wiley and Sons, 1982). This state-of-the-art summary of personality styles is a companion volume to the recently revised *Diagnostic and Statistical Manual*, the official psychiatric handbook for diagnosis.
6.
Arthur Conan Doyle, "The Adventure of the 'Gloria Scott,'" *The Original Illustrated Sherlock Holmes* (Secaucus, New Jersey: Castle Books, 1980), 236–247. The case is of special interest to Holmes buffs, since it reveals some of his history before becoming the world's first private detective.
7.
The perceptual and logical powers of Sherlock Holmes are spelled out in greater detail by Marcello Truzzi and Scot Morris in "Sherlock Holmes as a Social Scientist," *Psychology Today*, December 1971, 62–86.
8.
My description of The Detective owes much to David Shapiro's sketch of the paranoid type and Theodore Millon's depiction of the paranoid personality's suspicious pattern.
9.
Shapiro, op. cit., 61.
10.
Ibid., 57.
11.
Theodore Millon, op. cit., 381.
12.
Jerry Adler, "The Ludlum Enigma," *Newsweek*, April 19, 1982.
13.
Shapiro, op. cit., 96.
14.
The shoot-out microevent, reported in Susan Quinn, "The Competence of Babies," *Atlantic Monthly*, January 1982, 54–60, is from the reserach of Dr. Daniel Stern, a psychiatrist at Cornell University Medical Center in New York City.
15.
Selma Fraiberg reported this case at a symposium held at the University of California Medical Center, June 5–7, 1981, in San Francisco.
16.
Jenny's battle with her mother is in Daniel Stern, *The First Relationship: Infant and Mother* (Cambridge: Harvard University Press, 1977), 110–113.
17.
Stern, ibid., 114.
18.
Theodore Millon, *Disorders of Personality* (New York: John Wiley and Sons, 1981), 90.

19.
Morton Schatzman, *Soul Murder* (New York: New American Library, 1974).
20.
Schreber, quoted in Schatzman, 26.
21.
This formulation of the anger at the root of paranoia is more fully elaborated in W. W. Meisner, *The Paranoid Process* (New York: Jason Aronson, 1978).
22.
Gisela Zena, "Mistreatment of Children and Children's Rights," quoted in Alice Miller, *For Your Own Good* (New York: Farrar, Straus and Giroux, 1983), 89.
23.
Ibid.
24.
Adapted from Miller, op. cit., 106.
25.
Double-bind theory is spelled out in Gregory Bateson, Don D. Jackson, Jay Haley, and John Weakland, "Toward a Theory of Schizophrenia," *Behavioral Science* 1 (1956), 251–286.
26.
R. D. Laing, *Self and Others* (London: Tavistock Publications, 1969), 127–128.
27.
Ernest Schachtel, *Metamorphosis* (New York: Basic Books, 1959).
28.
Erving Goffman, *The Presentation of Self in Everyday Life* (New York: Doubleday & Co., 1959).
29.
Lilly Pincus and Christopher Dare, *Secrets in the Family* (New York: Pantheon, 1978).

Part Five

1.
Sigmund Freud, *Group Psychology and the Analysis of the Ego* (New York: Bantam Books, 1965), 13–16.
2.
Manfred Kets deVries and Danny Miller, *The Neurotic Organization* (San Francisco: Jossey Bass, 1984).
3.
David Reiss, *The Family's Construction of Reality* (Cambridge: Harvard University Press, 1981).

4.
Robert Merton's 1949 study typed individuals; Reiss extends the local/cosmopolitan typology to families.
5.
Reiss, op. cit., 21.
6.
Reiss, op. cit., 66.
7.
David Reiss and Marry Ellen Oliveri, "Sensory Experience and Family Process: Perceptual Styles Tend to Run in but Not Necessarily Run Families," *Family Process* 22 (1983), 289–316.
8.
Ibid., p. 226.
9.
Jill Metcoff and Carl A. Whitaker, "Family Microevents: Communication Patterns for Problem Solving," in Froma Walsh, ed., *Normal Family Processes* (New York: Guilford Press, 1982), 258–259.
10.
Eric Bermann, *Scapegoat* (Ann Arbor: University of Michigan Press, 1973).
11.
The case of Roscoe is reported in Reiss, op. cit., 231, based on Bermann's account.
12.
Hume Cronyn told this story in an interview with Timothy White, "Theater's First Couple," *The New York Times Magazine*, December 26, 1982, 22.
13.
R. D. Laing, *The Politics of the Family* (Toronto: CBC Publications, 1969), 40.
14.
Ibid., 41.
15.
Ibid.
16.
Ibid., 29
17.
Michael Weissberg, *Dangerous Secrets* (New York: W. W. Norton and Co., 1983).
18.
Sandra Butler, *Conspiracy of Silence: The Trauma of Incest* (San Francisco: New Glide Publications, 1978).
19.
The case of Margaret is described in Butler, op. cit. Though Butler interviewed hundreds of incest perpetrators and victims, the case of Margaret reads like a composite. While it may be somewhat apocryphal, it nonetheless makes the point here.

20.
Weissberg, op. cit., 26.
21.
Ibid., 108–109.
22.
Irving Janis, *Victims of Groupthink* (Boston: Houghton Mifflin, 1972; revised edition, 1983).
23.
Ibid., 3.
24.
Ibid., 205.
25.
Arthur S. Golden, "Groupthink in Japan Inc.," *The New York Times Magazine,* December 5, 1982, 137.
26.
Janis, op. cit., 13.
27.
Ibid., 37–38.
28.
My conversation with Harry Levinson was printed, in part, as "Oedipus in the Board Room," in *Psychology Today,* December 1977, 45–51.
29.
Charles C. Manz and Henry P. Sims, Jr. "The Potential for 'Groupthink' in Autonomous Work Groups," *Human Relations* 35 (1982), 773–784.
30.
Eugene M. Fodor and Terry Smith, "The Power Motive as an Influence on Group Decision Making," *Journal of Personality and Social Psychology* 42, 178–185.

Part Six

1.
Goffman's theory of frames is described in *Frame Analysis* (Cambridge: Harvard University Press, 1974.). The interpretation of frames as simultaneously activated shared schemas is my own, not Goffman's.
2.
Herb Caen, *San Francisco Chronicle,* November 29, 1967.
3.
"A Conversation with Roger Schank," *Psychology Today,* April, 1983, 32. Some cognitive psychologists—notably Ulric Neisser—are not so sanguine as Schank about scripted computers mimicking human behavior. Neisser points out that most of the information by which we navigate through a situation remains out of awareness, and is practically endless. His point is that it would be virtually impossible to program a computer with as much information as a human uses in a situation—for one thing, the human cannot even tell you completely what that information is.

4.
William James, *The Principles of Psychology* (New York: Dover, 1950; originally published 1910).
5.
Alfred Schutz, *Philosophy and Phenomenological Research,* is quoted in Goffman, op. cit., 4.
6.
Peter Berger and Thomas Luckmann, *The Social Construction of Reality* (New York: Doubleday & Co., 1966), 22.
7.
Luigi Pirandello, *Tonight We Improvise* (London: Samuel French, 1932), 7–8.
8.
John Barth, *Lost in the Fun House* (New York: Doubleday & Co., 1968), 127.
9.
Kathryn Hulme, *The Nun's Story* (London: Frederick Muller, 1957), 37–38.
10.
J. L. Mannond and Barbara Hammond, *The Town Labourer* (London: Longmans, Green, and Co., 1918), 19–21.
11.
Shoshana Zuboff, "Work and Human Interaction in Historical Perspective," Harvard University, January 1979. The insights in this section are based on Zuboff's incisive studies of the social organization of experience in the workplace.
12.
Sebastian DeGrazia, *Of Time, Work, and Leisure* (New York: The Twentieth Century Fund, 1962), 60.
13.
Reinhard Bendix, *Work and Authority in Industry* (Berkeley: University of California Press, 1974), 87.
14.
Harold Wilensky, "The Uneven Distribution of Leisure," *Social Problems* 9 (1961).
15.
Jean-Paul Sartre, *Being and Nothingness,* trans. by Hazel E. Barnes (New York: Philosophical Library, 1956), 59.
16.
Wallace Shawn and André Gregory, *My Dinner With André,* (New York: Grove Press, 1981), 66.
17.
Ibid., 80–81.
18.
I owe my knowledge of the American rule—that eyes be averted at about eight paces—to Goffman, in a graduate seminar he taught at Berkeley in 1967. I no longer recall whose study he was citing. The difference between American and Middle Eastern gaze rules has a better-known parallel in

the distance at which people feel comfortable standing from each other while talking. In Arab countries the preferred distance is close enough to see the iris dilate; in America it is arm's length. Thus, as Calvin Hall reports in *The Silent Language* (New York: Doubleday, 1959), over the course of talking while standing, an Arab will edge closer and closer to an American, who will in turn back up. The result is that—given a free range—the Arab will back the American against a wall.

19.
Erving Goffman, *The Presentation of Self in Everyday Life* (New York: Doubleday & Co., 1959), 230.

20.
Ibid., 231–232.

21.
Ibid., 52–53.

22.
Margot Slade, "Reacting to Boorish Manners," *The New York Times*, May 23, 1983, B12.

23.
Mihaly Csikzentmihalyi, "Attention and the Holistic Approach to Behavior," in Kenneth S. Pope and Jerome L. Singer, eds., *The Stream of Consciousness* (New York: Plenum, 1978).

24.
Charlotte Selver, "Sensory Awareness and Total Functioning," *General Semantics Bulletin* 20 and 21 (1957), 10.

25.
Paul Theroux, *The Kingdom by the Sea* (Boston: Houghton Mifflin, 1983) 12–16.

26.
The New York Times, September 17, 1983.

27.
J. M. Darley and D. Batson, ". . . From Jerusalem to Jericho," *Journal of Personality and Social Psychology* 27 (1973), 100–108.

28.
Much of this research has been done by two Rosenthal protégés in particular, Miron Zuckerman and Bella DePaulo. The full reports of the research reported in this section can be found in: Bella M. DePaulo, Miron Zuckerman, and Robert Rosenthal, "Humans as Lie Detectors," *Journal of Communications*, Spring 1980; Miron Zuckerman, Bella M. DePaulo, and Robert Rosenthal, "Verbal and Nonverbal Communication of Deception," *Advances in Experimental Social Psychology* vol. 14 (Academic Press); and Robert Rosenthal and Bella DePaulo, "Sex Differences in Eavesdropping on Nonverbal Cues," *Journal of Personality and Social Psychology* 37 (1979), 2, 273–285.

29.
Rosenthal and DePaulo, op. cit., 280.

30.
Personal communication with author, Harvard University, 1981. See also Judith A. Hall, *Nonverbal Sex Differences* (Baltimore: Johns Hopkins University Press, 1984).
31.
Bella DePaulo, "Success at Detecting Deception: Liability or Skill?" *Annals of the New York Academy of Sciences* 364 (June 12, 1981).
32.
Goffman, op. cit.
33.
In Lawrence Altman, "The Private Agony of an Addicted Physician," *The New York Times*, June 7, 1983, C8. Also "Medical Groups Rebut Charges Against Doctors," *The New York Times*, February 25, 1983.
34.
Leo Tolstoy, "The Death of Ivan Illych," *Collected Works* (New York: New American Library, 1960), 137. The frames that keep the facts of death from intruding into social awareness are detailed in David Sudnow, *The Social Organization of Dying* (Englewood Cliffs, New Jersey: Prentice-Hall, 1967).
35.
Clyde Haberman, "Controversy Is Renewed Over Japanese Textbooks," *The New York Times*, July 11, 1983.
36.
Jane Kramer, "Letter from Europe," *The New Yorker*, February 28, 1983.
37.
John Ogbu, *Minority Education and Caste* (New York: Academic Press, 1978). I was told about Ogbu's work—and his study of my childhood schools—by Ulric Neisser.
38.
Neal Ascherson, "Ghost Waltz," *The New York Review of Books*, March 5, 1981, 28. Ingeborg Day, *Ghost Waltz* (New York: Viking, 1981).
39.
Bini Reichel, "Tell Me About Nazis, Daddy," *Village Voice*, May 10, 1983, 9. Also, Reichel's interviews with members of the Third Reich in "What Did You Do in the War, Daddy?" *Rolling Stone*, March 31, 1983. The collective repression of postwar Germans is described in Alexander and Margarite Mitscherlich, *The Inability to Mourn* (New York: Grove Press, 1975).
40.
Harrison Salisbury, "Stalin's Tactics at Home," *The New York Times Book Review*, January 17, 1982. Review of Anton Antonov-Ovseyenko, *The Time of Stalin* (New York: Harper & Row, 1982).
41.
David K. Shipler, "Russia: "A People Without Heroes," *The New York Times Magazine*, October 15, 1983, 95, 106.
42.
Ibid. 106.

43.
George Orwell, *1984* (New York: New American Library, 1961, Appendix).
44.
Floyd Abrams, "The New Effort to Control Information," *The New York Times Magazine,* September 25, 1983.
45.
Walter Reich, "Psychiatry in Russia," *The New York Times Magazine,* Janaury 30, 1983.

Conclusion

1.
Buddhaghosa, *Visuddhimagga: The Path of Purification,* Nanamoli Thera, trans. (Berkeley: Shambhala, 1976).
2.
Sigmund Freud, "Recommendations to Physicians Practising Psychoanalysis," *The Collected Papers of Sigmund Freud,* vol. 2, James Strachey, ed., (New York: Basic Books, 1963).
3.
Joshua Lederberg, "David Hamburg: President-Elect of AAAS," *Science,* June 23, 1983.
4.
Theodore Lidz, *The Person* (New York: Basic Books, 1976).
5.
Dennis D. Kelley, in Eric Kandel and James Schwartz, eds., *Principles of Neural Science* (New York: Elsevier, 1981).
6.
"Shedding a Chinese Veil," *The New York Times,* August 18, 1981.
7.
Irving Janis, *Victims of Groupthink* (Boston: Houghton Mifflin, 1983).
8.
Allen Wheelis, *The Illusionless Man: Fantasies and Meditations* (New York: W. W. Norton, 1966).

INDEX

ABOUT THE AUTHOR

Daniel Goleman writes regularly on the behavior sciences for *The New York Times*. He holds a B.A. degree from Amherst College and an M.A. and Ph.D. from Harvard University. Dr. Goleman is a former visiting professor at Harvard and senior editor at *Psychology Today*.